In this powerful book F. A. Nazir deploys a wealth of historical and legal scholarship to show how legislation originally drafted with the utilitarian purpose of protecting India's various religious communities from words and actions calculated to bring offence has, in the very different context of an Islamic theocratic state, become an instrument of oppression against all religious minorities. Nazir raises issues of fundamental importance for Christians, Muslims, and all those concerned with religious freedom and stability in the contemporary world.

Brian Stanley, PhD
Professor of World Christianity,
University of Edinburgh, Edinburgh, UK

The Evolution of Legislation on Religious Offences

A Study of British India and the Implications for Contemporary Pakistan

F. A. Nazir

© 2019 F. A. Nazir

Published 2019 by Langham Monographs
An imprint of Langham Publishing
www.langhampublishing.org

Langham Publishing and its imprints are a ministry of Langham Partnership

Langham Partnership
PO Box 296, Carlisle, Cumbria, CA3 9WZ, UK
www.langham.org

ISBNs:
978-1-78368-542-4 Print
978-1-78368-572-1 ePub
978-1-78368-573-8 Mobi
978-1-78368-574-5 PDF

F. A. Nazir has asserted her right under the Copyright, Designs and Patents Act, 1988 to be identified as the Author of this work.

All rights reserved. No part of this publication may be reproduced, stored in a retrieval system or transmitted, in any form or by any means, electronic, mechanical, photocopying, recording or otherwise, without the prior written permission of the publisher or the Copyright Licensing Agency.

British Library Cataloguing-in-Publication Data
A catalogue record for this book is available from the British Library

ISBN: 978-1-78368-542-4

Cover & Book Design: projectluz.com

Langham Partnership actively supports theological dialogue and an author's right to publish but does not necessarily endorse the views and opinions set forth here or in works referenced within this publication, nor can we guarantee technical and grammatical correctness. Langham Partnership does not accept any responsibility or liability to persons or property as a consequence of the reading, use or interpretation of its published content.

Contents

Introduction 1

Part I: Origin, Development and Application of the Legislation on Offences Relating to Religion in the Indian Subcontinent

Chapter 1 27
The Legislation on Religious Offences of the Indian Penal Code
    1.1 The Primary Amendments in Chapter XV in British India 33
    1.2 Chapter XV of 1860 36
    1.3 Section 295 to Protect the Places and Objects of Worship 36
        1.3.1 The Accusation of Defiling a Place or Object of Worship 37
        1.3.2 The Meaning of a Sacred Place of Worship 38
        1.3.3 The Meaning of a Sacred Object 39
        1.3.4 The Meaning of "Intention" of Section 295 41
    1.4 Section 296 of IPC to Protect Religious Assemblies 43
        1.4.1. Main Ingredients of Section 296 44
        1.4.2. Voluntarily Causing Disturbance in Religious
            Worship or Religious Ceremonies under Section 296 45
        1.4.3. Lawful Engagement of Assembly for the
            Performance of Religious Worship 50
    1.5 Section 297 of IPC: Protecting Funeral Rights and the
        Human Corpse 52
        1.5.1. Intention as Essence of the Offence under Section 297 53
        1.5.2. Trespass and Prosecution 54
    1.6 Section 298 of the IPC to Protect Against Acts Wounding
        Another Religion 56
        1.6.1. Religious Freedom of Discussion under Section 298 57
        1.6.2. The Meaning of Deliberate Intention of Wounding
            Religious Feelings under Section 298 61
        1.6.3. Prosecutions and Cases under Section 298 66
    1.7 Conclusion 68

Chapter 2 69
The Issue of Offensive Writing and Publication and Amendments to Religious Offences Laws in British India
    2.1. Offensive Publications and the Historical Setting of
        Amending Chapter XV in 1920s 71
    2.2. Section 295-A of the IPC 76
        2.2.1. The Main Ingredients and Procedures of Section 295-A 77
        2.2.2. Deliberate and Malicious Intention of Section 295-A 78
        2.2.3. The Intention to Outrage and Insult in Section 295-A 79
    2.3. The Application of Section 295-A after 1927 82
    2.4. The Controversial Application of Section 295-A to Ban *Angare* 85
    2.5. Conclusion 97

Part II: Implications of Offences Relating to Religion from Post-1947 in the Independent Subcontinent (India and Pakistan)

Chapter 3 101
The Legacy of British Law in Independent India and Pakistan
    3.1 The Application of Chapter XV of Religious Offences in
        India post-1947 104
        3.1.1 The Impact of Conversion Acts on Chapter XV:
            Of Offences Relating to Religion 107
    3.2 The Application of Chapter XV: Of Offences Relating to
        Religion in East Pakistan post-1947 112
    3.3 Chapter XV in Bangladesh 119

Chapter 4 123
The Application of Chapter XV: Of Offences Relating to Religion in West Pakistan from 1947 to 1979
    4.1 Religious Communities of West Pakistan 125
    4.2 Ahmadi-Muslim Controversies and Religious
        Offences from 1947–1954 129
    4.3 The Application of Chapter XV from 1956 to 1979 141
        4.3.1 Protection of Sacred Places of Different
            Classes under Section 295 141
        4.3.2 Protection of Christian Community from Offensive
            Publications under Section 295-A 143
        4.3.3 Protection and Discussion of Islamic
            Publications and Faith under Section 295-A 145
    4.4 The Anti-Ahmadi Riots and Religious Offences from 1974 158
    4.5 Conclusion 164

Part III: Implications of Offences Relating to Religion from Post-1947 in the Independent Subcontinent (India and Pakistan)

Chapter 5 169
   The Legislation on Offences Relating to Religion and Islamization of Pakistan (1979–1988)
     5.1 The Political Power of Zia-ul-Haq and Religious Offences 170
     5.2 Islamization, Law and Order and the Creation of Federal
        Shariat Court 172
     5.3 Amendments in Chapter XV of Pakistan Penal Code from
        1980 to 1986 174
     5.4 Section 295-B 186
        5.4.1 The Meaning of Defile and Damage in Section 295-B 186
        5.4.2 The Meaning of "Wilful" Action in Section 295-B 189
        5.4.3 The Prosecution on Suspicion under Section 295-B
            and Mob Violence... 191
     5.5 Section 295-C 194
        5.5.1 The Discussion over the Death Sentence and Life
            Imprisonment and the Issue of "Intention" in Section
            295-C 195
        5.5.2 The Meaning of Defiling the Prophet in
            Speech and Writing in Section 295-C 200
     5.6 Conclusion 214

Chapter 6 219
   The Blasphemy Law and the Question of the Protection of Religious Communities and Their Religious Rights
     6.1 The Protest of Religious Communities for their Protection 220
     6.2 Judicial Concern over the Misuse of the Blasphemy Law
        and the Safety of Religious Communities 225
     6.3 Political Efforts to Bring Changes in the Legal Procedure of
        Blasphemy Accusations.. 228
     6.4 Critical Implications of Blasphemy and Proposal for the
        Amendment Bill of Blasphemy from 2007–2012 235
     6.5 Amendments to the Blasphemy Laws Act 2010 240
     6.6. Reaction to the Amendment Bill.. 246
     6.7 Conclusion 248

Bibliography... 255

Introduction

> We have to see the reasons behind the incident [in Joseph Colony, Lahore]. If anyone has committed an offence, the law is there [but] what about the riot and arson. Where is your [Punjab government's] writ? Nothing has been produced to establish causes of the incident . . . Whose responsibility is it to protect life, property and dignity of the citizens?
>
> <div align="right">Chief Justice Iftikhar Muhammad Chaudhry
(<i>The Nation</i>, 11 March 2013)</div>

On 11 March 2013, the Supreme Court of Pakistan took note of an incident which occurred in Joseph Colony in Badami Bagh, Lahore, on 9 March, in which over 175 houses, a church containing religious books, and all the belongings of the Christian community were burnt and torched by a mob over a blasphemy accusation, defiling the Prophet Muhammad, which had not yet been prosecuted. The Supreme Court rejected the Punjab provincial government and police authorities' reports on the accusation, and declared that the blank reports and totally unsubstantiated stories about the incident could not be accepted and, moreover, that the Christian community of the colony was damaged despite having nothing to do with the incident. The Court also raised another important concern: no one had the right to take the law into his hands. The disastrous consequences could have been controlled but why, asked the court, did officials stay inactive, unable or uninterested in protecting the Christians of Joseph Colony?

This is just one example of many where Christians are prosecuted under what is commonly known as the blasphemy law. The offence of blasphemy and its application to all religious communities such as Ahmadis, Christians and Hindus, and including some Muslims, is one of the most critical issues in Pakistan today. Various reasons behind the cases such as insult or personal advantage or animosity, which are readily labelled as religious conflict, have become a matter of life and death in Pakistan. The nature of religious conflict and legal efforts to avoid or reduce it in Pakistan is not a sudden or very modern religious problem glossed as "blasphemy," as contemporary news and media imply today. The issue is rooted in the history of Pakistan.

Religious conflicts historically occurred between religious communities or within one religious community. For example Hindu-Muslim communalism regarding religious practices and religious differences was critically appraised in the Indian Subcontinent ruled by the British. In post 1947 Pakistan, animosity between Hindus and Muslims comparatively dropped but religious conflicts remain, yet in different modes and with different outcomes. Before approaching the contemporary pattern of religious conflicts it is important to see what the geopolitical context of Pakistan is in South Asia.

In 1947 Pakistan became an independent and Islamic nation of South Asia, but its known history actually began in the third millennium BCE with the Indus Valley civilisation and its cities Mohenjo-doro and Harapa.[1] The Indus Valley was first settled by Aryans in the north-west of the Indian subcontinent from 1500 to 1200 BCE.[2] The development of Hinduism, and significantly the caste tradition, started with the Aryans. In 712 Arab Islam entered through Sindh. Mehmud Ghazni invaded in the year 1001 and later conquered Punjab after having a vision of Islamic dominance. Some regions were almost completely Islamized by Hindu converts to Islam, helping Islam become a major religion in India.[3] By 1707 many Muslims, particularly under the Mughal Empire, ruled over north India but their power declined after the death of the sixth Emperor, Aurangzeb.[4] The British came as merchants "for trade, but the constitution of the [East India] Company began in commerce and ended in empire."[5] During the era of Islamic supremacy in India, the Hanafi school of law was the legal code employed under the

---

1. Stephen Neill, *A History of Christianity in India: The Beginnings to AD 1707* (Cambridge: Cambridge University Press, 1984), 3–5.
2. John C. B. Webster, *The Dalit Christians: A History* (Delhi: ISPCK, 1992), 3.
3. Neill, *History of Christianity*, 8, 63–67.
4. Akbar S. Ahmed, *Pakistan Society: Islam, Ethnicity and Leadership in South Asia* (Karachi: Oxford University Press, 1997), 6–7
5. Ahmed, *Pakistan Society*, 11.

Ghaznavids (975–1187 CE),⁶ though some scholars such as Fayzee and Zaman suggest that the Hanafi law was well established and practiced under the Mughal emperors (1500–1700 CE). They further note that the Islamic law known locally as the Muhammadan law is described in well-known texts such as the *Hedaya* and the *Fatwa Alamgiria*, which were the paramount authorities in Hanafi law in India.⁷

British rule brought new political institutions, and when indigenous mechanisms were adapted to colonial purposes, they were incorporated within new systems of law. Peters argues that between 1790 and 1807, the British transformed Islamic criminal law. Certain homicide acts, stoning to death for *hadd* crimes including apostasy, were repealed and strict rules of evidence and the notion of doubt (*shubha*) were introduced.⁸ Some sources note that it was not that easy for Muslims to accept India under non-Muslim governance, for they were being colonized and lost much power. Various *fatwas*, for example, were declared by Shah Abd al Aziz, a Muslim scholar, against the British as non-Muslim rulers in India, although by the 1820s, scholars in Delhi agreed that as long as the practice of the Muslim faith was guaranteed by the political regime, Muslims could peacefully remain in a non-Islamic country.⁹

---

6. Antony Black, *The History of Islamic Political Thought* (Edinburgh: Edinburgh University Press, 2001), 48–49; Joseph Schacht, *An Introduction to Islamic Law* (Oxford: Clarendon, 1982), 65.

7. The *Hedaya* was written by Burhanuddin Marghinani (d. 1197 CE) who lived and wrote in Marghinan, a small town Farghana, in Russian Turkestan. The *Hedaya* has achieved its legal authority in India. The *Fatwa Alamgiria*, composed by Shaykh Nizam Burhanpuri and his companions, is a collection of *fatwas*, the replies of juriconsults to the questions addressed to them. The work was done by the orders during the reign of the Emperor Aurangzeb Alamgir (1685–1707) in Delhi. Muhammad Qasim Zaman, *The Ulama in Contemporary Islam: Custodians of Change* (Princeton, NJ: Princeton University Press, 2002), 22; Asaf Ali Asghar Fyzee, *Outlines of Muhammadan Law* (Delhi: Oxford University Press, 1974), 37, 50; Asaf Ali Asghar Fyzee, *Cases in the Muhammadan Law of India and Pakistan* (Oxford: Clarendon, 1965), xvii; Schacht, *Introduction to Islamic Law*, 57.

8. Rudolph Peters, *Crime and Punishment in Islamic Law: Theory and Practice from the Sixteenth to the Twenty-First Century* (Cambridge: Cambridge University Press, 2005), 118–119; Zaman, *Ulama in Contemporary Islam*, 22–23.

9. Muhammad Khalid Masud, "The World of Shah Abd al Aziz (1746–1824)," in *Perspectives of Mutual Encounters in South Asian History 1760–1860*, ed. Jamal Malik (Leiden; Boston: Brill, 2000), 307–314; Barbara D. Metcalf, *Islamic Revival in British India: Deoband, 1860-1900* (New Delhi: Oxford University Press, 2002), 49–52; William W. Hunter, *The Indian Musalmans* (London: Trübner, 1876), chapters 3 and 4.

It was a challenge to see whether all communities could be protected when the criminal law was formally replaced with the new Indian Penal Code in 1860, which contrasted with what could seem certain arbitrariness in Hindu and Muslim law. The *shari'a* was then restricted exclusively to the realm of the laws of personal status such as the law of marriage, divorce, children and inheritance for Muslims. This research is limited to discuss the control of religious conflicts during British rule of the region, written in Chapter XV: Of Offences Relating to Religion, of the Indian Penal Code, a code which continued to be practised in South Asia – India, Pakistan and Bangladesh – after the British had gone.

British governance was criticized and challenged by Hindus and Muslims to get independence from British domination. In 1909 the Muslim League was founded to protect the political and religious rights of Muslims in India. Under the direction of Muhammad Ali Jinnah, the founder of Pakistan, the Muslim League effectively capitalized on the elections of 1945–1946, helping Pakistan constitute itself as an independent country on 14 August 1947.[10] Soon after this, religious communal violence started pushing minority groups in the western region to migrate to one or the other of the newly formed nations to join their co-religionists.[11] Among those co-religionists, Ahmadis, Hindus and Christians went to, or stayed, in what is now Pakistan as they were promised that they would be protected in Pakistan. How can the current context regarding religious conflicts between and within religious communities be evaluated in the post-colonial period?

Religious Conflicts in Pakistan

During the post-colonial period, the category of religious offences took different directions under the new geo-political and socio-political status of India and Pakistan. The major concern regarding the issue of conversion and application of the conversion acts affected the application of religious offences in some Indian states. However, Pakistan faced major ethnic and religious conflicts within the Islamic community of East and West Pakistan

---

10. Akbar S. Ahmed, *Jinnah, Pakistan and Islamic Identity: The Search for Saladin* (London: Routledge, 1997), 55, 112.

11. Ahmed, *Jinnah, Pakistan and Islamic Identity*, 166.

based upon differences in religious views on shaping the constitution. The religious differences in the theological beliefs of Ahmadis and Muslims remained critical in West Pakistan. It was a theological argument, particularly related to the finality of the Prophet Muhammad, which finally split both sects, with the majority declaring Ahmadis non-Muslims in 1974. Pakistan's Islamic reformation in the 1980s brought major changes in the constitution and law including changes such as blasphemy laws which affected religious arguments, differences, discussions, conversion and even social quarrels and banal disputes among different religious communities. It changed the nature of the 1860 law against "insulting religious feelings" which have particularly affected non-Muslims of Pakistan and impacts on the entire country.

This research is also influenced by my own personal experience and search for identity as a non-Muslim in Pakistan when I found myself silent, unable to answer questions about Christianity in some religious conversations and discussions with fellow students, mostly Muslims and one Ahmadi, in 1992–1996. We were a happy group of young women enjoying and celebrating Christmas and the Muslim Eid: but given the religious difference I was usually regarded as the one lacking true religion. They raised various apologetic questions: the Bible is not pure but is an altered and corrupted book; Jesus did not die on the Cross and did not rise from the dead; British and American Christians with whom I usually associated do not keep themselves in *parda* veil, and similar issues. I was unable to answer freely and if I attempted to respond, I deliberately kept my voice flat, especially when comparing Christianity to other religions.

I was shocked one day when one of my friends brought me an Urdu book written about Christianity especially comparing it with Islam. I read the book, checking all biblical references, and realized that many references were misquoted. I took that book back and asked whether misquoting the bible was a religious offence or not? They were somewhat embarrassed, but no-one answered. I was aware if any Christian had commented in such way in respect of Islam without taking care and respect, the situation would have been different. Misquoting or changing the context of some biblical references was not a big deal for my friends but it wounded my religious feelings and indeed changed my life. Initially I became interested to learn more about Christianity and the social issues Christians face in Pakistan. Later, I started to research the historical roots and causes of religious conflicts among religious communities: the result is this book. Though my initial interest was to understand the nature of present religious injury, I eventually saw that the roots of religious conflict injury lay not in the last few years, but rather far back, in the law, colonial legacy, religious protest, political power and religious conflicts among and within religious communities, and that it affected not only Christians, but variously Hindus, Ahmadis including some Muslims.

It is understandable that discussions arise when two different religions confront each other, as I experienced as a girl, but in contemporary Pakistan, religious conflicts have been turned into a very volatile affair, quickly resulting in legal accusations claiming religious disturbance, whatever the facts of the case. For example, one of the recent blasphemy cases gained national and international attention in the news when eleven-year-old Rimsha Masih, an illiterate Pakistani Christian girl with Down's syndrome was accused under section 295-B of committing blasphemy for burning pages of *Nurani Qaida* containing verses of the Qur'an and was arrested on 16 August 2012. It is important to see what kind of religious tension or conflict lay in the background to such an accusation. After Rimsha's arrest, Khalid Jadoon, a Muslim local cleric, said in a television interview that he was disturbed by the church music and prayers of the local Christian community and had warned them that they will suffer if they continue such practices. He called for the eviction of all Christians from the neighbourhood because "Pakistan is an Islamic country given by Allah."[12] During the investigation of the case, Khalid Jadoon came under suspicion for changing the evidence, especially mixing pages of the *Qaeda* in the ashes coming from Rimsha's home on 22 September 2012. The main reason for doing this was, as Zubair the witness asserted: "Jadoon said that it is evidence against the Christians and a way to get them removed [from the area]."[13] Rimsha was later released by Islamabad High Court on the basis of lack of evidence or of the intention to commit blasphemy.[14] Now she is free from the charge but actually not free from

---

12. Khalid Jadoon's Interview on *Geo News*, 30 August 2012 at PST 20:00.
13. Jadoon interview,.
14. "No Evidence Against Pakistan 'Blasphemy Girl,'" *BBC News Asia*, posted on 22 September 2012, https://www.bbc.co.uk/news/world-asia-19686941.

the fear of further attacks and has moved with her family to Canada. This case attracted much attention and was mostly condemned by Muslims and non-Muslims alike. It was the first time when members of Pakistan *Ulama* Council stood up for non-Muslims especially to condemn misusing the law against an innocent girl.[15] Such condemnation, though showing the world that Pakistan is concerned that the law should not be misused, does not mean the country has safeguarded the future of the minorities who have little or no power to protect themselves today.

The Aims of the Research and Current Literature on the Issue

The issue of religious offences and their implications for Pakistan, especially from the 1980s to the present, has been discussed in contemporary sources. Over the last thirty years, current approaches have tended to describe Pakistan as an intolerant state especially in terms of not providing adequate protection for its religious communities from violence. Some sources claim that the Islamic reformation brought under the military rule of Zia-ul-Haq caused the recent intolerance while others dignify his intentions of reforming Pakistan. Though elements of his laws have been changed, the most debated issue is the application of the law of blasphemy which prescribes the death sentence for defiling the name of the Prophet Muhammad under section 295-C and life imprisonment for defiling the copy of the Qur'an under section 295-B. The implication of this law has not only led communities themselves to protest for their security and human rights but also directed others to write on human rights and freedom of expression. However, there is an absence of any examination of the historical roots of the law which would show how gradually not only the law but also the mode of its prosecution has been changed.

Yet the focus of this thesis is not limited to blasphemy law in modern Pakistan, easy though it would have been to do that. The thesis does not aim to give details and arguments about the scales of punishments such as death sentence or life imprisonment for assaulting God, Prophets and

---

15. "Ulama Council Chief Demanded Bail for Rimsha," *The Express Tribune*, 4 September 2012.

beliefs in Judaism, Christianity and Islam. The major reason for doing this research is to set out the historical promulgation and objectives of Chapter XV: Of Offences Relating to Religion, of the Indian Penal Code. Thomas B. Macaulay (1800–1859), an English Christian, historian and legislator, and a member of the Supreme Council of India, played an important role in introducing English education and preparing the penal code for British India between 1834 and 1838.[16] This research particularly reviews how the legislation on religious offences was revised from 1837, applied in 1860 and practised till 1947 under colonial rule and in the post-colonial era in South Asia.[17]

One of the important foci is to examine the actual application and procedure of the law. What kind of religious issues were tried under this law in the various eras since promulgation: the nineteenth century; the run-up to Independence; the early years of Pakistan; and the Zia-ul-Haq era and beyond? How were these various laws and clauses used, dropped, or annulled by later amendments? This discussion covers a range of case studies to show the early objectives and procedure by taking a careful historical approach, especially the setting out and use of "intention" necessary when prosecuting anyone for religious offence.

Before embarking on this evolutionary procedure it is significant to note that Macaulay and his legislation for the Indian Territory were inspired by the ethical and political theories of utilitarianism usually associated with British social and philosophical reformers such as Jeremy Bentham (1748–1832) and J. S. Mill (1806–1873). The general concept of utilitarianism is based on the view that the nature of each human being includes the desire to obtain happiness and avoid pain. To ensure each relationship with other individuals will enable that outcome, specifically targeted legislation is

---

16. Stephen Evans, "Macaulay's Minute Revisited: Colonial Language Policy in Nineteenth-Century India," *Journal of Multilingual and Multicultural Development*, 23, no. 4 (2002): 260–281; Wing-Cheong Chan, Barry Wright and Stanley Yeo, eds., *Codification, Macaulay and the Indian Penal Code: The Legacies and Modern Challenges of Criminal Law Reform* (Surrey: Ashgate, 2011), 20, 34.

17. Thomas B. Macaulay, *A Penal Code Prepared by Indian Law Commissioners* (Calcutta: Bengal Military Orphan Press, 1837); Thomas B. Macaulay, J. M. Macleod, G. W. Anderson, and F. Millet, *The Indian Penal Code as Originally Framed in 1837* (Madras: Higginbotham, 1888); Thomas B. Macaulay, *Complete Works of Thomas Babington Macaulay*, vol. 3 (London: Longmans, Green and Co., 1866).

necessary. Bentham, in his *Essays on the Influence of Time and Place Matters of Legislation*, urged that India be reformed through utilitarian ideology, by promulgating and reforming laws and judgments[18] based on moral principles, hence his famous phrase, "the greatest happiness of the greatest number" in Indian society.[19] Though Mill's theory, discussed in his book *Utilitarianism*, was influenced by Bentham, it was slightly different.[20] For example, one of the examples of Mill's utilitarianism is based on a standard of morality which is different from Bentham's who reviews all forms of happiness: Mill argues for the importance of intellectual and moral pleasures as superior to physical pleasure.[21]

It is not relevant to discuss the whole theories of early utilitarianism. However, it is sufficient to note that Macaulay, influenced by Bentham's principles of utilitarianism for reforming Indian law and social life, used this as the basic principle for a rational and efficient legal system, as admirably set out in Eric Stokes's, *The English Utilitarians and India*.[22] Through Macaulay, utilitarianism thus played an important part not only in the drafting of the Penal Code but also in modernizing and reforming British rule in India.[23]

---

18. Bentham, "Essay on the Influence of Time and Place in Matters of Legislation," in Kartik Kalyan Raman, "Utilitarianism and the Criminal Law in Colonial India: A Study of the Practical Limits of Utilitarian Jurisprudence," *Modern Asian Studies* 28, no. 4 (October 1994): 739–791.

19. Jeremy Bentham, *The Principles of Morals and Legislations* (Oxford: Clarendon, 1879), chapter 1; Jeremy Bentham, *A Fragment on Government* (Oxford: Clarendon, 1776), preface (available at http://www.efm.bris.ac.uk/het/bentham/government.htm).

20. John Stuart Mill, *Utilitarianism: Liberty and Representative Government* (London: Dent, 1909).

21. Mill, *Utiliarianism*, 16–17.

22. For detail see "Macaulay as Law Member," discussed by Eric Stokes in, *The English Utilitarians and India* (Oxford: Clarendon, 1959), 192, 225–229; modern scholars such as John Clive argue that Macaulay cannot labelled as merely a disciple of Bentham and that if one were to characterize him in that way, Macaulay would have to be identified as one of the last representatives of the Scottish School. See John Clive, *Thomas Babington Macaulay: The Shaping of the Historian* (London: Secker & Warburg, 1973), 473; Leader-Elliot argues that Macaulay was closer to Adam Smith than he was to Benthamite utilitarianism particularly when reviewing Smith's work, *Theory of Moral Sentiments*, published in 1759. For details see Ian D. Leader-Elliott Professor, "Macaulay's Penal Code, Adam Smith and the Jurisprudence of Resentment," working paper (January 2012), available at: http://works.bepress.com/ian_leader-elliott1/1.

23. Stokes, *English Utilitarians*, 227; Barry Wright, "Macaulay's Indian Penal Code: Historical Context and Originating Principles," in *Codification, Macaulay and the Indian*

Macaulay's Penal Code was accepted, subject to revision in 1837 and finally enacted in 1860. It cannot be denied that the Indian Penal Code remained an impressive example of comprehensive law reform, despite retrograde changes introduced in the 1860 enacted version.[24] Together with later colonial amendments, it was used in British South Asia and other British Asian areas until and beyond independence.[25] Stokes argues that later reforms in the law resulted in the loss of some of his radical innovations, which will be set out in the following discussion of the legislation concerning "Offences Relating to Religion."[26]

Macaulay's designation of Chapter XV: Of Offences Relating to Religion shows his concern to foster multicultural understanding by attempting to ensure that the laws imposed by the colonial power matched the expectation of its colonial subjects. Therefore, in the context of religious diversity, the law's major objective was to bring harmony among religious communities and to control religious conflicts which occurred through "the differences among communities of feeling."[27] This aim encouraged the legislature to protect religious places, worship or objects including all funeral rites and to prevent religions discussions from causing violence. Various rules and regulations, case studies and judgments and procedures have been found in legal documents published in the "Indian Legal Reports" of British India and in commentaries written on the Indian Penal Code (IPC) in order to discuss the historical period and practice of religious offences in British India.[28]

Penal Code: The Legacies and Modern Challenges of Criminal Law Reform, eds. Wing-Cheong Chan, Barry Wright, and Stanley Yeo (Surrey: Ashgate, 2011), 19–56.

24. Chan, Wright, and Yeo, *Codification, Macaulay*, 3.

25. K. J. M. Smith, "Macaulay's 'Utilitarian' Indian Penal Code: An Illustration of the Accidental Function of Time, Place and Personalities in Law Making," in *Legal History in the Making*, eds. W. M. Gordon and T. D. Fergus (London: Hambledon, 1991), 145–164.

26. Stokes, *English Utilitarians*, 224.

27. Chan, Wright and Yeo, *Codification, Macaulay*, 294–295; Gauri Viswanathan, *Outside the Fold: Conversion, Modernity, and Belief* (Princeton, NJ: Princeton University Press, 1998), 250–251.

28. Among those commentaries are: Mahabir Prashad Jain, *Outlines of Indian Legal History*, 2nd ed. (Bombay: N. M. Tripathi, 1966); Hari Singh Gour, Gyanendra Kumar, M. C. Desai and R. B. Sethi, *The Penal Law of India: Being an Analytical, Critical & Expository Commentary on the Indian Penal Code (Act No. XLV of 1860), As Amended Up to Date*, 10th ed., vol. 1 (Allahabad: Law Publications, 1982); W. R. Hamilton, *The Indian Penal Code with Commentary* (Calcutta: Thacker, Spink and Co, 1895); William Morgan and A. G. Macpherson, *The Indian Penal Code: Act XLV of 1860* (Calcutta: G. C. Hay, 1861);

Macaulay was aware that there were bound to be deficiencies in the interpretation and application of the Code, and therefore proposed some careful revisions, which were effected between 1837 and 1858. However, after his death, his basic principle could be said to have remained as the cornerstone of reforms of the law in British India and the early post-colonial era.[29] For example, the law to control religious offences was amended and reformed in the 1920s to punish the person who "with deliberate and malicious intention of outraging the religious feelings of any class . . . by words, either spoken or written, or by visible representation, insults or attempts to insult the religion or the religious beliefs of that class . . ."[30] This law (section 295-A) was an addition to the earlier clauses of Chapter XV of IPC, and was especially included to protect the Muslim community from offensive publications written against the Prophet Muhammad. However, a change to the philosophy and intention of Macaulay's law came after 1980 in Pakistan, when further amendments were made to protect the sanctity of the Prophet. The law, originally intended to avoid religious conflicts in India, was very different from the blasphemy laws then existing in England and used in British history to protect Christianity. Indeed that first British India law of 1860 as it has evolved in Pakistan has only been referred to as the "Blasphemy law" for at the most the last thirty years. The outcome, therefore, of these recent changes has been to restrict and arguably to diminish the 1860 Penal Code.

Setting out the variations between English law, the British India 1860 law, and its outworking over the years proved all the more necessary in order to understand the later picture, the application and amendments of the law in the last thirty years, which are usually discussed in modern sources with at best a very limited assessment and incomplete or irrelevant historical evaluation. For example, Linda S. Walbridge gives adequate information

---

J. O'Kinealy, *The Indian Penal Code and Other Laws Relating to the Criminal Courts of India* (Calcutta: S. K. Lahiri, 1900); M. H. Starling, *Indian Criminal Law and Procedure* (London: W. H. Allen, 1869); Charlton Swinhoe, *The Case-Noted Penal Code: The Indian Penal Code (Act XLV of 1860 as Amended)* (Calcutta: Thacker, Spink and Co, 1909); Clive, *Thomas Babington Macaulay*; Frank Normandy, *A Dictionary and Manual of the Criminal Law* (Madras: Lawrence Asylum Press, 1883); John D. Mayne, *Commentaries on the Indian Penal Code*, 7th ed. (Madras: Higginbotham, 1872).

29. Chan and Wright and Yeo, *Codification, Macaulay*, 6–7.

30. Nand Lal, *The Indian Penal Code, Act XLV of 1860*, vol. 1 (Lahore: Krishan Lal, 1929), 1328, 1330.

about the historical existence of Christianity with her main focus on how Bishop John Joseph came to commit suicide in protest in order to encourage reform of the blasphemy law in Pakistan in 1998. However, she not only gives insufficient information but also gives an incorrect background for the legislation of Offences Relating to Religion in the Indian British subcontinent. For example, she notes that "section 295-A was added in 1980" to the Pakistan blasphemy law to punish offensive speech and writing, adding her unsubstantiated assumption that the law "may have been an attempt to prevent intra-Islamic violence since Sunnis and Shia's have different opinions . . ."[31] This is a totally inadequate conclusion as the historical setting of section 295-A, applied by the British in 1927, is an addition to Chapter XV to protect Muslims from offensive publications and speech. Regarding the concern of Walbridge, that section 295-A could be used for Sunni-Shia conflicts, it must be noted that section 295-A successfully protected the Christian community before the law was amended in 1980s. However, it cannot be denied and will be argued that application of this law was significantly limited in Pakistan.[32] Major sectarianism did not start in 1980s but began with the birth of Pakistan, as exemplified by the Ahmadi-Muslim conflicts in the 1950s and 1970s, which gradually affected Chapter XV: Of Offences Relating to Religion and later came to affect all religious communities, making Christians, in the same way as Ahmadis and now Shias, more vulnerable to accusation today in Pakistan as discussed in the second part of the thesis.

Significantly, reviewing the early judicial dealing regarding some cases in West Pakistan deemed religious, makes clear that contrary to Walbridge's assumption, Chapter XV did indeed bring justice to protect different classes. Contrary to the later application of the law, which discourages communities from discussing religious matters freely, some historical cases took the prosecution of religious matters very seriously, discussing and judging without any disorder or violence. In one of the cases, for example, Christian beliefs

---

31. Linda S. Walbridge, *The Christians of Pakistan: The Passion of Bishop John Joseph* (London: Routledge, 2003), 89.

32. Mohammad Munir, and M. R. Kayani, *Report of the Court Inquiry Constituted under Punjab Act 11 of 1954 to Enquire into the Punjab Disturbances of 1953* (Lahore: Government Print, Punjab, 1954).

which had been insulted by a Muslim were discussed and protected[33] and, even more important for this research, that religious rights of religions were protected provided the issue of intention was clear. In two other cases, two books were judged inoffensive, despite containing matter which might be offensive to Muslims, because they were judged as not having been written maliciously to offend Muslims.[34]

Pakistani lawyers and writers, who have reviewed the historical background of the law in British India, are important to mention. Ismail Qureshi, a Muslim writer and a senior advocate of the Lahore High Court, is one of the important sources mentioned in this research. From an Islamic perspective, he argues that blasphemy against the Prophet Muhammad is punishable with death in Islam, as discussed in detail in *Namoos-e-Rasalat or Qanoon-e-Toheen-e-Rasalat* (The honour of the prophethood of Muhammad and the law of blasphemy) an Urdu book published in 1994. This book states that Pakistan changed its law to protect the sanctity of the Prophet which was not protected in British India.[35] Qureshi wrote another book *Muhammad the Messenger of God and the Law of Blasphemy in Islam and West* published in 2008 in English, especially to address the readers in the West and also for those interested in Islamic laws. In his book the research "was done with historical details and judicial aspects of law of blasphemy in Islam and other religions: Christianity and Judaism."[36] Furthermore he discussed in this book how punishments for blasphemy as prescribed in the Bible were implemented in the past in European countries and America. Qureshi commented, while discussing the Salman Rushdie case which was *not* tried under British and European Blasphemy law, that Europe is conservative in maintaining its own orthodox laws while Pakistan's Government "proposed

---

33. In the matter of the Book "Jesus in Heaven on Earth" and in the matter of Woking Muslim Mission and Literary Trust, Lahore and of the Civil and Military Gazette, Limited, Lahore v. The Crown, PLD (1954) Lahore 724.
34. The Punjab Religious Book Society v. The State, PLD (1960) Lahore 629; Muhammad Khalil v. The State, PLD (1962) Lahore 850.
35. Muhammad Ismail Qureshi, *Namoos-e-Rasalat aur Qanoon-e-Toheen-e-Rasalat*, 2nd ed. (Lahore: Nashran-o-Tajran Kutub, 1999), 53.
36. Muhammad Ismail Qureshi, *Muhammad: The Messenger of God and the Law of Blasphemy in Islam and the West* (Lahore: Nuqoosh, 2008), ix.

to make amendments in the just equitable law of blasphemy in an attempt to show the country as a secular, modern state."[37]

Qureshi provides adequate detail about European Blasphemy laws but gives little of the historical implementation of Chapter XV: Of Offences Relating to Religion in 1860 (amended in 1920s in British India and then in Pakistan in 1980s). He does not detail, for example, that religious conflicts, generally occurring between Muslims and Hindus, came under the law especially regarding the protection of religious worship, places of worship, religious assemblies and freedom of religious discussions. Qureshi put much more focus on the events which occurred in 1920s and 1930s and argues that the main reason for religious violence over the offensive writings in this period – which brought extra-judicial judgment such as killing of two Hindu blasphemers, Rajpal and Ram, by young Muslim men – was the absence of a proper law to protect Muslim feelings in British India.[38] This is demonstrably not the case, as will be discussed in detail in the first half of the thesis, and briefly clarified here. The issue is to what extent the British were successful or unsuccessful in bringing religious tolerance, to what extent all religious communities and their religious objects were protected, including Muslims, and how the British dealt with offensive publications which assaulted the Prophet Muhammad.

Qureshi does insist that Muslims should refrain from taking the law into their own hands as "an adequate remedy is available against the offender through due process of law."[39] According to Qureshi, an accusation of blasphemy should be judged only by the "intention" which is the most important element introduced by the Islamic law. He can be regarded as the first who tried to amend the blasphemy law, especially to revise the death sentence carried out according to Islam, and to add mention of "intention" in section 295-C as the basis of prosecuting anyone accused of defiling the Prophet. However, his proposal was withdrawn by the ruling Government of Nawaz Sharif in 1991.[40] He also argues that Pakistani non-Muslims should

---

37. Qureshi, *Muhammad: The Messenger*, 92–93.
38. Qureshi, *Muhammad: The Messenger*, 193; Qureshi, *Namoos-e-Rasalat*, 34.
39. Qureshi, *Muhammad: The Messenger*, 193.
40. Discussed in detail in Muhammad Ismail Qureshi v. Pakistan through the Secretary of Law and Parliamentary Affairs, PLD (1991), FSC 10.

not be afraid as the law of blasphemy is not aimed against them. He further notes that "no non-Muslim has been convicted under this law so far due to strict observation of the law of evidence."[41] The blasphemy law itself and its proper use may not be harmful to any religious community and indeed all communities can be accused under this law. However, he does not discuss or give any example of this law providing proper legal or social safety to religious minorities. There are numerous examples to illustrate how in various cases non-Muslims in the last thirty years have been accused on mere suspicion and were punished by the local community without any trial and formal accusations in Pakistan.

While Qureshi does not include the contemporary implications of the law of blasphemy in Pakistan, other sources have provided much information about the contemporary application of the law. Some of these sources will be carefully discussed to show how political leaders and lawyers have not only condemned the misuse of the law and declared that it violated religious rights, but that it also indicates why the blasphemy law results in extra-judicial consequences in contemporary Pakistan. Therefore, they have all made suggestions to reduce the misuse of the law, although each of them faces threats when they defend and deal with minorities' cases in Pakistan. Asma Jahangir, a Muslim writer, human rights activist and lawyer, who served as the first woman president of the Supreme Court Bar Association of Pakistan, has defended not only Muslims but also religious minorities. Various blasphemy cases are discussed in her book *From Protection to Exploitation: The Laws Against Blasphemy in Pakistan*, discussed later in the thesis. She notes that the blasphemy laws of Pakistan have "controlled and silenced the liberal lobbies," dissuading them from discussing religious matters or the need to bring about changes to the post-1980s laws.[42] She further argues that the law has affected society as a whole and minorities in particular, but that, "the core issue is that while laws based on religion are easy to enact, they are virtually impossible to repeal."[43] Therefore the gap between liberals and

---

41. *Muhammad Ismail Qureshi v. Pakistan*; Ismail Qureshi, *Judgment of Yousaf Kasab Blasphemy Case* (Lahore: Al-Maarif, 2000), 12.

42. Asma Jahangir, *From Protection to Exploitation: The Laws Against Blasphemy in Pakistan* (Lahore: AGHS Legal Aid Cell, 2008), 13–15.

43. Jahan, *From Protection to Eploitation*, 13–15.

conservatives remains and the communities continue to suffer. She has often been strongly opposed for fighting for minorities' rights, religious freedom and security, as discussed in chapter 5 of this research.[44]

It is essential to point out at the outset that the career of politicians of any religious background in Pakistan can be ended by threats of violence if they discuss the post-1980s laws with the intention of reforming them to reduce their misuse. Sherry Rehman, a Pakistani Muslim journalist and politician, is one of the examples discussed later in this research.[45] Rehman, in her political career (2002–2007 and 2008–2011) as a member of parliament, was regarded as a democrat and liberal Muslim who had taken bold steps and decisions on contentious issues of Pakistan such as passing key legislation to protect religious communities and human rights.[46] One especially bold step was tabling a Blasphemy Bill of 2010 to bring further changes in Chapter XV: Of the Religious Offences law to reduce its misuse and to protect the minorities of Pakistan; this action is discussed in the third part of the thesis.[47] Though Jahangir and Rehman have clearly said that the law of blasphemy has threatened the justice system, human rights and politics of Pakistan, they have also put more emphasis on the contemporary application and misuse of the law, and made little attempt to anchor their views in the past.

As well as these major figures who will be discussed where appropriate in the thesis, there are a host of minor modern sources which it may be helpful to mention here: Mathews George Chunakara and Naeem Shakir,[48]

---

44. Rana Ranveer, "Asma Targeted in Ahmadi Hate Campaign," *The Express Tribune*, 27 October 2010; Asma Jahangir, "Walking Together for Freedom," lecture presented at the, *Breaking Barriers: What It Will Take To Achieve Security, Justice and Peace*, conference hosted by the Joan B. Kroc Institute for Peace & Justice at the University of San Diego, 27 September 2012.

45. "Profile: Pakistan's New US Envoy Sherry Rehman," *BBC News*, 23 November 2011, https://www.bbc.co.uk/news/world-asia-15858462.

46. Some of her important Bills tabled in the parliament were: Women Empowerment Bill, Anti-Honor Killings Bill, Domestic Violence Prevention Bill, Affirmative Action Bill and Hudood Repeal Bill, available at http://www.jinnah-institute.org.

47. Sherry Rehman, "Amendments to the Blasphemy Laws Act 2010," 30 November 2010, available at https://www.jinnah-institute.org/images/amendments%20to%20the%20blasphemy%20laws%20act%202010.pdf.

48. Mathews George Chunakara, ed., *The Blasphemy Law in Pakistan and Its Impact* (Hong Kong: International Affairs, Christian Conference of Asia, 1998).

some publications by the National Council of Peace and Justice,[49] Charles Amjad-Ali,[50] Patrick Sookhdeo,[51] Usama Sadiqque,[52] Clement John,[53] reports and articles by Amnesty International,[54] and reports published by the Jinnah Institute.[55] All of these people have tackled the issue, but have limited their approach to contemporary applications. Although some of these authors attempt to review the historical application, they rely on just one of the incidents of Rajpal's prosecution for writing *Rangila Rasul* which led the British to amend Chapter XV: Of Offences Relating to Religion in the 1920s. This research, in contrast, has included other cases prosecuted for offensive publication such as "Saor-i-Dozakh" (Trip to Hell), *Risala-i-Vartman*, *Vichitra Jiwan* and *A Trip to Islam*, which give another insight into the historical aspects of the issue, noting especially the amendments brought in Chapter XV: Of Offences Relating to Religion, when still under the British, to protect anti-Muslim publications and subsequently other communities. In particular, this argument has been developed by researching and discussing cases mentioned above, and the historical revision of

---

49. National Commission of Peace & Justice, a Christian organization has previously responded to and engaged with the application of blasphemy law in academic publications: mostly regarding the current issues including that the law was not misused in British India. Emanuel Yousaf Mani, *Human Rights Monitor 98, A report on Religious Minorities in Pakistan* (Lahore: National Commission of Justice and Peace, 1999); Felix Qasir G. M. Amritsari, *The Blasphemy Law*, vol. 2, *Death sentence, Acquittal and exile* (Karachi, Idar-e Amn-O Insaf, 1995); Felix Qaisr G. M. Amritsari, *The Blasphemy Law*, vol. 3, *From Commitment to Hara-Kiri* (Karachi: Idara-e Amn-O Insaf, 1998); Peter Jacob Dildar and Aftab Alexander Mughal, *Section 295-C Pakistan Penal Code: A Study of the History, Effects and Cases under Blasphemy Laws in Pakistan* (Faisalabad: National Commission for Justice and Peace, 1995); Khalid Asi Rashid, ed., *A Peaceful Struggle: A Collection of Bishop John Joseph's Writings against Laws and Discrimination* (Faisalabad: National Commission of Justice and Peace, 1999).

50. Chris E. Toffolo and Charles Amjad-Ali, "Christians in Pakistan Confront Charges of Blasphemy," *The Christian Century* 115, no. 21 (July 1998).

51. Patrick Sookhdeo, *A People Betrayed: The Impact of Islamization on the Christian Community in Pakistan* (Fearn: Christian Focus, 2002), 238–302.

52. Osama Siddique and Zahra Hayat, "Unholy Speech and Holy Laws: Blasphemy in Pakistan – Controversial Origin, Design Defects, and Free Speech Implications," *Minnesota Journal of Int'l Law* 17, no. 2 (2008): 303–385.

53. Clement John, *Religion, State and Intolerance: Pakistan – 60 Years' Intermix of Religion and Politics* (Geneva: World Council of Churches, 2009).

54. Amnesty International, "Pakistan: Use and Abuse of the Blasphemy Law," 26 July 1994, AI Index: ASA 33/08/94; Amnesty International, "Pakistan: Insufficient Protection of Religious Minorities," 1 May 2001, AI Index: 33/008/2001.

55. Mariam Faruqi, ed., *A Question of Faith: A Report on the Religious Status of Minorities of Pakistan* (Karachi: Jinnah Institution, 2011).

offensive publications discussed by Barrier and Thursby.[56] Even the controversial action of banning *Angare* (embers) in the 1930s, demanded by the Muslims of Lukhnow, has been discussed to show the early misuse of their law by the British, which followed a very similar application to practices in contemporary Pakistan.[57]

The Research Approach and Time Scope

The thesis briefly discusses the period 1837–1860, especially the origins of and amendments to the legislation in Chapter XV of the religious offences law. It is not my intention to comment much on the issue of caste practices and culture in the Indian context, although it is important to note that caste practices were initially included but later deleted. Though caste practices were omitted, their legacy remained in major ethnic and social practices which can still be seen in contemporary accusations in Pakistan.

1860–1920 is a significant period in terms of seeing the application of the law, especially the extent to which it brought the tolerance that British law enforcers claimed. Some cases discussed in this period will show the main objectives of the law. However, some cases also reveal that people in some ways misunderstood the context of the law and brought accusations to use the law to settle their personal scores, but such intentions were by and large negated by judges who saw through the personal animosity. Apart from this it is also important to show that the British policy of encouraging freedom of discussion under section 298, though revealing its own religious interests

---

56. N. Gerald Barrier, *Banned: Controversial Literature and Political Control in British India 1907-1947* (Columbia, MO: University of Missouri Press, 1974); G. R. Thursby, ed., *Hindu-Muslim Relations in British India: A Study of Controversy, Conflict, and Communal Movement in Northern India 1923-1928* (Leiden: Brill, 1975).

57. Ahmad Ali and N. M. Rashed, "The Progressive Writers' Movement in its Historical Perspective," *Journal of South Asian Literature* 13, no. 1/4 (1977–1978): 90–97; Carlo Coppola and Sajida Zubair, "Rashid Jahan: Urdu Literature's First 'Angry Young Woman,'" *Journal of South Asian Literature* 22, no. 1 (1987): 166–183; Shabana Mahmud, "Angāre and the Founding of the Progressive Writers' Association," *Modern Asian Studies* 30, no. 2 (1996): 447–467; Geeta Patel, *Lyrical Movements, Historical Hauntings: On Gender, Colonialism, and Desire in Miraji's Urdu Poetry* (Stanford, CA: Stanford University Press, 2002); Priyamvada Gopal, *Literary Radicalism in India: Gender, Nation and the Transition to Independence* (London: Routledge, 2005).

and advantages, gave freedom to all religious communities to cherish and speak of their views.

1920–1947 is one of the important eras that shows how the British were threatened by critical events occurring in Hindu-Muslim communalism, both illustrated and incited by offensive publications. This is the period when two communities were trying to legitimize their arguments on the one hand to protect their rights and on the other to defend their beliefs. It is demonstrated how the British, as mediators, dealt with the issue of offensive speech and publication and brought in amendments to Chapter XV. The 1920s and 1930s also show some examples of extra-judicial judgements and murders of those who insulted the Prophet Muhammad, the legacy of which remains later in Pakistan. One of the important revisions of this period shows how the British government struggled to maintain their power threatened by the freedom movement which brought a controversial application of the law. Finally the application of the law shifted to new political powers: India and Pakistan from 1947.

The major reason for examining Chapter XV in the post-colonial period (1947–1979) is to see how it played an important role in protecting all communities in India and Pakistan (East and West). Initially with independence, all the countries promised to protect all communities, and adopted the British era law in its entirety with necessary changes of nomenclature. However, it was a struggle to maintain Pakistan and India as secular states, which increasingly affected the original objectives of the legislation on religious offences. Amid such conflicts, India gradually revised the original application of religious offences by the promulgation of the Conversion Act, and Pakistan took a significant direction in Islamizing its constitution which affected its ability to deal equitably with all religious communities. In post-1947 Pakistan, animosity between Hindus and Muslims dropped, despite around 20 percent of East Pakistan's population remaining Hindu; however, in West Pakistan tension between Ahmadis and Muslims rose, which affected religious offences.

Post-1980s is the era that shows how the entire application of the legislation on religious offences was changed. Since the law of blasphemy had been applied it annulled the earlier British Religious Offences legislation. The blasphemy law appears to be applied in contexts which may seem beyond the religious reach even of Islam. The major aim of this research is to study what is commonly called the law of blasphemy, the historical and legal frame of this law in Pakistan, and the application of the law. It is necessary to see whether all religious groups are equal and safe before the state law and how they are protected under the law of blasphemy. If they are not, and the hypothesis is that they are not, the thesis will examine who suffers under this law and how judicial, political and religious communities struggle to deal with religious prosecutions.

Thus the main argument of this thesis is to describe, discuss and analyze historical claims to toleration and protection of communities from religious motivated offences and violence, seeing how they gradually shifted from one political authority to another with different understanding and application of religious offences. Such shifts show how religion became a political slogan for authorities and how it changed the pattern of everyday living within and between communities, still current in Pakistan today. All of the concerns regarding the law of blasphemy, especially its historic and gradual evolution at the hands of different governing officials and protesters, require exploration and discussion on a broad front.

Approaches and Methodology of the Research

The thesis has achieved its goal through field research including archives, library, personal interviews and the collection of various legal reports and case studies. First, the primary source material on the British promulgation of the Indian Penal Code of 1860 and its objectives were viewed and used from the Bodleian Law Library of Oxford University, Edinburgh University Law Library, National Library of Scotland, and the British Library, London, which specifically contains sources, documents, archives, and banned books belonging to British India.

Second, the post-colonial application of the religious offences in India and Pakistan falls into six different categories:

1) To discuss the experience of East and West Pakistan's dealing with religious offences, some commentaries on Pakistan Penal Code, the historical Munir Report: *Report of the Court Inquiry Constituted under Punjab Act 11 of 1954 to Enquire into the Punjab Disturbances of 1953,* and other cases studies have been

used from Lahore High Court library.
2) Various reports and books published by Christian and Muslim organizations especially Human Rights Commission and National Council of Justice and Peace, written on the contemporary implication of the law were collected during my field research in Pakistan.
3) Some modern sources (Ahmad, Nasr, Mailk, Musk, Jalal, Lau, Zaman available at the University of Edinburgh) have also been utilized to discuss the period of Islamizing Pakistan. Contemporary scholarship on religious freedom of speech and blasphemy has been used from the main library of Edinburgh University and New College Library.
4) Pakistani newspapers: *Dawn, The News, The Daily Times* and *Nawa-e-Wakt* have also been utilized.
5) Online sources such as the *Encyclopaedia of Islam and Quran* (Brill Online) and information about the contemporary issues from the Jinnah Institute (www.jinnah-institute.org) and the Ahmadi website (www.thepersecution.org) have been used.
6) Various articles from journals such as *Almushir, South Asian History, Journal of Islamic Law and Culture, Indian Church History Review, American Centre for Law and Justice, Harvard Human Rights Journal, Rutgers Journal of Law & Religion, Law & Contemporary Problems, International Journal of Middle East Studies, Asian Survey, The Journal of Social Studies, Connecticut Journal of International Law,* and *The Christian Century* have been used.

The Structure of the Thesis

This thesis on Chapter XV: Of Offences Relating to Religion, presented in six chapters, has been divided in three historical parts covering the different periods. The first part discusses the law's origin, early amendments, development and application of Chapter XV in the era when the country was under British rule. The second part notes the adaptation and application of Chapter XV after 1947 in the Independent Subcontinent (India and Pakistan). The third part of the thesis discusses the amendments to, and changes in, the legislation on Offences Relating to Religion made from the 1980s and their implications for contemporary Pakistan.

The Division of Chapters

The first part of the thesis explores how the British dealt with the multi-religious background and religious conflicts of the Indian subcontinent. The first chapter discusses why this law, Chapter XV, was able to take root and was promulgated in the subcontinent with its essential objective of bringing tolerance and protection from religiously motivated insult and violence. The chapter shows various legal interpretations and case studies to explain the context of the legal procedure of religious prosecution under this law. The second chapter discusses the continuing religious issues particularly affecting the mode of prosecution expressed in religiously offensive "speech and publications" which became a religious, political and social threat to the colonial power. The chapter investigates how such religious conflict led the British to modify the law and shows how they attempted to use religious offences for their colonial advantages. The tendency of top-down control rather than support of the vulnerable, implicit in these modifications and actual prosecutions, remained after independence in the subcontinent in general and in Pakistan in particular: but it began under the British.

The third chapter gives a short review of Pakistan's and India's initial independent status, adopting religious offences laws and freedom of expression with the major aim of protecting all religious communities. However, both countries had difficulty in maintaining full secularism with consequent religious neutrality. The Conversion Act of 1950 affected religious offences in India, and the Islamic political and religious policies of Pakistan not only affected the relationship between the East and West wings of Pakistan but also affected the early application of religious offences intended to protect all religious communities. Having set out the common heritage in 1947, the chapter explains in some detail the evolution of India, and of West and East Pakistan.

The fourth chapter specifically examines religious offences and their application from 1947 to 1976 in Pakistan. It discusses the gradual procedure of Islamizing the constitution of Pakistan in which the goal of maintaining a common national identity among all religious communities was lost. It focuses on the limited application of Chapter XV, of the religious offences law, pointing out that on the one hand the Pakistan judicial system successfully protected some Christians and Muslims accused under religious offences laws, but on the other hand the application of these same laws became controversial as they were used to restrict rather than protect the very vulnerable Ahmadis. The process by which Ahmadi-Muslim conflicts became political protests, which later played an important part in changing the constitution of Pakistan, will be laid out. In describing this change, the chapter reconsiders the core question of just what priorities the Muslim *ulama*, Islamic religious parties and leaders and government strategies were seeking to fulfil, which led to the radical alteration in the religious offences law.

The fifth chapter aims to explore the Islamic revolution of Islamic law from 1977 to 1986 and the introduction of the blasphemy laws in the constitution of Pakistan. It mainly focuses on the presidency of Zia-ul-Haq (1977–1987), when both the intentions of the blasphemy law and its penalties were significantly altered in Pakistan. The chapter particularly discusses the category of blasphemy against the Prophet Muhammad, (*Sabb al-Nabi* or *Qanoon-e-Toheen-e-Rasalat*, section 295-C) which prescribes a mandatory death sentence and fine for the accused, whether Muslim or non-Muslim, even when the offence in speech or publication was unintentional. The lesser charge of blasphemy against the Qur'an, usually attached to defiling or damaging a copy of the Qur'an (*Qanoon-e-Toheen-e-Quran*, section 295-B), which prescribes life imprisonment, is also disscussed. The implications of the blasphemy law will be discussed with some of the experiences of those who suffered, were imprisoned or prosecuted under it. The chapter examines how such changes in the religious offences have brought a different application of the law and how what can be seen as the procedural failure of Pakistan's legal system, given the absence of an independent judiciary, leads religious communities, particularly minorities, to suffer grievously under the law of blasphemy.

The sixth chapter shows the struggle and protest over the protection of religious communities and people alleged to have committed blasphemy, which has become a question of life and death in Pakistan. The issue of blasphemy has been greatly disputed among political officials and religious groups after Zia-ul-Haq's death and it remains a critical issue which has a deep impact on the community of Pakistan. The chapter discusses various political authorities, Muslims and non-Muslims, lawyers and religious groups, who have been appealing to make possible changes in the law but nothing has been done to protect the communities. One of the continuing struggles is how, on the one hand some are concerned with the critical application of the law which they wish to review and revise, and on the other are people who wish to protect the sanctity of the Prophet and of Islam. Officials, caught between the two and recognising the political and the brute strength of the latter group, do not try to change the law, either from fear that they, as others who have tried, will be killed, or because they are anxious not to be seen to oppose tenets of their own faith.

The conclusion indicates just how religious and political interests have historically changed the direction of Pakistan and the application of the legislation on religious offences. The politically powerful class now seems powerless to bring any further changes if it also wishes to protect its own political interest and power, and can be pressured by the mob, incited some time ago to lead historical protest and is now capable of bringing extra-judicial declarations, violence and lynching. Amid such conflict, and with little capacity to control the law and its misuse, all full citizens of Pakistan will continue to suffer, as Pakistan faces religious anarchy and fanaticism. Would that the pre-1920s version of Chapter XV was still in operation!

Part I

Origin, Development and Application of the Legislation on Offences Relating to Religion in the Indian Subcontinent

CHAPTER 1

The Legislation on Religious Offences of the Indian Penal Code

The Offences Relating to Religion, Chapter XV is one of the criminal codes of India, Pakistan and Bangladesh which was intended to prevent and control religiously motivated violence and in this has arguably been successful for much of its existence. It pre-dates the creation of these countries (1860–1947), coming from the Indian Penal Code (IPC) of 1860 when the sub-continent was under military rule by the British during the colonial period.[1] It was the period when the British regarded punishing crimes and maintaining law and order as the responsibility of the state, as proposed by Macaulay[2] who believed that no country ever stood in such need of a law as India.[3] Dealing with religious offences under the Penal Code was one of the significant strategies of the British law enforcers who claimed that "there is perhaps no country in which the government has so much to apprehend from religious excitement among the people."[4]

---

1. The Indian Penal Code was not only applied in 1860 in India but was later applied and reproduced in most other British Colonies and to date many of these laws are still in practice in places as far apart as India, Pakistan, Bangladesh, Sri Lanka, Nigeria and Zimbabwe. K. D. Gaur, *The Textbook on the Indian Penal Code*, 4th ed. (New Delhi: Universal Law Publishing, 2009), 7; Gour, *Penal Law of India*, 14–15.

2. In 1834 the first Law Commission of India was constituted with T. B. Macaulay as its president and Macleod, Anderson and Millet as commissioners to prepare the Indian Penal Code. Macaulay and his companions derived assistance for the construction of IPC from the French Code and from the decisions of the French Courts of Justice and the Code of Louisiana, prepared by Livingston. Macaulay, et al., *Indian Penal Code*, x.

3. Thomas B. Macaulay in Hamilton, *Indian Penal Code*, x; Macaulay, *Complete Works*, 139.

4. Macaulay, et al., *Indian Penal Code*, 409; Hamilton, *Indian Penal Code*, 285.

To keep religious harmony and tolerance, Chapter XV: Of Offences Relating to Religion, of the Indian Penal Code was able to take root in the Indian subcontinent and become a significant piece of legislation. Chapter XV has been constantly tested, amended and criticized at different instances by lawmakers as well as enforcers for much of the period and with varying intensity. For example, it was criticized before and after the initial application of this law and the new amendments to it, during the colonial period between 1837 and 1858. One of the major areas of discussion of Part 1 is how judicial and political forces came together to bring about significant changes and amendments to the law. Before discussing this, however, we must review what kind of religious issues appeared to be the problem that the promulgation of Chapter XV was designed to alleviate, and what was the distinctive understanding and objective of British law enforcers to protect all religious communities of the Indian subcontinent.

Overall, with regard to the Offences Relating to Religion for India, it seems the Legislature, in enacting Chapter XV of IPC, intended to ensure religious freedom and "to punish, in a country populated by persons of widely different religions, deliberate acts or offences perpetrated by persons of religious persuasion."[5] However, the potential for clashes among religious traditions meant the role of the foreign government was not an easy task. The British government observed with concern religious tensions and contradictions among various religions in the subcontinent. Addressing religious issues was not new for the British Empire as "Christianity is part and parcel of the law of the land [England]."[6] Various religious offences known as blasphemy were included in the law to protect Christianity. For instance, according to the (English) Christian Blasphemy Act 1679, it was a crime for any Christian to deny publicly that Christianity is true or deny publicly the scriptures to be of divine authority.[7] For the British, offences relating to writing and publication were statutes restricting objectionable

---

5. R. A. Nelson, *The Indian Penal Code*, vol. 2 (Lahore: Law Publication, 1970), 1358.

6. The phrase that Christianity is "part and parcel" of the law apparently means that as a great part of the securities of the legal system consists of judicial and official oaths sworn upon the Gospels, Christianity is inextricably interwoven with the law. Hamilton, *Indian Penal Code*, 284.

7. S. Sharifuddin Pirzada, *Fundamental Rights and Constitutional Remedies in Pakistan* (Lahore: All Pakistan Legal Decisions, 1966), 316.

material about religion which had long been part of English Common Law. Blasphemous writing as a category was developed by judges there between 1676 and 1922 to prevent anti-Christian writing and speech in Britain.[8]

A review of this legislation suggests that the sections of the Chapter XV: Of Offences Relating to Religion of the Indian Penal Code follow the intention of English law. For example, most of the religious statutes of English law were aimed at preventing disturbances in worship and church, disturbing the congregation, assaulting Christian ministers, breaking church windows or laying violent hands on a consecrated place, and that can also be seen in the Indian legislation on Offences Relating to Religion.[9] These issues will be mentioned in the discussion of the various sections of Chapter XV later in this chapter. The legislature, in enacting Chapter XV, apparently had it in view that most of these English statutes deal with the offences against the established church, and offences against religious peace. They further note that: "for obvious reason the Indian religious offences in the Penal Code has no provision regarding offences against Christianity or against the church and the few sections in this chapter are directed against certain acts which are most likely to excite people to commit a riot or other breach of peace."[10]

Given that religious offence may be regarded as a serious crime within one religion, the practicalities become more complex and critical when multi-faith communities are encountered. Before passing the religious offences section of the Indian code, law enforcers viewed the different kinds of insults that could happen in the religious communities of the subcontinent. Consideration of minority and majority status as well as the supposed superiority and inferiority of different religions and different classes and castes

---

8. There were several cases regarding writing deemed blasphemous in Britain. For example, Thomas Woolston was prosecuted for writing the book, *Six Discourses on the Miracles*, in which he denied the miracles and was imprisoned in 1728 until he died in 1733. In 1763 Peter Annet was prosecuted and imprisoned for writing a magazine, *The Free Inquirer*, which denied the Pentateuch. In 1792 Thomas Paine was prosecuted and exiled for writing the book, *The Age of Reason* but his influence remained substantial in the country, where new editions of his book were published and prosecuted, Thomas William being so prosecuted in 1797, Daniel Eaton for publishing the third edition and prosecuted, imprisoned for eighteen months and pilloried in 1812. Nicolas Walter, *Blasphemy in Britain: The Practice and Punishment of Blasphemy, and the Trial of Gay News* (London: Rationalist Press Association, 1977), 1–2; Hamilton, *Indian Penal Code*, 284.

9. J. W. Cecil Turner, *Russell on Crime*, vol. 2 (London: Stevens, 1964), 1519–1529.

10. Hamilton, *Indian Penal Code*, 283; Lal, *Indian Penal Code*, 1323.

could be one reason to insult another religion, especially if the discussion went into religious matters and claims of its sole truth and assertion that others were untrue or false. This point is made in the review report by Macaulay:

> The question whether insults offered to a religion ought to be visited with punishment, does not appear to us at all to depend on the question whether that religion be true, or false. The religion may be false but the pain which such insults give to the professors of that religion is real. It is often, as the most superficial observation may convince us, as real a pain, and as acute a pain as is caused by almost any offence against the person, against property, or against character. Nor is there any compensating good whatsoever to be set off against this pain. Discussion, indeed, tends to elicit truth. But insults have no such tendency. They can be employed just as easily against the purest faith as against the most monstrous superstition. It is easier to argue against falsehood than against truth. But it is as easy to pull down or defile the temples of truth as those of falsehood. It is as easy to molest with ribaldry and clamour men assembled for purposes of pious and rational worship, as men engaged in the most absurd ceremonies. Such insults, when directed against erroneous opinions, seldom have any other effect than to fix those opinions deeper, and to give a character of peculiar ferocity to theological dissension. Instead of eliciting truth they only inflame fanaticism.[11]

It was debated that religious encounter is sensitive and significantly it was suggested that the consequences of an insult could turn into violence, which may have led to the classifying of religious offences, which was intended to respect the religious susceptibilities of persons of different religious beliefs. For example, it was discussed in the early report on the law that British Christians are numerically a very small minority of the Indian population possessing the high government posts and "under their rule are placed millions of Mahomedans, of different sects . . . strongly attached to the fundamental articles . . . [and] creeds, and millions of Hindus strongly

---

11. Macaulay, et al., *Indian Penal Code*, 136; Macaulay, *Penal Code Prepared*, 49.

The Legislation on Religious Offences of the Indian Penal Code   31

attached to doctrines and rites."[12] Contradictions accrued where religious communities followed different doctrines and beliefs as well as different practices of rituals. Following different beliefs derives from the holding of distinct understanding, as where a religion such as Christianity proclaims that Jesus is the only way of salvation and invites others to embrace it. However, contest also arises not only through holding different beliefs but also through sharing some apparently similar beliefs differently understood. For example, in Islam, anyone who believes in God, the prophets of God, Gospel, final judgment and angels is counted a believer. However, conflict may exist when Muslims realize that Christians regard Christ as the son of God, which Muslims see as the sin of polytheism (*shirk*), associating partners with God or giving his characteristics to others beside him. Not only do conflicts of beliefs bring critical discussion but conflict is also significantly linked with religious conversion, the religious duty of the two main monotheistic religions in South Asia, Islam and Christianity, which will be discussed later in this chapter.

This research evidences the fact that religious rituals and practices remained critical sources of accusation and it was to control such issues that the British applied Chapter XV of religious offences. For example, some riots occurred and intensified Hindu-Muslim relations when it was observed that practising different rituals such as slaughtering a cow and playing music of religious communities were contested and critical issues, especially where it is a sacred act for Muslims to sacrifice a cow, which is intolerable to Hindus who worship the cow. Likewise music and singing disturbs Muslim worship but is a sacred practice of Hindus and Christians who use these elements during their worship. Such issues led some of both communities to disgrace and damage the others' places of worship, some accusations of which will be set out below.

Likewise, places of worship were also vulnerable to damage where it was observed that building a certain mosque or temple had violated the sacredness of a certain religion. For example, one of the riots which occurred in

---

12. The First Report in Macaulay, *Indian Penal Code*, 409; The word Muhammadan, introduced by European scholars and lawyers, was a convenient expression for Muslims as well as Islamic Civil Law known as Muhammadan Law. Fyzee, *Outlines of Muhammadan Law*, 37; Jain, *Outlines of Indian Legal History*, 660–667.

Banaras in 1809, on the issue of defiling the place of worship, when it was observed that a mosque was built by Aurangzeb in sight of the old Hindu temple. In this conflict about fifty mosques were destroyed and hundreds of people lost their lives.[13] The intensity of such practices was present before the application of Chapter XV which was intended to deal with the practice of different cases of the religious communities, as the authors noted:

> ... No offence in the whole Code is so likely to lead to tumult, to sanguinary outrage, and even to armed insurrection. The slaughter of a cow in a sacred place at Banaras in 1809 caused violent tumult, attended with considerable loss of life. The population of a mosque at Bangalore was attended with consequences still more lamentable and alarming. We have therefore empowered the Courts in cases of this description, to pass a very severe sentence on the offender.[14]

Though various religious rituals, practices and controversies were already present before the enforcement of Chapter XV: Of Offences Relating to Religion in British India, later performances of such rituals can be clearly linked to political and religious animosity among religious communities, discussed later in the chapter. Therefore based on these principles and discussions, the law enforcers declared that "such a state of things is pregnant with dangers which can only be averted by a firm adherence to the true principles of toleration."[15] According to Macaulay, controlling conflict among religious communities was the principal aim of Chapter XV of religious offences, which declared:

> The principle on which this chapter has been framed is a principle on which it would be desirable that all Governments should act, but from which the British Government in India

---

13. N. C. Saxena, "The Nature and Origin of Communal Riots in India," in *Communal Riots in Post-Independence India*, 2nd ed., ed. Asghar Ali Engineer (Hyderabad: Sangam Books, 1991), 51; Gyanendra Pandey, "The Colonial Construction of Communalism," in *Writings on South Asian History*, Subaltern Studies vol. 6, ed. Ranajit Guha (Delhi: Oxford University Press, 1994), 132–169.

14. It was said in note J being the note on revision on "the chapter of offences relating to the religion and caste" before the application of the law. Macaulay, *Penal Code Prepared*, 49–50.

15. Macaulay, 49.

cannot depart without risking the dissolutions [*sic*] of society. It is this, that every man should be suffered to profess his own religion, and that no man should be suffered to insult the religion of another.[16]

It can be said that an early concern of the enforcers of the law was to bring religious tolerance to all communities and to punish acts such as insulting another religion that could endanger public tranquillity, which was a major concern of the law. Generally this principle required every person to be liable to punishment without distinction of nation, rank, caste and faith provided the offence had been committed in British India.[17] Despite declaring the general objective of Chapter XV fairly swiftly, editing and criticism continued to be concerned with whether the structure and the categories listed under Chapter XV would be flexible enough to cover all possible conditions of religious crimes and laws in the Indian subcontinent. There was a long delay (1837–1860) in passing it into law as the British Indian Government was concerned over uniformity and diversity in all issues relevant in an Indian context.[18] The criticisms and amendments of the chapter during this pre-promulgation period will now be discussed.

1.1 The Primary Amendments in Chapter XV in British India

Some caste practices were considered to include religious crimes which could be taken under the law. The original title of Chapter XV of IPC was "Offences Relating to Religion and Caste" which included eight sections and punishments.[19] In framing the caste practices Macaulay claimed that though the Hindu caste system was rooted and practised in India, where actions which would otherwise be considered criminal were based on caste traditions and practices, they were not an offence in any part of India. The

---

16. The first and second report of the Indian Penal Code quoted in Macaulay, *Indian Penal Code*, 136, 409.
17. Ratanlal Ranchhoddas and Dhirajlal Keshavlal Thakor, *The Indian Penal Code*, 20th ed. (Bombay: Bombay Law Reporter Office, 1951), 1–13.
18. Macaulay in Clive, *Thomas Babington Macaulay*, 426.
19. Sections: 275, 276, 278, 280, 282, 283, 284, and 285 were included in the original chapter of the law. Macaulay, *Indian Penal Code*, 48–50.

Hindu caste system is a wide subject beyond the present brief, but it is relevant to review some caste customs to which the British objected or which they saw as discriminatory which were initially included but then omitted from Chapter XV.

Macaulay added section 283 in Chapter XV, punishing caste practices such as *dhurna*, a method of obtaining justice such as the payment of a debt, by sitting and fasting before the door of the Charan person from whom reparation is sought, or even killing a child or adult. Another caste practice, *traga*, was included which is self-immolation and the self-shedding of blood to enforce demands, practised by the Bards (the high class poets or writers) and castes. There had long prevailed in India the practice of hiring a person of a particular religious caste to threaten to injure himself unless redress is given. Any person who practises this would have committed a religious crime under section 283.[20] J. Awdry, one of the British critics of the law, suggested that section 283 related to these practices, is ". . . likely to suggest modes of annoyance to persons of adverse sects against each other."[21] M. Lewin observed that the punishment of such caste practices as *dhurna* or *traga* "should not be made to depend on the name of the Deity being invoked, or should any absurd alarm or belief be held to excuse an act in itself wrong."[22] Both critics advised omitting section 283 from the chapter as they were adequately dealt with elsewhere in the chapter.[23]

The use of food to create conflict was included in sections 284 and 285, the former making it a religious offence to intentionally cause anyone to lose caste by eating food polluted by those of a lower caste[24] and the latter making it an offence intentionally to cause food belonging to any person to be in a

---

20. Macaulay, *Indian Penal Code*, 49, 137.
21. J. Awdry in Macaulay, 415.
22. M. Lewin in Macaulay, 415.
23. M. Lewin in Macaulay.
24. The full version of section 284 is:
    Whoever with the intention of causing any person to lose cast, commits any assault which causes that person to lose cast, or induces that person to do ignorantly anything whereby that person incurs loss of cast, shall be punished with imprisonment of either description for a term which may extend to six months, or fine which may extend to two thousand rupees, or both.
Macaulay, *Indian Penal Code*, 49–50.

state in which that person cannot use it as food.[25] Macaulay made clear that this was especially crucial for the high caste Brahmins, if lower castes intentionally mixed beef in food, causing the former to lose caste. He argued that intentionally depriving a Hindu of his caste by assault or by deception was not an offence in any part of India, and proposed to make this "an offence, but not to deal with it severely."[26] It was argued by the reviewing committee that caste and what constitutes the loss of it should be clearly defined and fully explained in the legislation on religious offences. J. F. Thomas suggested that losing caste could be dealt with in the religious sphere. For example, Brahmins had a remedy in civil action to recover the amount necessary to procure the indemnification for temporary loss if someone intentionally added meat to their food. Apart from these suggestions it was also observed that the section would only uphold the Brahmins' privilege of caste, high castes being able to misuse such a law by accusing lower castes without a genuine religious offence being committed.[27] Eventually, all sections relating to caste, including in the chapter title, were omitted, and it was limited to four sections on Offences Relating to Religion and passed into Law in 1860 throughout India.

Even though all caste sections were removed from the chapter, there were however some cases where lower castes were accused of offending high castes which were brought under the legislation on Offences Relating to Religion in British India, an issue which will be seen later in the chapter. It is also important to note that this is a legacy that has remained for religious ethnic groups who, for example, converted to Christianity but remained lower class and untouchable: in some cases they are still being accused of committing a religious offence which can be seen in a few such cases taken as religious offences under Chapter XV. It is now necessary to consider just which offences could be prosecuted as religious offences in Chapter XV of IPC in British India.

---

25. The full version of section 285 is: "Whoever intentionally causes any food belonging to any person to be in a state in which that person, according to the rules of his religion or cast, cannot use it as food, shall be punished with fine which may extend to fifty rupees." Macaulay, *Indian Penal Code*, 50

26. Macaulay, 50, 137.

27. Macaulay.

1.2 Chapter XV of 1860

In the final edited Chapter XV of 1860, injuring or defiling a place of worship with intention (section 295), disturbing a religious assembly (section 296), trespassing on a place of worship and graveyard (section 297), uttering words or making gestures with intent to wound religious feelings (section 298) were among the offences so defined. For British law enforcers, the edited Chapter XV covered all possible conditions and contested actions relating to religion which, when promulgated, would be enough to maintain the major objective of bringing tolerance among all religious communities in the Indian subcontinent. It was certainly a hard aim to put into practice, as indicated by long and frequent juridical discourses which both criticized and insisted on the difficulty of deciding how the legislation on religious offences was to be applied in specific conditions and cases. Despite the problems, there was no major change in the edited Chapter XV from 1860 till 1927, although during this period various "rules and regulations" were declared to clarify the context of the law, such as what kind of "intention" could be accepted to prosecute certain religious offences, discussed below, after the different sections of Chapter XV were applied in British India.

1.3 Section 295 to Protect the Places and Objects of Worship

This section makes punishable acts of destruction, damage or defilement committed by anyone, even if the person is a worshiper of the sacred place which they have defiled. Originally the punishment for defiling places was seven years imprisonment but was later reduced to two years.[28] This section is similar to the English law that protects church property and its surroundings from damage or theft of the property belonging to the church.[29] According to Russell the law related to:

> Affrays in a church or churchyard have always been esteemed very heinous offences, as being very great indignities to the

---

28. Macaulay, 48.

29. R. H. Helmholz, *The Oxford History of the Laws of England*, vol. 1, *The Canon Law and Ecclesiastical Jurisdiction from 597 to the 1640s* (Oxford: Oxford University Press, 2004), 494–498.

Divine Majesty, to whose worship and service such places are immediately dedicated; and upon this consideration all irreverent behaviour in these places has been esteemed criminal by the makers of our laws. Several statutes have been passed for the purpose of preventing disturbances in places of worship belonging to the Established Church[30]

The objective of the English Blasphemy Law was to protect Christian sacred places and churches, but the religious offences in the British Indian subcontinent, especially section 295, had a broader application used to protect sacred places or objects such as churches, mosques, temples and sacred tombs, and signs or figures representing gods.[31]

Section 295 of IPC requires two things for a prosecution. First, there must have been some destruction, damage or defilement to a place or worship or object held sacred, including inanimate objects such as idols in Hindu temples or in churches or the like, and animate objects such as cows or bulls.[32] Second, such destruction must have been done with the intention to insult and with the knowledge that a person is likely to consider such destruction as an insult to religion in that place.[33] Both points will be discussed in detail in the following sections.

1.3.1 The Accusation of Defiling a Place or Object of Worship

Continuing the discussion of the first requirement of section 295, mentioned above, it is necessary to explore what kind of destruction, damage or defilement counted for an accusation to be taken seriously. The words "destroy" and "damage" mainly indicate material objects and acts which are designed to cause a particular result. It was held by Muthuswami Airye that the word "defile" has a broader meaning that does not only mean to make a sacred place unclean or dirty but to render a place or an object ceremonially or ritually impure.[34] For the accusation under section 295 the place or object

---

30. Turner, *Russell on Crime*, 1766.
31. Ranchhoddas and Thakor, *Indian Penal Code*, 224.
32. Gour, *Penal Law of India*, 2178.
33. Nelson, *Indian Penal Code*, 1361.
34. Nelson, 1362.

must be sacred. Here the meaning of the sacredness of "place" and sacredness of "object" is different and cannot be merged.

1.3.2 The Meaning of a Sacred Place of Worship

Considering the sacredness of place, common examples of such sacred places are mosques, churches, or temples, but in addition to these other designated places may be considered sacred. A case lacking proof of a "sacred place" cannot be brought under this section. If people consider any other place sacred, the place must have been consecrated for worship or for some sacred ritual. For example, Hindus, apart from having properly built temples, consecrate some places by placing a stone painted with ochre to mark the spot and also regard the water of the Rivers Ganga and Narbada as sacred. There are many other local places that can be considered sacred but in all such cases the prosecutor must have proof that the "defiled" place was actually held sacred. Considering this issue, Hari Singh Gour notes one of the cases under section 295, when after having a quarrel with a relative in 1898 the accused threw cooked food (fish, fowl and rice) into a well. He was convicted under section 295 of IPC for desecrating the sacredness of the well but that case was annulled on appeal as no evidence was found that the well was a sacred place or object.[35]

In the case of Islamic sacred places, apart from mosques, certain Muslims fly a green flag from places such as tombs called *dargahs* or burial grounds which they regard as objects of veneration. Such places could be as sacred as a mosque, clearly a place of worship, if a declaration of *waqf* has been made in *Shari'a* law, which blocks off a property and allows the revenue from that particular area to be used for the cause of Allah or worship.[36] For example, one of the cases which occurred in the colonial era was made by the few Muslims of Kujra North India in 1941 regarding a hut used for prayers without the permission from the landlord. It was declared that the use of any place like that hut for public call to prayers, called *azan*, could not be converted into a place of worship or object as contemplated by section 295. It was also held that the owner of that hut had a right to allow either

---

35. Gour, *Penal Law of India*, 2180.
36. R. D. McChesney, *Waqf in Central Asia: Four Hundred Years in the History of a Muslim Shrine 1480-1889* (Princeton: Princeton University Press, 1991); Syed Ameer Ali, *Muhammadan Law*, vol. 1 (Calcutta: Thacker, Spink & Co., 1917), 201–202.

Muslims or Hindus to use the hut as a place of worship but if the owner had not dedicated such place for worship, it could not be said that the place had been consecrated for the public worship. Therefore no one can be convicted for insulting the sacred place when there is no evidence to show that such place was an accepted place of worship.[37]

The reason for the accusation as described in the above cases shows the misreading or misuse of the context where "dishonouring places of worship" has been raised. Notably most of the cases like this were said not to show a genuine religious offence even though courts had clearly discussed the context and dismissed the case. It can also be seen that courts review the background of the cases: Hindu-Muslim tension based on religious differences, for example, was one of the major causes of bringing accusation, such as where the hut had been used as a place of worship. The court significantly examined and dismissed the case in which Hindus of that community had become apprehensive that the hut might be converted into a mosque and second, the more serious historical issue where the Hindu community of Kujra was concerned that the slaughter of the cow might have violated the Hindu belief. It is for this reason that special care was taken to clarify the term sacred object in each case within the meaning of section 295 of IPC.

1.3.3 The Meaning of a Sacred Object

There are different explanations of the meaning of the word "object." According to the Calcutta High Court, the term "sacred object" means "something with an object of worship, such as an idol or a picture, something that is capable of destruction in the sense in which that word is ordinarily used, or of damage or defilement."[38] For instance, custom ordains that an untouchable whose touch, in the opinion of Hindu belief, is impure should not enter the enclosure surrounding the shrine of any Hindu god: any untouchable with the knowledge of this belief who deliberately enters temples and defiles sacred objects commits an offence and can be prosecuted under section 295.[39] One example is a Hindu temple practice in which persons

---

37. Bechan Jha v. Emperor, AIR (1941) Patna, 492; similar judgement was also passed in1886 in Ratna Mudali, ILR (Indian Law Reports) 10 Madras 126.

38. Lal, *Indian Penal Code*, 1324; Nelson, *Indian Penal Code*, 1363.

39. Atma Ram v. Emperor, (1924) 25 Cr. LJ 155 in Lal, *Indian Penal Code*, 1325; M. H. Nizami, *Supplement to Commentary on the Pakistan Penal Code* (Karachi: Law Book

especially appointed for the purpose and observing set rules touch the idol or pour coconut water on it (*abishkam*). Anyone who performs the *abishkam* deliberately with the object of openly ridiculing the established rule can be convicted under section 295.[40]

Apart from including the rituals as an object, it was debated whether animals such as bulls or cows, sacred animals according to Hindu faith, constitute "objects" under section 295 of IPC. The High Court of Allahabad and the High Court of Calcutta held that the word "object" in the section 295 includes inanimate objects such as sacred places and rituals but does not include animate objects like cows and bulls. The argument was discussed in a case in which Imam Ali and Amiruddin were convicted by the magistrate of Shahjahanpur under section 295. They were prosecuted for killing a cow on 30 August 1887, at Tilhar municipality, Muazampur Street on the side of the public highway. The magistrate found that they knew well that the killing of the cow was considered an insult by Hindus who consider it a sacred object, and he fined them Rs 25 each. The case was appealed and the sole question was whether the word "object" could be extended to animate objects such as priests, cows, bulls or any other objects that are sacred in the sacred place of worship.[41]

The Chief Court of Punjab held the meaning and usage of the word "object" of section 295 was not limited to inanimate objects, and was wide enough to include animate objects like cows or bulls.[42] But like the sacred place, the object has to be sacred and should be worshiped or capable of so being, the decision being made carefully by the courts, and a distinction made between objects that, on one hand, can be sacred and on the other, ones which are merely venerated while not being sacred. For instance, a tomb of a Muslim saint is an object of veneration but it is not a sacred object unless it shows evidence of consecration and is so used by Muslim worshippers.[43] J. Brandt observed:

House, 1954), 214.

40. Lal, *Indian Penal Code*, 1325.
41. Imam Ali and others v. Queen Empress (1887) ILR Allahabad, 152.
42. Hakim v. Emperor 1884 P. R. 27 quoted in Nelson, *Indian Penal Code*, 1363.
43. Ratna Mudali, ILR 10 Madras 126.

There is a distinction, not arbitrary, between objects which are objects of respect and even veneration and objects which are held sacred; as an example of the former, I may refer to a sepulchre . . . as distinguished from a place of worship to the deity, or where an idol; or altar is kept; and such distinction appears to have been kept in view by the Legislature, for while section 295 deals with the latter class of objects and places.[44]

The mere defilement or destruction of a sacred place or object which was clarified by courts is not an offence under the section 295. In order to sustain a conviction, there must be an *intention* of thereby insulting which is the most important component of this section. Notably, all religious communities are entitled to be punished according to the nature and intention of the offence. Intention includes the mental capacity and knowledge to insult through such an act and, separately or at the same time, through words uttered, gestures assumed, threats given or the determination expressed.[45] Legal action cannot be taken to punish an accused unless and until the status of intention is clear.

1.3.4 The Meaning of "Intention" of Section 295

Before any conviction can be secured under section 295, the "intention of insulting" a religious place or object must be clear.[46] For the act must be intended to cause, or knowingly be likely to cause, wrongful loss or damage to any person by injuring any property, whether it belongs to that person or not.[47] For example, a case brought under section 295 was rejected on the grounds that the appellant was not aware that removing some materials from a small old disused fallen-down building would hurt the feelings of Muslims.[48] Likewise, the *Sheo Shankar* appeal was allowed, in which the high-caste accused had destroyed a sacred thread worn by a *Sudra*, a lower caste of Hindus. The accused was judged not to have insulted Hindu religion

---

44. J. Brandt in Ratna Madali, ILR 10 Madras, 127–128.
45. Nelson, *Indian Penal Code*, 2178.
46. Morgan and Macpherson, *Indian Penal Code*, 218.
47. That has been explained in section 425 of India Penal Code of 1860.
48. Jan Muhammad v. Narain Das, (1883) AWN 39 in Gour, *Penal Law of India*, 2178; Nelson, *Indian Penal Code*, 1364.

because in the court's view *Ahria* and *Sudra* castes are not entitled to wear it, wearing it is not a part of their religion and as such destroying a thread worn by them in assertion of a mere claim to a rank could not amount to an insult to their religion. However, the court stated that if a Muslim, Christian or atheist tore off the sacred thread worn by a Hindu who was entitled to wear it, this would be likely to be considered as a disrespectful insult and thus an offence against the Hindu religion dealt with by section 295 of IPC. The court observed that the matter was not truly a religious matter for the plaintiff but rather an injury to his dignity and status as a high caste Hindu. Therefore a conviction under section 295 of IPC was dismissed.[49]

In the first instance, certain acts cannot be prosecuted where the intention of insulting the sacred place or object is not involved. Second, certain acts may offend another religious community but cannot be regarded as a religious offence because of the other's having religious legal rights. For example, there are many cases where Muslims slaughtering cows, sheep and goats were looked down on by Hindus who insisted that any cow slaughter was intolerable to them and causing them to riot, yet Muslims insisted upon their right to sacrifice cows.[50] It is significant to note that the claim of protecting or sacrificing the cow was one of the critical issues which became a political icon for Hindus in their conflicts with Muslims. Muslims fought successfully to have their religious freedom ritually to sacrifice a cow.[51] Yet while the legal right to sacrifice existed, this was voided when Muslims deliberately and intentionally offended Hindus by actions surrounding the slaughter, the moral obligation not intentionally to insult applying. For such acts, specific rules and regulations of sacrificing were added to the Code of Criminal Procedure: cows should be slaughtered in the slaughter house, any procession or parades of sacrificial and decorated animals indicating impending slaughter was prohibited, and any exhibiting of the flesh was prohibited, unless covered. All these rules were declared to control outrageous intention which "hurt the feelings of others [Hindus]."[52]

---

49. Sheo Shankar v. Emperor, AIR (1940) Oudh 348.
50. Thursby, *Hindu-Muslim Relations*, 102–108.
51. Thursby, 78–79.
52. Rules and regulations were issued under section 144 of the Code of Criminal Procedure which gives the power to issue order in urgent cases of nuisance of apprehended

In such regulations any Muslim who killed a cow in the presence of other Muslims, not in the slaughter house, only to use its meat and skin, cannot be accused of religious offence under section 295, although had it been done intentionally in front of Hindus, especially if the flesh was exposed; police may arrest the accused without warrant under section 295.[53]

After discussing all clauses of section 295 of IPC, it is clear that no case can be proceeded with unless the basic ingredients such as the sacredness of the place of worship *and* the intention of doing the act as a religious insult are proven. It is also worth noting that new rules and regulations were brought in to clarify the notion of intention. Hindu-Muslim tension based on the cow issue remained in British India, although it seems the colonial courts were by and large successful in excluding personal animosity behind accusations under section of 295, although the exclusion of personal motives cannot be certain.

After protecting the sacred places and objects, Chapter XV: Of Offences Relating to Religion advanced in another direction to prevent voluntarily causing disturbance to any assemblies lawfully engaged in religious worship under section 296. The aim of the following discussion is to view the context of religious assembly and worship of any religious class which was generally protected from external interruption and disturbance. What kind of intention of disturbance could be prosecuted and the extent to which interference in religious assembly was allowed is the focus of the next section.

1.4 Section 296 of IPC to Protect Religious Assemblies

Whoever voluntarily causes disturbance to any assembly lawfully engaged in the performance of religious worship or religious ceremonies shall be punished with imprisonment of

---

danger. Regulations discussed above were extended in 1925 by district Magistrate Lincoln in Delhi. Thursby, 87–88.

53. O'Kinealy, *Indian Penal Code*, 188.

either description for a term which may extend to one year, or with fine, or with both.[54]

According to Gour, section 296 corresponds with the English law under Mary I, the Queen of England (1516–1558) in the statute (I Mary, sess.2. c. sec. 2) against disturbance during the time of church service.[55] Under that statute, the church in the reign of Mary Tudor in early reformed England saw the restoration of Catholic worship and assembly.[56] In order to be punished under that statute, the disturbance of the assembly had to be shown to have been caused intentionally and presumably by dissenting Protestants.[57] Later the Toleration Act of 1689 of England permitted Roman Catholics and Dissenters under certain conditions to worship according to their own agreed forms, any following a different form being "not lawfully engaged in worship," and thus not protected.[58]

This condition in English law such as voluntarily disturbing a lawful assembly of worship is included in section 296 of IPC, the only difference being that section 296 in the subcontinent applies to disturbance caused to religious assemblies among the diverse religious communities of British India. In the Indian context the issue of disturbing religious assemblies is not only based on external interruption or changes to the assembly's worship or tradition but also on giving religious freedom to discuss religious matters in religious gatherings and assemblies as discussed in section 296 of IPC.

1.4.1. Main Ingredients of Section 296

To constitute an offence under section 296, (1) there must be a voluntary and intentional disturbance to an assembly engaged in religious worship or

---

54. The crime under this section is cognizable but a summons should be issued in the first instance. The offence can be tried by the magistrate (Presidency or of first class officials). Normandy, *Dictionary and Manual*, 314; Morgan and Macpherson, *Indian Penal Code*, 218–219.

55. Gour, *Penal Law of India*, 2191.

56. Mary I was the eldest daughter of Henry VIII and only surviving child of Catherine of Aragon. During her reign, she repaired the severed relationship with Rome and returned England to Catholicism. Many persecutions were carried out during her reign against religious reformers mostly known as Protestants, 300 of whom were burnt. R. H. Pogson, "Revival and Reform in Mary Tudor's Church: A Question of Money," in *The English Reformation Revised*, ed. Christopher Haigh (Cambridge: Cambridge University Press, 1987), 139–156.

57. Gour, *Penal Law of India*, 2191.

58. Hamilton, *Indian Penal Code*, 287.

religious ceremonies; and (2) the assembly must be lawfully engaged in such worship or ceremony, that is, it must be doing what it has a right to do as discussed in the following points.

1.4.2. Voluntarily Causing Disturbance in Religious Worship or Religious Ceremonies under Section 296

The general objective of this section is to secure freedom from molestation when people get together for their religious ceremonies. The original section 296, submitted in 1837 before its promulgation, was limited to describe the disturbance intentionally done in the "place of worship" which was later replaced by "whoever voluntarily disturbs the ceremony of worship."[59] However, the final edited version of section 296 referred to whoever voluntarily disturbs religious ceremonies which may or may not take place in a place of worship.[60] So what is this offence that has been done "voluntarily" within the meaning of section 296? According to section 39 of the IPC, an act can be done voluntarily when the person "causes it by means whereby he intended to cause it, or by means which, at the time of employing those means, he knew or had reason to believe to be likely to cause it."[61] Describing wilful disturbance, the English Criminal Law Commissioners said:

> We have included within the predicament of wilful offenders not only such as directly intend to inflict a particular injury, but also all such as wilfully and knowingly incur the hazard of causing it . . . the proper suggestion of guilt in such cases is . . . that a man is presumed to intend the natural or probable consequences of his own act, gives to words which denote intention, the meaning here annexed to "voluntarily."[62]

In a "voluntary disturbance" case it was still not clear whether it includes interrupting a service of religious worship or ceremony or interrupting certain acts to harm or harass people. Missionaries had objected to section 296 and raised two concerns regarding the meaning of "voluntarily causing

---

59. Macaulay, *Indian Penal Code*, 49.
60. Vijairaghava Chariar v. Emperor, (1903) ILR 26 Madras 554.
61. Morgan and Macpherson, *Indian Penal Code*, 28.
62. The English Law Commissioners in Morgan and Macpherson, *Indian Penal Code*, 28–29.

disturbance," particularly where their intention was not to hurt but to share religious matters and to proselyte others. First, it was argued that places of worship are not the only places where people gather for religious worship as other people, mostly Hindus, use places such as *melas*, festivals and places like *Juganath* and *Ganga Sagar* for religious observance. It was discussed whether missionaries committed an offence when they:

> Quietly commence the reading of an inoffensive tract, and when curiosity or some other motive has gathered around him a small number of persons, may proceed to proclaim the message of the Gospel of God our Saviour, and thereby become liable to what hitherto he was not, an accusation of wilfully causing disturbance to an assembly lawfully engaged in the performance of religious worship.[63]

That observation generally meant that missionaries could not be convicted for sitting and sharing calmly the Christian faith unless they insulted or threatened to insult the religious assembly of any religious group. This concern was not only based on interfering in other religious assemblies but also being interfered with or interrupted by Hindus and Muslims during church worship without any aggression and threat to them, as discussed by law enforcers:

> Supposing him to speak with all the calmness and moderation ascribed to the missionary, would not the whole assembly be moved with indignation? Would not the mere fact of his raising his voice in such an assembly on such an occasion and to such purpose be justly felt as an aggression, an insult? And would it not be thought that there was a defect in the law which did not provide for the punishment of the aggression.[64]

The committee of law enforcers, bearing in mind the meaning of "voluntarily," decided that "the section did not apply to persons who engage in friendly discussion together, and that a disturbance caused by the interference of third persons in such discussions is not a disturbance voluntarily

---

63. Macaulay, *Indian Penal Code*, 414.
64. Second Law Report, Macaulay, 414.

caused by the missionary or his hearers."[65] Second, it was proposed that while it should not be a crime to enter with moderation and calmness, a conviction was possible only if those entering did so to insult, or threaten to insult, or even assault non-Christians engaged in religious ceremony. The law commissioners declared that "nobody can be convicted . . . who has not been guilty of aggression."[66]

Therefore according to the arguments given above, the section on voluntarily causing disturbance was not intended to exclude people from taking part in religious worship, but rather to prosecute where someone has actually intended to disturb or interrupt with aggression or to harm. The offence under section 296 cannot be dismissed where this intention is due to religious animosity and hostility, or other cause[67] for it would be a religious crime under section 296 of IPC if an accused voluntarily and knowingly actually caused a disturbance.[68] It should also be clear what "disturbed" constitutes in section 296 of the IPC. The word "disturbance" here means molest, let, vex or trouble, or in any other unlawful way to disquiet a religious assembly.[69] It means the peace of the assembly should not be interrupted, whether by sound, noise, or any other diversion that can disturb the assembly as illustrated in one of the cases. In 1885, a mosque in Muhalla Madanpura, Banaras was used by Hanafis[70] according to whose tenets the word *amin* (amen) is spoken in a low tone of voice.[71] The accused, Ramazan, Muhammad Husain, and Abdul Rehman, who formerly belonged to Hanafis

---

65. Hamilton, *Indian Penal Code*, xiii.
66. Macaulay, *Indian Penal Code*, 414.
67. Muhammad Hussain v. Emperor, AIR (1919) Allahabad 188.
68. The Public Prosecutor v. Sunuku Seethiah, (1911) ILR 34 Madras 92.
69. Nizami, *Supplement to Commentary*, 216.
70. Hanafi is the first Islamic School of Law, founded by Imam Abu Hanifa (699–766 CE) in Kufa, Iraq. It is the oldest and regarded as the most liberal of the four schools. Abu Hanifa was one of the earliest Muslim scholars who established new ways of applying Islamic tenets to everyday life (Joseph Schacht, *Introduction to Islamic Law*, 57). This school of law was practised in India during Moghul rule; see Ali ibn Abi Bakr Marghinani, *The Hedaya, or Guide: A Commentary on the Mussulman Laws*, trans. Charles Hamilton (Lahore: Premier Book House, 1975).
71. The word *amin* is of Semitic origin, being used both in Arabic and Hebrew. It has been adopted in prayers by Muslims as much as by Christians, Muslims deriving it from the *Sunna*, the practice of Prophet Muhammad as a word representing earnestness in devotion or prayer. Queen Empress v. Ramazan, (1885) ILR 7 Allahabad 461.

but had lately become Wahabi, were using that mosque, and in the course of prayer they called the word *amin* in a loud tone as required by the tenets of their new sect. They were not held liable under section 296 as there was no voluntary disturbance of any assembly.[72] The main ground for the prosecution was of a different sect saying the word *amin* loudly.[73]

The full Bench ordered the case to be re-tried to investigate whether there was a lawful assembly and whether it was, in fact, disturbed act or behaviour by the accused. The court was bound by section 57 of Act 1 of 1872 (Evidence Act) to take judicial account of "Islamic Law." It was held by J. Mahmood that Islamic law should be used in all questions regarding any religious usage or institution. The act of the accused took place during the interval when prayers were not going on and at that time the assembly was not engaged in the performance of religious worship and was not actually disturbed voluntarily within the meaning of section 296.[74] It was also held that there is no indication in the Islamic law schools that pronouncing the word *amin* can be a cause of injury to the prayers of any other person. Regarding the question of the new Islamic Wahabi sect it was held that all Muslims are entitled to enter a mosque and perform their worship or prayer and say the word *amin* and when this word is pronounced loudly in the honest exercise of conscience it is not an offence and cannot be prosecuted under section 296. However, if any Muslim goes into the mosque not for religious purposes but to create a disturbance and to interfere with the devotion, he is criminally accountable under section 296.[75]

---

72. Wahabism was founded by Muhammad ibn Abd al-Wahhab (d.1792 CE) who was influenced by the work of Ibn Taymiyya (1263–1328), the Hanbali scholar. This sect is known for its strict observance of the Qur'an. H. Laoust, "Ibn Abd al-Wahhab," in *Encyclopaedia of Islam*, 2nd ed., eds. P. Bearman, Th. Bianquis, C. E. Bosworth, E. van Donzel and W. P. Heinrichs, Brill Online, 20 June 2013, http://dx.doi.org/10.1163/1573-3912_islam_SIM_3033.

73. According to *Hedaya* which is the text book of Hanafi School of law, one of the four schools of Islamic Law, lays down that the word should be pronounced in prayer after *Sura-e-Fateha*, or the fist chapter of Qur'an in a low voice. On the contrary, the followers of the Shafi, Malik and Hanbal, schools of law, follow that the word *amin* should be pronounced aloud. *Queen Empress v. Ramazan, (1885).*

74. Swinhoe, *Case-Noted Penal Code*, 228; R. A. Nelson, *The Pakistan Penal Code: With Commentary*, vol. 3 (Lahore: Law Publishing Company, 1975), 1306.

75. *Queen Empress v. Ramazan, (1885).*

In reviewing this case it could be argued that breaking traditional practice by, for example, saying *amin* in the worship loudly could in certain circumstances be regarded as religious offence, but this case concerned personal advantages as well as religious conflict. According to the statement of Ramazan (the accused in this case) there was a dispute between him and Abdullah, who was in charge of the mosque, regarding the Mosque accounts. The court held that saying of *amin* aloud had been made the pretext for the prosecution with the object of stopping the accused from requesting the prosecutor to ask Abdullah to render accounts of the disbursement of the income of the property belonging to the mosque. It was held that this case was not liable under the section 296 as no one voluntarily disturbed the assembly.[76] It can be seen that section 296 in this case was used as a tool to settle a personal score. It can be argued that the majority of the worshipers may bring an accusation to deprive the minority, the accusers in this case, of the right of worship or to make them silent, a point which had been brought up earlier in the pre-promulgation discussions cited above.

It has also been seen that particular social and political circumstances of British India impacted on society in ways related to the religious issue of disturbing religious assembly. For example, in the cases of *Kolimi Mahabub v. Sri Sidheswaraswami*, permission was given to the Muslim community between 1904 and 1905 to build a new mosque in the village, on a particular site. Tensions started only in 1939 when Muslims objected to Hindu processions that had long been accustomed to passing by with music. Hindu residents of the village sued for their rights to pass in procession to the accompaniment of music, which they achieved given that the music was a legal and appropriate religious accompaniment to these processions.[77]

Considering the contemporary political circumstances of the case it cannot be denied that the subcontinent was struggling for independence from the British Empire. The growth of Muslim separatism from the late nineteenth century and the rise of communal violence from the 1920s were major contributory factors to independence. However, it was only from the late 1930s that independence was felt to be possible by partition, creating two

---

76. *Queen Empress v. Ramazan*, (1885); Swinhoe, *Case-Noted Penal Code*, 228.
77. Kolimi Mahabub v. Sri Sidheswaraswami, AIR (1945) Madras 496.

sovereign nations of India and Pakistan.[78] It has been argued that religion was one of the powerful tools that was a driver for independence.[79] Considering this background it can be argued that the case of *Kolimi Mahabub v. Sri Sidheswaraswami* straddles two different periods. It probably was not an issue when the mosque was built, between 1904 and 1905, when the Muslim community was not disturbed by Hindus as they customarily passed by with the music. However, it became an issue between 1938 and 1945, when the question of gaining independence of the subcontinent from Britain arose and the question of a separate state for Muslims was at its peak. However contemporary social and political issues did not support the conviction under the case, as has been discussed above. It was held that playing music before a mosque was not an offence and could not be taken under section 296 which demands a substantial and not fanciful disturbance of religious worship.[80]

Apart from the voluntarily causing of a disturbance in a religious assembly in section 296, it is also necessary to review whether the assembly is lawfully engaged in religious worship or not. Like the meaning of voluntarily disturbance, religious worship of any class can only be interrupted if it was lawfully constituted.

1.4.3. Lawful Engagement of Assembly for the Performance of Religious Worship

To come within the protection afforded by section 296 of the IPC the assembly must be essentially a religious assembly rather than any unlikely gathering.[81] An assembly of three being adequate, although if it is not a religious assembly – even if carrying out its proceedings under such a rubric – it would not be protected under this section,[82] due to an assembly being a meeting where people are together for a common and formal purpose of worship.

---

78. Robin W. Winks and Alaine M. Low, eds., *The Oxford History of the British Empire: Historiography*, vol. 3 (Oxford: Oxford University Press, 2001), 214–242.

79. Lawrence James, *The Rise and Fall of the British Empire* (London: Abacus Books, 2005), 412.

80. *Kolimi Mahabub v. Sri Sidheswaraswami*.

81. The judgement has been discussed in *Chrishnachari v. Emperor, (1889) 1 Weir 259* in Gaur, *Textbook on the Indian Penal Code*, 423.

82. Swinhoe, *Case-Noted Penal Code*, 228; Nizami, *Supplement to Commentary*, 216; Nelson, *Pakistan Penal Code*, 1307.

For example, it is a practice among Hindus to meet at each other's house to hear *Bhajans* (religious songs) and *Kathas* (religious stories), but this would not be considered religious worship or a religious ceremony. Macaulay had proposed that this section should apply to disturbance "in a place of worship" and the missionaries who objected to the section were answered by the Indian Law Commissioners that it was restricted to a place of worship where persons of other religions have no right to enter and where they would be trespassers.[83] However, it was also added that, just as the missionaries would resent the intention of Hindus and Muslims impugning their faith, so too would the latter be offended by the intention of the missionaries.

It is also necessary that the assembly is lawfully gathered for worship according to their faith or religion. The word "lawfully" applies when the assembly meets together in a proper place to do what is considered proper. It was declared that no particular religious sect or class has a right to appropriate a public highway for worship even temporarily as it causes obstruction, inconvenience or annoyance to the public. However, considering religious gatherings outside worship places, all religious communities are entitled to have religious processions through public streets, but they should not interfere with the ordinary use of such streets. However, equally the public should not interfere by disturbing the religious procession that is being held in the streets.[84] In the case of *Vijairaghave Chariar v. Emperor*, Justice Bhashyam Ayyangar (13 M. LJ 171) was inclined to the view that within the meaning of this section, no assembly can be lawfully engaged in the performance of religious worship or religious ceremony on a highway unless it is established, or can be reasonably so presumed, that the dedication of the highway included such use. For example, a procession during the Islamic Muharram can be lawfully done on a highway and such assembly cannot be convicted under section 296.[85]

The British legislation on Offences Relating to Religion moves from protecting religious assemblies for worship to other areas of protecting religious funeral ceremonies from disturbance and preventing trespass in places of

---

83. Macaulay in Hamilton, *Indian Penal Code*, 287.

84. Muhammad Jalil Khan v. Ram Nath Katua, AIR (1931) Allahabad 341.

85. Dhalu Ram v. Emperor, 10 Cr. LJ 445 (1909) in Lal, *Indian Penal Code*, 1332–1333; The similar judgment has been passed in *Masit v. Emperor (1912) ILR 34 Allahabad 78*.

worship. It is significant to note that the practice of section 297 does not refer to religious feelings in particular but is based on the emotions of the bereaved and respect for the dead in British India as discussed later.

1.5 Section 297 of IPC: Protecting Funeral Rights and the Human Corpse

Whoever, with the intention of wounding the feelings of any person, or of insulting the religion of any person, or with the knowledge that the feelings of any person are likely to be wounded, or that the religion of any person is likely to be insulted thereby, commits any trespass in any place of worship or on any place of sepulchre, or any place set apart for the performance of funeral rites or as a depository for the remains of the dead, or offers any indignity to any human corpse, or causes disturbance to any person assembled for the performance of funeral ceremonies, shall be punished with imprisonment of either description for a term which may extend to one year, or with fine, or with both.[86]

Section 297 of the IPC extends the principle laid down in section 295 concerning sacred places, following English Common Law, which declares it is a crime to remove, without lawful authority, a corpse from a grave in a burying ground belonging to a congregation of Protestant Dissenters.[87] Places reserved for the cremation or burial of the dead are universally to be regarded with veneration as sacred to the memory of the dead and that is certainly the case for followers of different religious communities.

Section 297 initially only applied to a sepulchre, but its scope was extended in accordance with the recommendation of the British Law Commissioners who thought the word "sepulchre," the proper meaning of which is burial

---

86. The crime under this section can be tried by the magistrate (Presidency or of first class officials or second class). The offence under this section is cognizable but a summons shall issue in the first instance. The offence is bailable but not compoundable under sender section 297. Morgan and Macpherson, *Indian Penal Code*, 219–220; Normandy, *Dictionary and Manual*, 315.

87. Reg v. Sharpe, Dears & B. 160; 26 LJ M. C 47 in Lal, *Indian Penal Code*, 1340.

or interment, was not sufficiently comprehensive to encompass the Indian context. It was declared that section 297 punishes a person who commits trespass in any place of worship, any place of burial, any place set apart for the performance of funeral rites or a depository for the remains of the dead, offends any dignity of any human corpse, or causes disturbance to any person assembled for the performance of funeral ceremonies.[88] Degrees of criminality under section 297 depend upon "intention" or knowledge.

1.5.1. Intention as Essence of the Offence under Section 297

Intention is again the substance of the offence under section 297. The act must relate to the religion or hurting the feelings of any person by the commission of an act. Mere suspicion of malicious intention is insufficient to prosecute the case.[89] Therefore the essence of section 297 is an "intention" to offend feelings, or insult religion which can be prosecuted "when with that intention either (i) trespass on a place of sepulchre, (ii) indignity of corpse, or (iii) disturbance to persons assembled for funeral ceremonies, is committed."[90]

Any person who destroys or disturbs a place of religious worship or a sepulchre with the intention of wounding the feelings of any another person, or with the knowledge that the feelings of a person are likely to be wounded, is liable.[91] For example, in one such case in 1896, the accused, Subhan, entered a burial place and ploughed up a grave with the permission of the owner, but here the perpetrators were held liable under section 297 of the IPC as the act was done intentionally to hurt the feelings of others and the knowledge of potential injury was sufficient. In the court, considering these elements of section 297, J. Knox, delivering the judgement, said that "the act of petitioners was an act of injury of sepulchre, and it was an act which they must have known would have been likely to wound the feelings of others."[92]

---

88. Macaulay, *Indian Penal Code*, 414–415; Gour, *Penal Law of India*, 2196.
89. Hajee Muhammad Ghouse (1903) 1 Weir 287 in Gaur, *Textbook on the Indian Penal Code*, 425.
90. Burhon Shah v. Emperor (1887) P. R. N0. 26 quoted from Gaur, *Indian Penal Code*, 2197–2198 and Lal, *Indian Penal Code*, 1335.
91. Gaur, *Textbook on the Indian Penal Code*, 424.
92. Queen v. Subhan ILR 1896 Allahabad 395–6.

Though "intention" in section 297 is significant, the offence occurs when the action also involves "trespass" in a place of sepulchre, an indignity to a corpse, or disturbance to people assembled for a funeral ceremony.

1.5.2. Trespass and Prosecution

The term trespass as defined in section 297 of the IPC means any violent or injurious act committed in such a place and with such a knowledge or intention as stated in the section.[93] In various cases the trespass is committed within the sepulchre or sacred place and dishonours the dead body or remaining part of it in the grave.

First, "trespass of sepulchre" can be seen in the case where, in 1915 Umar Din, the accused, dug up and levelled certain graves existing on a plot of land, called Khasra No. 383 which is described in the Revenue Records as graveyard and *waqf* property in Lahore. It had been sold to him by the owners of an adjoining shrine of Shah Abdul Maali in Lahore and the case was successfully prosecuted under section 297. Notably, "a cemetery or graveyard is consecrated ground and cannot be sold or partitioned . . . but when a place is found not to be a *maqbra* (a burial ground) but only one or two bodies are buried there, the actual spot is where the bodies lie buried is consecrated."[94] It was held that the act of destroying or disturbing a place of sepulchre hurts the religious feelings of the persons whose relatives were buried in the graves no matter whether the land on which the sepulchre is does or does not belong to the person guilty of the alleged act.[95]

Second, "trespass of assaulting sacred place or place of worship" with the knowledge and intention that the feelings of persons would be wounded falls under section 297.[96] According to Allahabad Court (*Queen v. Subhan* 1896 I. L. R. Allahabad 395) and Calcutta Court (*Jhulan Sain v. Emperor* 40 c.548) the question of the true meaning of the word "trespass" as used in section 297 was directly involved, and the view expressed by the judges was

---

93. Abdul Kader v. Abdul Kasim AIR (1932) Calcutta 459.
94. Ali, *Muhammadan Law*, 406.
95. Umer Din v. Emperor, AIR (1915) Lahore 409. Contrary to the judgment passed in Umer Din's case an accused cannot be judged where he had not actually disturbed a grave, nor was it shown that any portion of the plot had been set apart as a sepulchre. Khoja Muhammad Hamid Khan v. Emperor, (1881) ILR 3 Madras 178.
96. Maqsood Hussan v. Emperor, AIR (1940) Patna 4141.

that this word in this section has not the same meaning as in the expression "criminal trespass" which is defined in section 441 of the IPC.[97] In section 297 it must be taken to have been used in its original meaning, covering any injury or offence done coupled with entry upon property which is sacred for religious worship.[98]

Third, "trespassing in the burial ground, dead body or its remaining parts" is another kind of religious offence under section 297. Considering this aspect of section 297, a burial ground of any religious community can also be protected for a certain religious community, even if it is not clearly in use.[99] Any act of trespass with the specified intention or knowledge by which the feelings of the relations of the dead are wounded would come under section 297.[100] For example, in a case in 1911, Ram Prasad entered a grove in Sindhauli and dug up certain graves, and exposed the bones of the bodies, that were residents of the village of Sindhauli who were buried there. He was convicted under section 297 because the accused, as well as the joint owner of the land, had entered the land with the intention or knowledge that what he was about to do was offensive to his fellow-residents.[101]

Apart from trespassing on a corpse or burial ground, anyone can also be prosecuted if they disturb a group gathered for a funeral, though the word disturbance is only relevant where there is actual interference or hindrance to the performance of the funeral ceremonies.[102] Chapter XV: Of Offences Relating to Religion, after protecting sepulchre and burial places and ceremonies in section 297, moves to the last section, 298, which protects against outraging words and acts that wound any religious class. Under section 298,

---

97. Criminal Trespass according to section 441 defined as follows: "Whoever enters into or upon property in possession of another with intention to commit an offence or to intimidate, insult or annoy and person in possession of such property, or having lawfully entered into or upon such property, unlawfully remains therewith intent thereby intimidate, insult or annoy any such person, or with intent to commit an offence." Lal, *Indian Penal Code*, 2266, 1336–1337.

98. Queen Empress v. Bhagya, Bat. Un. Or. C. 148 in Lal, *Indian Penal Code*, 1338.

99. Mohidin v. Shivlingappa, 23 B. 666 in Lal, *Indian Penal Code*, 1340.

100. Jhulan Sain v. Emperor, 40 C. 538=18 I. C. 677; Jailal Jha v. King Emperor, ILR 256 (1925) Patna 537 in Lal, *Indian Penal Code*, 1339.

101. Ram Prasad and others v. Emperor, (1911) ILR 33 Allahabad 773.

102. Mangat v. Emperor, AIR (1919) Lahore 433; Ghosita v. Kalke, (1885) AWN 49 in Lal, *Indian Penal Code*, 1340.

the nature of wounding the religious feelings of another religious class has changed somewhat from the earlier clauses, which reveals the wide scope of the section including freedom of religious discussion in British India. It is important to note that section 298 also demonstrates political interests and the religious advantages given to monotheistic religions to discuss their religious views freely. Therefore it is needed to consider to what extent religious freedom was given to religious communities under section 298 and who could be accused under it.

1.6 Section 298 of the IPC to Protect Against Acts Wounding Another Religion

> Whoever, with the deliberate intention of wounding the religious feelings of any person, utters any word or makes any sound in the hearing of that person, or makes any gesture in the sight of that person, or places any object in the sight of that person, shall be punished with imprisonment of either description for a term which may extend to one year, or with fine, or with both.[103]

Section 298 of IPC is the last section that punishes the doing of certain acts with the deliberate intention of wounding the religious feelings of any person. This section follows English law which sought to protect only Christian faith and doctrine. At one time to write against Christianity was an offence in English Common Law. From the sixteenth century to the mid-nineteenth century, blasphemy against Christianity (mainly applying to the Church of England) was held as an offence against common law: "to speak or otherwise publish any matter blaspheming God, e.g., by denying His existence or providence, or contumeliously reproaching Jesus Christ, or

---

103. Morgan and Macpherson, *Indian Penal Code*, 220–221. "This section is non-cognizable and the summons shall issue in the first instance. The offence under the section 298 can be tried by the Presidency magistrate or Magistrate of the fist class or second class. It is bailable as well as compoundable." Normandy, *Dictionary and Manual*, 316.

vilifying or bringing into disbelief or contempt or ridicule, Christianity in general, or any doctrine of the Christian religion, or the Bible."[104]

The English blasphemy law supports the Established Protestant Church and therefore punishes all irreverence, which could include or be aimed at the state. In British Indian territory, the legislature was exercised greatly about what policy to sanction, but at last decided in favour of religious neutrality and freedom of religious discussions. The difference between section 298 of the IPC and English Blasphemy Law is that the former treats all religions alike and pays no attention to irreverent comment of any religion as long as it is not uttered to cause offence to the other's religious feelings with the intentions of insult. Section 298 was much discussed and criticized before its promulgation in 1860, particularly to clarify the legal status of religious discussion and proselytization, and is still of considerable interest in light of present practice in the north-western section of formerly British India.

1.6.1. Religious Freedom of Discussion under Section 298

Generally, section 298 relates to spoken words and religious discussion uttered in the presence of a person with the intention of wounding their religious feelings. It was felt difficult to discern the context and intention, particularly where section 298 makes it an offence for anyone who utters any word or makes any sound in the hearing of that person with the deliberate intention of wounding the religious feelings. Reviewing potential accusations of offensive religious conversation among religious communities under section 298, Norton observed that "it was impossible to say to what absurdities the criminality of uttering any word or making any gesture in hearing or sight of a person with the intention of wounding his religious feelings may be carried out." J. F. Thomas further observed that under such conditions there is "a dangerous novelty liable to extensive abuse . . . and there can be no limit to criminal prosecution or to variety of sentences."[105]

The missionaries of Protestant churches and other church bodies, mostly serving in Calcutta and its surrounding areas, had objected to section 298 relating to the persons who deliberately intend to wound the religious feelings

---

104. Turner, *Russell on Crime*, 1757; R. K. Webb, "From Toleration to Religious Liberty," in *Liberty Secured? Britain before and after 1688*, ed. J. R. Jones (Stanford: Stanford University Press, 1992), 162; Hamilton, *Indian Penal Code*, 284.

105. Norton and J. F. Thomas quoted by Macaulay, *Indian Penal Code*, 409–410.

of any person, but the committee thought there was no reason to worry that the magistrates would so interpret the meaning of the section as to interfere unduly with missionary efforts.[106] It was suggested that "provisions should be made in order that they should work no harm to those who merely desire by useful and friendly discussion to proselytise others to what they consider a purer and sounder faith."[107] The missionaries considered section 298 as calculated to:

> Operate injuriously to themselves and disastrously on the spread of Divine Truth—Deliberate and wilful intention will surely be as strenuously, and honestly too, disclaimed by the zealous missionary, as it will be attributed to him by those who deem their religious feelings wounded or insulted, when their understandings are simply reasoned with. If it be establishable at all, it can only be by inference. But inference may be variously drawn from the very same overt acts, according to the light in which they are beheld by the adjudicators—so, "any word or sound," will include all discussion or announcement whatever: "any gesture," all ordinary animation in the advocate of truths the most interesting. Assuredly, if tried by these rules, there is not a discourse or expostulation of Prophet or Evangelist in the New or the Old Testament, nay, not of our Divine Saviour himself, which not be thought to wound, and keenly to wound, the feelings of a zealous Jew, Mussulman [Muslim], or Idolater, and which, if so, must not be held forbidden, under the new Code, to be either recited or imitated in the discourses of the Missionaries.[108]

Notwithstanding this explanation, complaints against section 298 were numerous not only from the missionaries, but also from lawyers and judges. For example, Giberne, a Judge of the Bombay High Court said "this clause might, I think, be excluded, for it almost amounts to the prohibition of

---

106. Hamilton, *Indian Penal Code*, xiii.
107. Hamilton, xiii.
108. Macaulay, *Indian Penal Code*, 410.

preaching the Gospel."[109] In his speech Bernard Peacock, the Vice President, on the third reading of the Indian Penal Code in the Legislative Council of India, observed that under section 298 the British had gone beyond the proper bounds of legislation which would affect the missionary performing his duty. Peacock clarified that there was no objection to a person who argues about religious matters with the intention of convincing. He drew attention to section 298 because it appeared to him that there was a great misunderstanding about procedure.[110] In commenting upon these criticisms, the law commissioners noted that:

> We understand these instances to be mentioned as indicative of the strictness with which the definition is to be constructed, so as not to make a person criminally liable for words, etc., wounding the religious feelings of another, unless a deliberate intention so to wound his feelings be unequivocally manifested, as it would be by mere railing and abuse, and by offensive attack upon his religion, under the pretext of discussion, without any argument which an impartial arbiter could possibly believe to have been addressed to him in good faith merely for the purpose of convincing him of the truth. It is here to be observed, that it is not the impression of the offended party that is to be admitted to decide whether the words uttered deserve to be considered as insulting, and whether they were uttered with the deliberate intention of insulting; these are points to be determined upon cool and calm consideration of the circumstances by the judge.[111]

After the discussion of section 298 and its objectives, in framing section 298 and passing into the law in Chapter XV of the IPC, the law commissioners, Macaulay and others, described the main "object" of the section by declaring that:

---

109. Mayne, *Commentaries on the Indian Penal Code*, 222.
110. Bernard Peacock in Hamilton, *Indian Penal Code*, xxxv.
111. Second report on the Indian Penal Code by the Indian Law Commissioners submitted on 24th June 1847, in Macaulay, *Indian Penal Code*, 411–412.

> We wish to allow all fair latitude to religious discussion, and at the same time to prevent the professors of any religion from offering, under the pretext of such discussion, intentional insults to what is held sacred by others. We do not conceive that any person can be justified in wounding with deliberate intention the religious feelings of his neighbours by word, gesture, or exhibition. A warm expression dropped in the heat of controversy, or an argument urged by a person not for the purpose of insulting and annoying the professors of a different creed, but in good faith for the purpose of vindicating his own, will not fall under the definition contained in this clause.[112]

It was declared that religious discussion among religious communities was not a crime under section 298. From the commissioners' observation, it appears the grounds for distinguishing such offences under section 298 were to preserve the general policy to bring religious harmony, peace and the protection of all religious communities in the free exercise of their particular form of religion.[113] It is important to note that not only missionaries but all religious communities could take an advantage of the freedom of religious discussion and be argued out of their cherished views on almost any religious subject in British India.

Though all religious communities were given freedom of discussion, on the question of what constituted an offence under section 298 it was declared that it is necessary for everyone to refrain from insults. If, in the discussion, any religious arguments or words are used which do wound the religious feelings of any person, they do not constitute an offence, because they would not be uttered with the deliberate intention of wounding the religious feeling of any person. Section 298 is probably the one law in this cluster under which there is at least room to explain the reasons behind the act of the accused if convicted for religious discussion. However, it was concluded that an insulting intention is necessary to constitute the offence and that had not been sufficiently noted by the critics of section 298. It was declared that it could be considered offensive where ". . . insulting or

---

112. Second report, in Macaulay, 409.
113. Macaulay, 409–410

contumelious language is used and where it may be fairly presumed that the intent of the offender is not grave discussion but a mischievous design to wound the feelings."[114] Therefore the essence of this offence under section 298 consists in the "deliberate intention" of wounding the religious feelings of another, which becomes a significant ingredient in making an accusation.

1.6.2. The Meaning of Deliberate Intention of Wounding Religious Feelings under Section 298

"Deliberate intention" was to be inferred from the words spoken, the place in which they were spoken, the people to whom they were addressed and other surrounding circumstances. In the first place, there can be no offence without deliberate intention of religious discussion as defined in section 298. These words have been explained by the law commissioners who observed:

> The intention to wound must be *deliberate*, that is, not conceived on the sudden in the course of discussion, but premeditated; it must appear, not only that the party, being engaged in a discussion with another on the subject of the religion professed by the other, in the course of the argument consciously used words likely to wound his religious feelings, but that he entered into the discussion with the deliberate purpose of so offending him. In other places in the Code a party is held to be guilty if [it] causes a certain effect the causing of which is an offence, intending to cause that effect, *or knowing that his act was likely to cause it*. Here there is a marked difference. Although the party uttering offensive words might be conscious at the moment of uttering them that they were likely to wound the feelings of his auditors, yet if it were apparent that he uttered them on the spur of the occasion, in good faith, simply to further his argument—that he did not take advantage of the occasion to utter them in pursuance of a deliberate purpose to offend—he would not, we think, be liable to conviction [under section 298]. If however a party were to force himself upon the attention of another, addressing to him, an involuntary hearer, an insulting

---

114. Macaulay, 136, 409.

invective against his religion, he would, we conceive, fall under the definition, for the reasonable inference from his conduct would be that he had a deliberate intention of wounding the religious feeling his hearer.[115]

The commissioners conceded, in the view of the High Court of North-West Province, that there would be difficulty drawing the line and that different religious people would be apt to take very different views of what ought to be considered as evidencing a deliberate intention of wounding the religious feelings. But they added:

> When a man in a course of an argument uses insulting words to another it is impossible to suppose that he does so without the intention of insulting him—it is not to be believed that he uses them in good faith simply for the purpose of convincing or persuading the person with whom he is arguing. In such a case the intention is to be inferred from the character of the words. Again when words not positively insulting in themselves are used in a manner clearly evidencing a deliberate intention to insult the religious feelings of another, the case will fall within the clause. But it will not be an offence when any person arguing with another on the subject of his religion says what is likely to wound his religious feelings, in good faith, simply for the purpose of convincing the person with whom he is arguing of what he believes to be the truth.[116]

Intentions can be inferred from "words" that can lead to religious discussions intended to convict or convert. The law commissioners agreed to declare that discourse addressed to anyone with the intention of converting the person, however it may wound religious feelings, should not be considered a religious crime.[117] Though the British government proclaimed neutrality in all religious matters, it later played a significant and pre-eminent role

---

115. The law commissioners' second report in Macaulay, *Indian Penal Code*, 412.
116. Macaulay, *Indian Penal Code*, 142.
117. Macaulay, 412–413.

in the religious history of the sub-continent.[118] During colonialism, giving knowledge of the faith of Christianity to Indian religious communities was British "policy, not only as Christians, but as statesmen."[119] With regard to the intention of this section the Indian law commissioners observed:

> In England an attempt to convert any one from the religion of the country by the most gentle and dispassionate address, is by law is an offence; to attempt the same thing by contemptuous or vituperative language is an offence which would be severely punished in practice. But the reason is that conversion is not recognized as a legitimate object. The law assumes the truth of Christianity. But it is manifest that the law and the legislature of this country cannot assume the truth of any religion. And, as free discussion, or, in other words, attempts to conversion, is the best criterion of the truth of anything the truth or falsehood of which is not already assumed by law to be beyond controversy, it seems to follow that a *bona fide* attempt to convert ought not in this country to be treated as a crime, even though the intention to convert be an intention to do so by wounding the religious feelings of the persons addressed. We apprehend it is almost impossible to convert a sincere or ardent votary of any faith without wounding his religious feelings in the early stages of the process. And if that be so, and if it is admitted that attempts at conversion from one faith to another ought not to be punished in British India, then the wounding of religious feelings ought not to be punished when the wound is inflicted with that legitimate object.[120]

The first conclusion to be drawn is that British policy was to maintain freedom of religious discussion. Second, section 298 allowed all religious communities, particularly but not only English or any foreign Christian missionaries, to discuss their faith which could lead anyone to convert. All

---

118. J. Rooney, *On Heels of Battles: A History of Catholic Church in Pakistan 1780-1886* (Rawalpindi: Christian Study Centre, 1986), 8–9.

119. H. F. Lechmere Taylor, *In the Land of the Five Rivers: A Sketch of the Work of the Church of Scotland in the Punjab* (Edinburgh: R. & R. Clark, 1906), 8.

120. The second report in Macaulay, *Indian Penal Code*, 413.

shared enthusiastically in the advantages provided by British imperial power which protected missionary work in the subcontinent.[121] There is no record of cases brought concerning injury to feelings when non-Christians were invited by missionaries to embrace Christianity. Probably this resulted from the clarification of section 298 noted by Peacock that "it was a mistake to suppose that the intention of the missionary was to wound the feelings of the person whom he intended to convert."[122] Therefore with such intention:

> No missionary can come within the provisions of Section 298 . . . he must use and utter words with the deliberate intention of wounding the religious feelings of some person, which, if he is at all keeping within the limits of his office cannot be the case, as his intention is not to insult, but to convince.[123]

Statements such as these reveal that the British protected the missionary from accusation, although it cannot be said that missionaries did not face criticism. They might not be judged by the law under section 298 but indeed were judged by local religious communities and individuals.[124] Local judgments on the issue of conversion or religious discussion were not taken to the courts even though that could have provided legal aid to Indian religious communities. It is interesting to see above that when a missionary discussed religious matters to convince and convert, they could not be convicted unless an intention to insult has been found. Before discussing the difference between "insult" and "convince" it is important to note that the scope of section 298 was not limited to missionary work alone, for discussing and arguing religious faith applied to all religious communities and religious sects such as Ahmadi-Muslims who could proselytize in British India. Notably, it

---

121. Brian Stanley, *The Bible and the Flag: Protestant Missions and British Imperialism in the 19th and 20th Centuries* (Leicester: Apollos, 1990); Brian Stanley and Alaine Low, eds., *Missions, Nationalism and the End of Empire* (Cambridge: Eerdmans, 2003), 16, 23.

122. Bernard Peacock in Hamilton, *Indian Penal Code*, xxxv.

123. Starling, *Indian Criminal Law and Procedure*, 248; Mayne, *Commentaries on the Indian Penal Code*, 221.

124. In one of the incidents, in Gujarat city in present day Pakistan, Robert Paterson, a Scottish missionary during his missionary work from 1860 to 1869 had a trying time with the Muslim community who became violent, used threatening language, seized his horse by the bridle, and ordered him to leave that place. Paterson in John F. W. Youngson, *Forty Years of the Punjab Mission of the Church of Scotland 1855-1895* (Edinburgh: R. & R. Clark, 1896), 121–122.

was noticed that religious conflicts occurred between Ahmadis and Muslims especially on Ahmad's claim of calling himself the Prophet, *nabi*. This led to several *fatwas*, or decrees declared in religious matters and discussions by *ulama* and clerics, against him regarding him as a heretic, unfaithful, and a liar.[125] The outcome of these discussions did not come to a head, as Ahmadis were not declared non-Muslims in British India. One of the main reasons was the British willingness to allow all religious communities to discuss and propagate their beliefs.[126] Therefore the notion of "convincing" for religious views applies to all religious communities who might enthusiastically try to convince anyone, and if an accused claimed any intentional wounding was done to "save life" they may be safe from prosecution. The problems this could raise were troubling, as J. F. Thomas noted in the Law Report:

> One Judge may, in his charity, assume, that there could be no "deliberate intention" of wounding the feelings, and so absolve all offenders—another may adopt the maxim, that the act itself indicates such intention. And if the Criminal Courts are to be [at] all times open to the zealots of differing sects, on every trifling occasion, the result must be to foster bigotry, and to keep the religious animosity of sects at its height, as well as to interfere with individual security and peace.[127]

Though the possible consequences of discussing religious matters were reviewed, the question arises of the exact meaning of "insult" in religious discussion which could be prosecuted under section 298. One of the reasons given in the pre-1860 revision of section 298 was that abusive language must not be used for religious discussion. Thomas gave the example that under section 298, monotheistic followers, Christians and Muslims, "would be subject to penalty for the undisguised and natural expression of their views of the evil and folly of idolatry" in British India.[128] It can be said that while

---

125. Spencer Lavan, *The Ahmadiyya Movement: A History and Perspective* (Delhi: Manohar Book Service, 1973), 50–62.
126. Yohanan Friedmann, "Ahmadiyya," in *Encyclopaedia of Islam*, 3rd ed., eds. Kate Fleet, Gudrun Kramer, Denis Matringe, John Nawas and Everett Rowson, Brill Online, 4 December 2012, http://dx.doi.org/10.1163/1573-3912_ei3_COM_0007.
127. J. F. Thomas quoted by Macaulay, *Indian Penal Code*, 409–410.
128. Second law report in Macaulay, *Indian Penal Code*, 409–410.

arguing about idolatry in a respectful manner may seem legal, it can be insulting where any Hindu deity or idols representing gods are disgraced through hate or prejudice. For example, anyone who intentionally breaks a particular idol by claiming that it was part of his campaign against idol worship insults or disgraces Hindu idols as a class. However the question remains unclear how converts dealt with the previous idols they worship.

Abusive and aggressive action can also be considered offensive as well as insulting. Missionaries argued that section 296, interfering in religious assembly and section 298, wounding religious feelings in religious discussion, should not be considered insult particularly when done with moderation and calmness as discussed above. That discussion mainly shows the British assumption that particular care of language and manner of discussing religious arguments was enough to control controversies. Religious communities may have implied certain moderation or absence of intention to wound on various occasions in British India. However, the same application and rules for religious discussion reveal a very different application post-1947. Before seeing this application it is important to review that no case was registered under section 298 during British India concerning insult during conversion or religious discussions, cases remaining limited to certain issues as discussed in the following point.

1.6.3. Prosecutions and Cases under Section 298

Given the careful pre-promulgation discussions about this section, the question arises on which issues were included in section 298 of the 1860 Indian Penal Code. All religions were safe from prosecution under section 298 although specific "acts of an accused" could be prosecuted if they have been done deliberately to injure the religious feelings. For example, in 1893, the accused, Rehman was held liable under section 298 because after sacrificing a cow on *Bakr Eid*, he carried the flesh around the village in an uncovered condition,[129] despite Hindu fellow villagers having previously endeavoured

---

129. *Bakr Eid* or *Eid-ul-Adha* or is one of the most celebrated festivals among Muslims. The festival of sacrifice, when the Muslims sacrifice *bakra* (goat), is observed to commemorate the great sacrifice of prophet Ibrahim who was so devoted, faithful and obedient to God's will that he unhesitatingly agreed to sacrifice his only son Ismail at his behest. E. Mittwoch, "Id al-Adha," in *Encyclopaedia of Islam*, 2nd ed., eds. P Bearman, Th. Bianquis, C. E. Bosworth, E. van Donzel and W. P. Heinrichs, Brill Online, 2010, http://dx.doi.org/10.1163/1573-3912_islam_SIM_3472.

to persuade the *zamindar* (the landlord) to prevent the slaughter of cows.[130] It was held by the High Court of Allahabad that that there was no doubt that Rehman exposed the cow's meat with deliberate intention to wound the religious feelings of Hindus.[131] Actions judged offensive but not through deliberate insult was not a crime under section 298. For example, a case in which Muslims had driven cows for slaughter in the *Eidgah* through a street containing Hindu shops, the court held that driving cows through a public street did not constitute "placing an object" in sight of the Hindu shopkeepers; deliberately placing beef in front of Hindus is an offence but simply driving animals to slaughter is not.[132]

The issue of cows remained a critical issue that was commonly prosecuted under section 298 amid increased Hindu-Muslim tensions, discussed in the following chapter. However, section 298 was used *within* religions as well as between Hindu castes where the insult was deemed social rather than religious. For example, an accused gave birth to an illegitimate child, whereupon she went to the house of the person whom she alleged to be the child's father, and threw upon him a cloth which she had been wearing at the time of her confinement. She was prosecuted under section 298 by the complainant who alleged the act deprived him of his caste. It was held that section 298 did not include acts related to injuries to caste as distinct from religious susceptibilities so the accused could not be convicted under this section.[133]

---

130. *Zamindar* means holder or occupier (*dar*) of land (*zamin*). The word was widely used whenever Persian influence was spread by the Indian Mughals or the Indian Muslims. Irfan Habib, *The Agrarian System of Mughal India, 1526-1707*, 2nd rev. ed. (Oxford: Oxford University Press, 2000), 140.

131. Queen Empress v. Rehman, (1893) 13 AWN 144 in Lal, *Indian Penal Code*, 1344; The similar judgment was passed in *Mir Chittan v. Emperor*, AIR (1937) Allahabad 13.

132. Habibullah v. Crown, 4 P. R. 1890 in Lal, *Indian Penal Code*, 1344; the similar judgement can also be seen in *Kirpal Singh v. Emperor*, 13 Criminal Law Journals (Cr. LJ) 601; O'Kinealy, *Indian Penal Code*, 188.

133. Tukaram v. Zeli, 6 C. PLR 7 in Lal, *Indian Penal Code*, 1344–1345; The similar judgment was passed where two men were accused under section 298 for offending the religious feelings of other fellows for mere polluting food. Moti Lal v. Emperor, (1901) ILR 24 Allahabad 155; Swinhoe, *Case-Noted Penal Code*, 229–230.

1.7 Conclusion

The historical view of Chapter XV (sections 295 to 298) of the Offences Relating to Religion of 1860, shows that the legal foundations of the law date back to English Christian blasphemy law and the colonial period when British rule brought new political institutions and a new system of law to India. Through Chapter XV: Of Offences Relating to Religion, originally applied in 1860, the British protected sacred places of worship under section 295, religious assemblies lawfully gathered for worship under section 296, funeral and burial rights under section 297 and against offensive acts of wounding the religious feelings of any religious class under section 298. This historical review also reveals how the law was re-shaped for its procedure and application and was discussed by many lawyers and British enforcers with various objectives and implications. This review of sections 295–298 also reveals that in various cases much criticism and clarification as well as some rules and regulations were included, although no significant changes or additions to Chapter XV were made from 1860–1927.

One of the important objectives of Chapter XV under sections 296 and 298 was to declare freedom of religious discussion and conversion. Such discussions may have been enabled by the British but freedom of speech and writing became another issue as well as a threat in the early twentieth century when religious discussions went beyond criticism and close to or arguably over the line of insult in various religious publications. This period brought new changes to Chapter XV which is discussed in the following chapter.

CHAPTER 2

The Issue of Offensive Writing and Publication and Amendments to Religious Offences Laws in British India

In India, the British aimed to maintain religious harmony among the diverse religious communities, otherwise threatened by religious, political and patriotic controversial writings and publications. They increasingly faced the issue of offensive writing from the end of the nineteenth century as threats to harmony by religious controversies, especially amid political tension, led to further steps to control publications that created religious agitation, especially tensions between Hindus and Muslims. For example, literature on the sanctity of the cow and eating the meat of the cow (the most commonly prosecuted crime under Offences Relating to Religion) increasingly affected Hindu-Muslim relations. This is because Hindu cow societies had increasingly launched campaigns with songs, tracts and posters which were banned by the British government lest they heighten tensions and produce riots.[1]

The increased religiously linked tensions, resulting from and feeding these social and religious changes, led to several amendments to the 1860 Indian

---

1. Barrier, *Banned*, 60.

Penal Code such as section 124-A[2] and section 153-A[3] under Act IV of 1898. These were added and applied by the British authorities to contentious publications, permitting magistrates and authorities to prosecute publishers and publications that disseminated seditious matter under section 124-A. This also applied to publications that attempted to promote feelings of hatred between different classes under section 153-A, political and patriotic poetry, songs and books being banned under sections 124-A and 153-A.

With tensions increasing during the early twentieth century, related in large part to the jockeying for position between Hindus and Muslims as the end of foreign rule became increasingly likely, the situation had changed dramatically by 1929 as religious communal violence, including verbal and written controversies on religious beliefs, became a widespread issue. Throughout the 1920s the government dealt with religious offences amid 122 riots from 1923–1928, which the government of India classified as serious communal disorders. These were exacerbated by various controversial publications, with the loss of approximately four hundred and fifty lives and major injuries to five thousand people.[4] Part of the background to the riots was the effect of the Hindu reform movement, which as it evolved and organized itself into "one religion," rather than a plethora of local activities and attitudes, confronted the Muslim community that had long been more or less (with the exception of Ahmadi and Shia) one group.

The main such Hindu group, the Arya Samaj, led by Dayanand Saraswati in the late nineteenth century in Punjab and western Uttar Pradesh, reformed various issues such as child marriage, widow remarriage, idolatry and caste "within a framework of the assertion of Hindu supremacy over

---

2. Section 124-A reads as follows:
   Whoever by words, either spoken or written, or by signs, or by visible representation, or otherwise, brings or attempts to bring into hatred or contempt, or excites or attempts to excite disaffection towards Her Majesty, or the Government established by law in British India, shall be punished . . . imprisonment which may extend to three years, to which fine may be added, or with fine. (Barrier, *Banned*, 6).

3. The full description of section 153-A is: "Whoever by words, either spoken or written, or by signs, or by visible representation, or otherwise, promotes or attempts to promote feelings of enmity or hatred between different classes of Her Majesty's subjects shall be punished with imprisonment which may extend to two years, or with fine, or with both."

4. Thursby, *Hindu-Muslim Relations*, 72.

other religions."⁵ Thursby suggested that religious tension was a result of the Arya and Muslim counter-publications in the Punjab province which fed, and fed on, inter-religious tension. Beyond these publications the Arya Samajit Swami Shraddhanand and the Sufi Muslim Khwaja Hasan Nizami were well-known for their proselytizing work in the 1920s. Each was an effective publicist and each was criticized for offending the other religious community. From this and other causes, Hindu-Muslim tension increased critically, leading to violence, fuelled by controversial publications including sexual aspersion and character assassination of the sacred figures of the others' religion: the Arya, for example, attacked Islam through the personal life of the Prophet Muhammad, worsening Hindu-Muslim relations.⁶ Under such intense circumstances the British government had to take legal action by adding 295-A to the law of Offences Relating to Religion. In order to discuss this issue, it is necessary to discuss the historical setting of this new clause.

2.1. Offensive Publications and the Historical Setting of Amending Chapter XV in 1920s

Section 295-A was added in consequence of the abortive prosecution of Mahesh Rajpal who had published an Urdu pamphlet called *Rangila Rasul*, "The Amorous Prophet," in May 1924 in which he described the alleged sexual incontinence of the Prophet Muhammad.⁷ Barrier notes that before the pamphlet had been banned, after much religious criticism had been received, one thousand copies were in circulation.⁸ Rajpal was prosecuted and convicted under section 153-A of the IPC for creating feelings of hatred between Hindus and Muslims. The sessions judge on appeal held that the pamphlet read as a whole "was intentionally offensive, scurrilous, and wounding to the religious feelings of the Muhammadan community."⁹ The

---

5. Aysha Jalal and Sugata Bose, *Modern South Asia: History, Culture, Political Econmy*, 2nd ed. (New York: Routledge, 2004), 111.

6. Thursby, *Hindu-Muslim Relations*, 4, 34–35.

7. The authorship was not indicated on the pamphlet. It had been commonly assumed that Rajpal was its author. Arya Samaj in later years admitted that Pandit Chamupati was the author of *Rangila Rasul*. Thursby, *Hindu-Muslim Relations*, 42–43.

8. Rajpal's trial proceeded for three years because of extensive appeals. Barrier, *Banned*, 100–101.

9. Rajpal v. Emperor, AIR (1927) Lahore 590.

Lahore High Court overturned Rajpal's conviction on appeal, on the basis that the publication did not constitute an offence within the meaning of section 153-A, and an attack on the Prophet could not expose the accused to the penalty for an offence directed against class hostility.[10] The object of the section was given in the statement of Objects and Reasons as follows:

> The prevalence of malicious writing intended to insult the religion, or outrage the religious feelings of various classes of His Majesty's subjects has made it necessary to examine the existing provisions of the law with a view to seeing whether they require to be strengthened. Chapter XV of the Indian Penal Code, which deals with offences relating to the religion, provides no penalty in respect of writing . . . Such writing can usually be dealt under sec. 153A of the Indian Penal Code, as it is seldom that they do not represent an attempt to promote feeling of enmity or hatred between different classes. It must be recognised, however, that this is only an indirect way of dealing with acts which may properly be made punishable themselves, apart from the question whether they have the further effect of promoting feeling of enmity or hatred between classes. Accordingly it is proposed to insert a new section in chapter XV of the Indian Penal Code, with the object of making it a specific offence intentionally to insult or attempt to insult the religion, or outrage or attempt to outrage the religious feelings, of any class of His Majesty's subjects.[11]

The Lahore High Court proposed to add a new section to deal with the issue of offensive writing. However, in the case of *Rangila Rasul*, Justice Dalip Singh of Lahore High Court argued that section 153-A was intended to prevent attack on a community but not to stop polemics against religious leaders; therefore, Rajpal's conviction was illegal. After the protracted trial of Rajpal, his conviction was set aside and he was released on 4 May 1927.[12] This judgment brought chaos when around ten thousand Muslims

---

10. *Rajpal v. Emperor*.
11. *Gazette of India*, dated 27 August 1927, Part V in Nelson, *Indian Penal Code*, 1369.
12. Barrier, *Banned*, 99–100.

attended an open protest, sending telegrams and petitions to the Delhi and Lahore secretariats, and petitioning for a special law to protect the Prophet Muhammad, a significant pointer to later hopes and expectations in the region.[13] Though security was provided in Lahore to prevent violent riots against Hindus and Sikhs, the critical reaction against the *Rangila Rasul* judgment produced unpleasant repercussions in daily life across the North-West Frontier Province. Approximately four hundred and fifty Hindus, for example, were persecuted in 1927 and were forced to migrate to Peshawar (now in Pakistan), only returning to their homes in the following year.[14]

The Punjab's British Governor, William Hailey, prohibited public meetings to maintain public peace among the many offended Muslims who were agitating for the government to remedy the defect in the Law and increase the punishment for those who offend any religious class through malicious writing.[15] Discussing the situation following the release of Rajpal, Hailey noted that there was a "very serious danger of disorder, for an attack on the Prophet was a concrete offence against Islam that stung them to the quick, and they could not bear the thought that Hindus could repeat it with impunity."[16] To calm the riot, he also promised that the British (particularly Punjab and Indian) Government would make plans to prevent circulations of the book, *Rangila Rasul* that had so offended the Muslim community. To Hailey the only way to calm the Muslim community was the successful prosecution of publications similar to *Rangila Rasul*, and indeed *Rangila Rasul* was merely one of the cases picked up in narratives of religious communities and their opponents.[17]

Historically, the decade of 1920 was the most critical period in the history of religious tension between religious communities in British India, which brought various other offensive publications written on the life of the Prophet Muhammad. For example, in 1927 the court in Agra discussed *Vichitra Jiwan*, another book against the Prophet Muhammad that offended

---

13. Barrier, 101.
14. B. S. Nijjar, *The History of the United Punjab* (Delhi: Atlantic, 1996), 154.
15. William Hailey quoted in Barrier, *Banned*, 100; Gour, *Penal Law of India*, 2186.
16. Hailey to Vincent, 11 August 1927 quoted in Thursby, *Hindu-Muslim Relations*, 41; Barrier, *Banned*, 100.
17. Secretariat notes, telegrams from PG quoted in Thursby, *Hindu-Muslim Relations*.

the Muslim community and affected Hindu-Muslim relations. Therefore all copies were forfeited under Section 153-A of IPC.[18] Though all publications written about the Prophet Muhammad in 1920s were judged offensive, *Rangila Rasul* was the focus of attention at the judicial, communal and political level, producing widespread religious controversy and debate over how to control malicious religious writing. It was assumed that banning books that wounded the feelings of Muslims would calm the community, although banning or forfeiting offensive religious books was not the only way.

Therefore the British were still looking for the successful prosecution of publications similar to *Rangila Rasul* in the Punjab province before making any change in the law. In the hope that he would secure an opposite ruling from the Lahore High Court to that initially given in *Rangila Rasul*, Justice F. W. Skemp was appointed to a special bench to hear arguments against another offensive essay written on the Prophet Muhammad in the monthly journal, *Risala-i-Vartman*, written by Devi Sharan Sharma, published in Amritsar, Punjab, especially the article "Sair-i-Dozakh," (A Trip to Hell).[19] It was declared that the article "Sair-i-Dozakh" could not be regarded as merely an attempt at "Hindu missionary work" as was claimed, as liberty to make religious criticism did not include a licence to resort to vile and abusive language. Judge Skemp declared that "the article deals with the Prophet Muhammad not as an individual but as the founder of Islam, and attempts to emphasize the futility of the Prophet's claims as the 'intercessor' for his followers."[20] The Judge also rejected the defence accepted earlier by Justice Dalip Singh dealing with the case of Rajpal's writing *Rangila Rasul*, that an offence against the founder of a religion cannot be regarded a crime against the religion itself.[21]

---

18. Kali Charan Sharma was convicted, by the magistrate of Agra, under Section 153-A of an offence of writing a Hindi book entitled *Vichitra Jiwan,* meaning a peculiar topsy-turvy, which contained an offensive attack on Islam especially on the life of Prophet Muhammad. The Governor in Council hereby declared that the book *Vichitra Jiwan* contained matter which promoted hatred between Hindus and Muslims and that further publicity of the book would promote enmity between Hindus and Muslims. Kali Charan Sharma v. King Emperor, AIR (1927) Allahabad, 654.

19. Devi Sharan Sharma and another v. Emperor AIR (1927) Lahore 594.

20. Judge F. W. Skemp in *Devi Sharan Sharma v. Emperor.*

21. GIPOL (Government of India Home Political Proceedings) 1927, 603 in Barrier, *Banned,* 101; John W. Cell, *Hailey: A Study in British Imperialism 1872-1969* (Cambridge:

Therefore, the Judge passed judgements against the editor and publisher of *Risala-i-Vartman* on 6 August 1927 for writing the article with the deliberate intention of promoting hatred and enmity between Muslims and Hindus.[22] The publication of "Sair-i-Dozakh" affected Hindu-Muslim relations not only in Amritsar, Punjab but also in Khebar, Afridi, namely among the Khukhihal and Zakkakhell, whose Jirga decided on a Hindu boycott in July 1927 till judgement was passed against the author of *Risala-i-Vartman*. During this period, about four hundred to five hundred Hindus were expelled from their houses and forced to move to Peshawar from Khebar, most leaving in fear though some with the sympathy of their neighbours.[23] Thus religious tension did not stay within the legal and judicial system but also affected the social life of Hindus and Muslims who had nothing to do with controversial writings.

Under the circumstances, the secretary of state pushed for amendments and argued that the law on religious publications should be clarified, because as it was publishers had nothing to fear from the law.[24] Hailey added that unless the government faced the problem, the Indians would find their own solutions.[25] The British therefore started imposing legal restrictions on religious publications and made plans to amend the law after reviewing cases such as *Risala-i-Vartman* and *Rangila Rasul* in Punjab. Hailey, in his letter to the Home Department, recommended a draft to add a section encompassing attacks on the founder or principal personages of a religion and preventing a broad range of provocative writing, but considered that it would be problematic to undertake any attempt to draft a law which would be both specific and wide-ranging in its reference.[26] Another suggestion was given by Sivaswamy Aiyer to prevent "attacks of a blasphemous character against any religion or religious founder, or any reputed incarnation thereof,

---

Cambridge University Press, 1992), 145.

    22. The author was sentenced to rigorous imprisonment for a period of six months and payment of a fine of Rs 250 or in default further rigorous imprisonment for three months. *Devi Sharan Sharma v. Emperor.*

    23. Nijjar, *History of United Punjab*, 154–155.

    24. Barrier, *Banned*, 100–101.

    25. William Hailey in Barrier.

    26. Hailey's letter to Home Department 12 August 1927 in Thursby, *Hindu-Muslim Relations*, 67–68.

or any prophets, saints or spiritual leaders revered by any class or persons."[27] This suggested provision saw all sacred personages protected from malicious attacks. One of the suggestions was also given by a Muslim, Ali, who wished to include "protection of the Prophet Muhammad by name from written attacks."[28]

The Home Department of British India reviewed all suggestions put forward for this new section in the proposed bill. The debate on the "Religious Insult Bill" produced a significant opportunity for the members of the Legislative Assembly to offer their own interpretation regarding the amendments. On the one hand the bill was criticized by Hindu members who "termed the bill an undue concession to Muslims, who were said to remain the favourite wife of the British Government."[29] On the other hand, Muslim members of the assembly feared that the bill did not go far enough to stop attacks on the Prophet and predicted that the amendment would not be effective.[30] Critics of the government continued to be suspicious that this legislation could reduce the freedom of the press and criticism of religion. However, after much discussion, a new section 295-A was passed and introduced by the Criminal Law Amendment Act (XXV of 1927) in August 1927. Though in the new version no name of any sacred person within religions was mentioned, it has been argued that section 295-A was specially designed to protect Prophet Muhammad and subsequently other historical sacred figures of religious communities from publications written with malicious intention.[31] Before discussing to what extent malicious writings were actually prevented after its enforcement, it is important to note what it contains and how the section dealt with religious publications.

2.2. Section 295-A of the IPC

Whoever, with deliberate and malicious intention of outraging the religious feelings of any class of His Majesty's subjects, by

---

27. Sivaswamy Aiyer in Thursby, 68.
28. Muhammad Ali in Thursby, 68.
29. Thursby, *Hindu-Muslim Relations*, 69–70.
30. Thursby, 70–71.
31. GIPOL 1929 in Barrier, *Banned*, 101; Gaur, *Textbook on the Indian Penal Code*, 418.

words, either spoken or written, or by visible representation, insults or attempts to insult the religion or the religious beliefs of that class, shall be punished with imprisonment of either description for a term which may extend to two years, or with fine or with both.[32]

In the bill as originally framed this section was first introduced in the following words:

Whoever, by words, either spoken or written, or by signs, or by visible representations, or otherwise, intentionally outrages or attempts to outrage the feelings, of any class of His Majesty's subjects, shall be punished with imprisonment of either description for a term which may extend to two years, or with fine or with both.[33]

The Select Committee to which the bill was referred had disapproved of this provision, and examined all aspects and suggested modifications both in words used in the section and in procedures. It redrafted the section by qualifying the word "intention" with "deliberate and malicious," and changed "religious feelings" to "religious beliefs." The committee also limited the offence to verbal and written attacks by "visible representation" rather than the earlier vague clause "by signs."[34] It was assumed that people might misuse the law as they were still allowed to publish religious books. It is important to note that not all religious writings fall under section 295-A but just those with deliberate and malicious intention to offend. Before discussing the application of this section after its inception, it is significant to look at the main ingredients of and procedures concerning section 295-A in British India.

2.2.1. The Main Ingredients and Procedures of Section 295-A

Anyone proposing to start proceedings under section 295-A had to obtain the necessary sanction from the relevant government before proceeding. It was essentially a civil case, which made malicious acts insulting any religion,

---

32. Lal, *Indian Penal Code*, 1328, 1330.
33. Lal, 1328, 1330.
34. Barrier, *Banned*, 101–102.

or outraging the religious feelings of any class of citizens, punishable as offences relating to religion, whether or not they amount to attempts to promote feelings of enmity or hatred between religious communities.[35] To constitute an offence under section 295-A, it is essential that the act is done in words, either spoken or written, or visible representation. The reference to "words" might cover an attempt to write a book or to voice a religious opinion or that the accused had maliciously insulted or attempted to insult the religion or religious beliefs of such a class.[36]

2.2.2. Deliberate and Malicious Intention of Section 295-A

Section 295-A does not limit all publication or speech and published matter, for the "religious belief of class of persons will not amount to an offence."[37] Section 295-A requires that the act of insulting should have been done with both deliberate *and* malicious intention.[38] According to the law commissioners in the second report the intention to wound religious feelings must be deliberate that did not conceive all of a sudden in the course of a religious discussion, but was premeditated by the accused.[39]

Second for prosecution under section 295-A, the intention behind the act must also be malicious. The term malicious has not been defined in the Penal Code but has been borrowed from the English Law as generally applied in legal phraseology. According to *Stroud's Judicial Dictionary*, malice in the common sense means ill-will against a person; but in a legal sense, it means an intentionally done wrongful act without cause or excuse.[40] Malice in its legal import does not mean merely ill-will but the wilful doing of an illegal act or the intention to do an act which is wrongful and to the detriment of another. Where any person wilfully does an act injurious to another without lawful excuse he or she does it maliciously.[41]

---

35. Gour, *Penal Law of India*, 2189; Lal, *Indian Penal Code*, 1330.

36. H. A. D. Phillips, *Comparative Criminal Jurisprudence* (Calcutta: Thacker, Spink & Co., 1889), 130.

37. Shaukat Mahmood, *The Pakistan Penal Code (XLV of 1860)*, 3rd ed., vol. 1 (Lahore: Legal Research Centre, 1981), 784.

38. King v. Nga Shwe Hpi, AIR (1939) Rangoon in Nelson, *Indian Penal Code*, 1372.

39. The law commissioners' second report in Macaulay, *Indian Penal Code*, 412.

40. The meaning of malice according to *Stroud's Judicial Dictionary*, in Nelson, *Indian Penal Code*, 1372; Nelson, *Pakistan Penal Code*, 1302.

41. Peary Lal v. State, AIR (1917) Allahabad 317.

It is therefore important to be certain the action has been deliberately and maliciously to outrage the religious feelings, and to insult the religion or religious beliefs of any such class before proceeding to prosecute under section 295-A.

2.2.3. The Intention to Outrage and Insult in Section 295-A

This section does not apply if the accused has used neither words nor visible representations to outrage any religious beliefs. Outrage means to treat with gross violence and indignity.[42] Notably, the words "outraging religious feelings" were intended to bring those culprits to book, as discussed in Rajpal's case, whose attack was on the Prophet Muhammad held sacred by Muslims. In the case of *Sheo Sharma*, another text insulting the Prophet Muhammad, it was held in 1927 that the newly added section 295-A has no retrospective effect, but if a new edition of an offensive book is published after enactment of the section, the author of the book can be convicted under this section if his connection with the publisher is established.[43] Considering any further publication or writing on religious issues, it was declared "if the language is of a nature calculated to produce or to promote feelings of enmity or hatred the writer must be presumed to intend what his action was likely to produce."[44] For example, it is possible that someone may attempt to publish a book or pamphlet on a religious matter only in reply to the opposite side or party. Under section 295-A, however, the prosecution must prove that the insult was for the sake of gratuitous insult and with an intention which derives from malice and malice alone. For Gour it would be a good defence if the accused says: "I had no malicious intention toward a class, but I did

---

42. Nizami, *The Pakistan Penal Code: XLV of 1860*, 5th ed. (Lahore: All Pakistan Legal Decisions, 1963), 269.

43. The charge against Shive Sharma (Shib Sherma) was for writing *Chaman Islam ki Sair*, A Trip To Islam, printed and published in Lucknow in 1939 in which he insulted Islam and the founding Prophet, Muhammad, arousing the anger of Muslims. It was actually first published in 1922, the second edition in 1928 and the third, brought to trial, in 1939. The book contained objectionable passages against Islam said to increase enmity or hatred between Muslims and Hindus: Sherma was found guilty of an offence under S. 153A. The accusation of "deliberate and malicious intention to outrage the religious feelings of Muslims" was tried under Section 295-A. Shive Sharma v. Emperor AIR (1941) Oudh 310 in Nelson, *Indian Penal Code*, 1372.

44. *Kali Charan Sharma v. King Emperor*, AIR (1927) Allahabad 649.

intend to wound and shock the feelings of an individual so that attention might, however rudely, be called to the reform which I had in view."[45] The case under section 295-A, "is not so much the matter of discourse as the manner of it."[46] It can be difficult for the court to defend the charge under section 295-A if anyone pleads that "he was writing a book in reply to the one written by one professing another religion who has attacked his own religion."[47] If anyone chooses to write such a book or pamphlet, they must take particular care with the language and manner of writing. Regarding the case of Rajpal that has been discussed above, the Select Committee in 1927, who dealt with the issue of writing an offensive book in their report, stated that the essence of the offence is that:

> The insult to religion or the outrage to religious feelings must be the sole, or primary, or at least the deliberate and conscious intention. We have accordingly decided to adopt the phraseology of sec. 298 which requires deliberate intention in order to constitute the offence with which it deals.[48]

Section 295-A became law in 1927, but up to that time acts constituting the offence under it also fell within 298, which still forms part of the code and runs as follows:

> Whoever, with the deliberate intention of wounding the religious feelings of any person, utters any word or makes any sound in the hearing of that person, or makes any gesture in the sight of that person, or places any object in the sight of that person, shall be punished with imprisonment of either description for a term which may extend to one year, or with fine, or with both.[49]

The two sections still stand together in the IPC but the question arises of the relative scope of each section. The expression used in section 298 is

---

45. Gour, *Penal Law of India*, 2188.
46. Gour, 2188.
47. Shiv Ram Das Udasin v. Punjab State, AIR (1955) in Gour, *Penal Law of India*, 2188.
48. *Gazette of India*, dated 17 September 1927, in Nelson, *Indian Penal Code*, 1373.
49. Morgan and Macpherson, *Indian Penal Code*, 220–222.

"wounding religious feelings" while the expression used in 295-A is "outraging the religious feelings." The word "outrage" is stronger and more serious than the word "wound."[50] The select committee in their report stated:

> We think that to penalise even an intentional outrage or attempted outrage upon the religious feelings of any class would be casting the net too wide for the cases with particular reference to which the Bill has been introduced. At the same time, we realise that the reference to the outraging of religious feelings was inserted to provide for the case of an insult to the founder of a religion or person held sacred by the followers of a particular religion where such an outrage does not amount to an insult of the religion. It has in one instance been held that an insult to the founder of a religion is not necessarily an insult to the religion although it may outrage the feelings of the followers of that religion. We have therefore provided that the new section shall only apply in cases where a religion is insulted with the deliberate intention of outraging the religious feelings of its followers.[51]

The intention of causing outrage to religious beliefs "must be malicious as well as deliberate, and must be directed to the class of persons and not merely to an individual."[52] Under section 298 religious feelings can be deliberately wounded by an accused seeking to draw attention to certain convictions in need of reform. It also means that people are free to discuss religious issues but their intention should be based on convincing others in theological discussion or conversation. Under section 295-A, however, the prosecution must prove that the insult derived from deliberate and malicious insult. If this is proved, the offence is non-bailable and the Court of Session or President Magistrate who tries the case may declare any publication to be seized and forfeited on the ground of containing offensive matter which is punishable under section 295-A.[53]

---

50. Nelson, *Indian Penal Code*, 1373–1374.
51. *Gazette of India*, dated 17 September 1927, in Nelson, 1373–1374.
52. Gour, *Penal Law of India*, 2187–2188.
53. An offence under this section is not cognisable by a police officer, as under schedule II of the Criminal Procedure Code as amended by Act XXV of 1927 they are not permitted

After reviewing the historical facts, it is clear that Chapter XV: Of Offences Relating to Religion of 1860 and its procedure was revised in order to meet the changing nature of the legislation on religious offences, religious writing and speech in the 1920s. It can also be seen that such change in the addition to section 295-A was intended to safeguard and to prevent cases like Rajpal's that might endanger public peace by stirring up the feelings of people or provoking the community to protest their hurt religious feelings. Considering such intensity of religious expression in "publication and speech," the British government, by changing the procedure of the prosecution under the clause 295-A, also declared that critical religious cases such as those discussed above would be tried at the Sessions or at the Presidency Magistrates.[54] The question now arises whether all British endeavours regarding the addition in the law in 1927 actually calmed the situation and helped to prevent or reduce incidents of offensive writings affecting religious communities in British India.

2.3. The Application of Section 295-A after 1927

Barrier has observed that throughout the 1920s, religious communities' anger over what they variously felt were offensive publications was a problem for the British government in India, with some extreme reactions and consequences such as in the case of the publisher, Rajpal.[55] Though he had been acquitted by the High Court, and offered police protection after two assassination attempts,[56] on 6 April 1929, Illam Din, a young Muslim man, aged 19–20 years, of Lahore stabbed Rajpal in his book shop.[57] Illam Din was convicted and given the death penalty for the murder. In the appeal, Muhammad Ali Jinnah (1876–1948), his defending lawyer and later founder of Pakistan, pleaded that provocation due to the youth of the accused was

---

to arrest without warrant, and by the same schedule a warrant and not a summons shall not ordinarily issue in the first instance. See Lal, *Indian Penal Code*, 1328, 1330; Gour, *Penal Law of India*, 2189.

54. Barrier, *Banned*, 102.

55. The point has been discussed in detail by Barrier in *Banned*, 66–107.

56. Khuda Bakhsh and Abdul Aziz, two Muslims attempted to kill Rajpal in 1927 but he survived. Qureshi, *Namoos-e-Rasalat*, 399–400.

57. Illam Din v. Emperor AIR (1930) Lahore, 157.

a mitigating circumstance, added to which Jinnah held the trial-court evidence was insufficient, the youth's reverence for the Prophet clear and his anger against those who maligned him reasonable, and the prosecution story doubtful. He also noted that the death sentence is harsh for a young person and the punishment should be converted to life imprisonment.[58] The British Judges, however, dismissed the appeal and confirmed the death penalty of Illam Din for murder under section 302 of the IPC.[59]

Ismail Qureshi, a Muslim lawyer in Pakistan, notes a subsequent case with a similar outcome in which Nathu Ram, a Hindu, was prosecuted for writing a "History of Islam" in 1933 in Karachi, Sindh Province, later part of Pakistan, in which he reviled both Islam and the Prophet. He was imprisoned for a year with fine, but was bailed against his offence following his appeal to the judicial commissioners in Karachi in 1934. Nathu Ram was murdered by Abdul Qayum, a young Muslim, when he came to court for the hearing in 1934. Like Illam Din, Abdul Qayum also received the death sentence for murdering the offender and later became known as Ghazi Abdul Qayum *Shaheed* (the martyr), for murdering Ram, defiler of the name of the Prophet.[60]

Historically, both cases are crucial examples, showing how Illam Din and Abdul Qayum both judged the accused and took the law in their own hands, becoming popular figures in subsequent history. However, Illam Din is the most quoted and known in the region of Punjab, the province in which religious incitement remained critical. As Asma Jahangir, a Muslim lawyer, has recently commented, Illam Din became a role model among many Muslims of the subcontinent, especially in contemporary Pakistan, where believers are urged by Muslim clerics to follow Illam Din *Shaheed*, the martyr, by killing those who insult the Holy Prophet.[61] Some such as Qureshi argue that the fateful instances following occurrences of offensive publications in 1920s and 1930s such as the murder of Rajpal and Ram by

---

58. *Illam Din v. Emperor* (1930); Syed Sharifuddin Pirzada, "Quaid-i-Azam Mohammad Ali Jinnah as a Lawyer, *Pakistan*," *Journal of History & Culture* XXVIII:1 (2007): 12.

59. *Illam Din v. Emperor*, AIR (1930) Lahore, 157.

60. Qureshi, *Muhammad: The Messenger*, 191.

61. Asma Jahangir is the Muslim head of the Human Rights Commission of Pakistan. She struggles to provide a legal support to many Christian cases based on blasphemy and has recieved many death threats. Jahangir, *From Protection to Exploitation*, 19.

Muslims occurred because "there was no law to redress their grievance with regard to slanderous attacks on the holy Prophet with the malicious intention to outrage their religious feelings,"[62] a view negated in the Introduction to this thesis. The historical setting and assessment of cases such as *Vichitra Jiwan*, *A Trip to Islam* and "Sair-i-Dozakh" and the promulgation of section 295-A discussed above give a different insight into the historical period. However, while the historical record shows various cases brought to defend the Prophet Muhammad, there were no recorded cases of anyone having been killed extra-judicially for insulting the Prophet after Rajpal and Ram during British rule.

Though the British significantly and critically dealt with religious offences and circumstances throughout the 1920s as outlined above, Barrier notes that the 1930s brought a flood of controversial publications on religious, political and patriotic issues that shook the British government: half the printed matter banned between 1933 and 1935 dealt with religious controversy.[63] For example, in Punjab, ninety-eight of the 135 newspapers had been involved in religious controversies.[64] Religious tensions did not only occur *between* religious communities, particularly Hindus and Muslims, but also *within* religious sects or groups. For example, some of the most offensive discussions and publications among Punjabi Muslims, later banned by the British, were by or on the Ahmadiya sect in which the founder was criticized for claiming and calling himself a Prophet.[65] Apart from the religious controversies, the realities of Indian politics in that period cannot be denied, particularly communal religious protest, so-called terrorist attacks and challenges by freedom movements against colonial control. Barrier notes that the government's "focus was diverted from the Hindu-Muslim violence to another cloud that was graying the political skies—a resurgence of challenge by the Congress and revolutionists."[66] Most of the published matter was deeply inspired by the freedom movement, religious publications playing

---

62. Qureshi, *Muhammad: The Messenger*, 193.

63. The number based on religious publications in GIPOL, 1931–1935 in Barrier, *Banned*, 125–126.

64. *Report on the Punjab Press*, 1933 and 1934 in Barrier.

65. The banned books written on Ahmadi sect are listed in banned literature of British India. Barrier, *Banned*, 139–141, 172–175.

66. Barrier, 103.

an important role in encouraging the fight for freedom.⁶⁷ Such publications were considered a serious threat, within these religious communities as well, to the British Empire and policies. Some cases involving the banning of offensive publications in the 1930s aroused controversy over the application of section 295-A of the IPC, as clearly shown in the case of *Angare* (meaning embers or red hot coals).

2.4. The Controversial Application of Section 295-A to Ban *Angare*

Angare, a collection of short fiction stories in Urdu, was written by Sajjad Zaheer, Rashid Jahan, Ahmad Ali and Mahmuduzzafar and published by Sajjad Zaheer, printed by Muhammad Jawad at the Nizami Press, Victoria Street in Lukhnow in December 1932, but banned on 15 March 1933 by the British government, "on the ground that the said book contains matter the publication of which is punishable under section 295-A of the Indian Penal Code."⁶⁸ The reason given for banning the publication of *Angare* was for insulting the Prophet Muhammad and outraging the Muslim community within the meaning of section 295-A.⁶⁹ However, *Angare* also included comments on social and religious traditions and practices as well as issues related to colonial governance and criticism of Urdu literature, none of which fell under section 295-A. Before analyzing various aspects of the stories it is necessary to discuss which stories in *Angare* dishonour the Prophet Muhammad, and how, for not all were considered offensive to the local Muslim clerics and community of Lukhnow.

Not all the authors of *Angare* were criticized, just Sajjad Zaheer (1905–1973) and Rashid Jahan (1905–1952) were alleged to have insulted Islam in their stories. First it will be helpful to give a brief description of the stories

---

67. In 1930 a Muslim movement was influenced by socialist ideas and was started up in North West Frontier Province in 1931 to "win the freedom for the country." Mahmud, "Angāre," 455.

68. *United Province Gazette*, 1933 in Mahmud, "Angāre," 463. All copies were destroyed by the police. Only three copies were kept in the record in New Delhi now known as National Archives of India and others two were sent to London. The British Museum kept a copy of *Angare* in 1933, now held in the Oriental and India Office Collection, British Library. Mahmud, "Angāre," 450.

69. Mahmud, "Angāre," 447; Ali and Rashed, "Progressive Writers' Movement," 91.

which offended the religious feelings of Muslims. Zaheer's first story *Nind Nahien Ati* (Sleep doesn't come) concerns a person who is unable to sleep, his mind wandering over various thoughts and objects such as sex and religion. Zaheer again writes about religion and sex in the second story *Jannat ki Basarat* (vision of paradise). According to this story:

> [A] Pious Maulana Daud, whether out of fear of God or of importance, prefers to pray from his Koran rather than to sleep with his young wife. On the holiest night of Ramadan, while prostrated over the Quran, he dreams that he is about to engage in intercourse with *a houri* [a woman]. He is then abruptly awakened by his wife's laughter from the erotic dream[70]

The literal meaning of these stories may be offensive but before reviewing the intention behind them and people's reaction it is important to review the stories by Rashid Jahan, a female physician who was particularly criticized and was called a radical *Angare-Wali* (woman of *angare*): "Muslims have threatened to chop off her nose."[71] Her first story, *Delhi Ki Sair* (Sightseeing Trip to Delhi) is a story about a Muslim woman, Malika Begum, whose husband, in a mood of generosity, offers to take her out to see the city of Delhi. On the Delhi platform he meets with his friend and goes off with him leaving his veiled wife behind, on a hot day, to keep an eye on the luggage. She sits and observes things while waiting for her husband. On her husband's return, already having lunch with his friend, he offers to buy *puris* for his wife without realising her feelings. She says "no thank you . . . I think you better [take] me home. I have seen enough of Delhi."[72]

In another story, which is actually a play, entitled *Parde ke Peeche* (Behind the Veil), Muhammadi Begum, a Muslim married woman, gives birth to a baby girl every year because her western-educated husband insists on having a son. Muhammadi's sister-in-law comes to visit her and realizes Muhammadi's health problem. She requested a lady doctor to come and help, and she

---

70. Zaheer's stories, *Jannat ki Basarat* and *Nind Nahien Ati* in Coppola and Zubair, "Rashid Jahan," 169.

71. Lubna Kazim, ed., *A Woman of Substance: The Memoirs of Begum Khurshid Mirza, 1918-1989* (Delhi: Zubaan, 2005), 102.

72. *Delhi Ki Sair* in Coppola and Zubair, "Rashid Jahan," 173; Kazim, *Woman of Substance*, 101.

warns her about the danger of continuing such pregnancies. The play ends with the arrival of the long- awaited son who mistreats his sisters, pointing out the situation as self-perpetuating, for the son will treats his family and future wife in the same way he saw his father treat his mother.[73]

The reaction of the contemporary local Muslim community of Lukhnow, where the accusation was brought, and initial criticism shows that *Angare* was criticized by conservative Muslims as described in the Urdu newspaper *The Medinah*, published in Bijnor on 13 February 1933:

> We are grateful to exalted God that he has allowed us to live in a remote township to perform the duties of journalism, a town which is safe from the piety-destroying and faith-removing elements of civilization . . . We could not find in them [the stories of *Angare*] anything intellectually modern except immorality, evil character and wickedness. To mock at the creator of the world, to ridicule religious beliefs and to make indecent jokes are the main characteristics of this bundle of filth. There is no regard for the greatness and majesty of God nor [sic] any respect for the sanctity and honour of the prophets, nor any respect of the human dignity. Instead one finds a bold and shameless display of every kind of foul language.[74]

Angare was also regarded as a religious offence by local clerics, as Ahmad Ali notes: "Mullahs from the pulpit and priests from the minarets carried invectives against the book and the authors; semi-political and all-India organizations passed resolutions condemning it."[75] Not only condemnation, but also a demand for prosecution as mentioned in an article in the *Hindustan Times* on 21 February 1933, writing that the Central Standing Committee of the All Indian conference, Lukhnow:

> Strongly condemns the heart rending and filthy pamphlet called *Angare* . . . which has wounded the feelings of the entire Muslim community by ridiculing God and his Prophet and which is extremely objectionable from the standpoints both

---

73. *Parde ke Peeche* in Coppola and Zubair, "Rashid Jahan."
74. *Medinah Press* quoted by Mahmud, "Angāre," 448–449.
75. Ali and Rashed, "Progressive Writers' Movement," 91–97.

of religion and morality. The committee further strongly urges upon the attention of the UP Government that the book to be at once proscribed.[76]

Local Muslim clerics issued *fatwa* (decree) against the publications of *Angare* and its authors. Funds were collected for their prosecution, and the punishments suggested included "stoning to death" and "hanging by the neck."[77] It is important to note that, initially, demands for death sentences for publishers were declared by local clerics without understanding whether such sentences could be practiced or not for religious offences. The intensity of the issue can be seen in one of the statements of the authors of *Angare*, Ahmad Ali, who said that "we were reminded of the Rajpal and the *Rangila Rasool* case."[78] Such statement shows they realized the possibility that they too might face death like Rajpal who was killed for publishing a book which insulted the Prophet. Howeve, Rajpal's case was considered offensive by Muslims, the judiciary and religious communities alike. The question arises whether the case of *Angare* legally falls under section 295-A for outraging the feelings of Muslims and Islam or not.

According to the legal procedure, the case of *Angare* was liable under section 295-A for "trial and revision" to declare the nature of literature and most importantly the intention of the authors, whether outrageous as well as malicious, to wound the feelings of Muslims within the meaning of the section. Though *Angare* was banned, the authors issued their statement of defence which reveals the glimpse of their intention as expressed in words that they "have chosen the particular field of Islam, not because they bear any 'special' malice, but because being born into that particular society, they felt themselves better qualified to speak for that alone."[79]

The intention of the writers was not seen as offensive by the entire Muslim community of British India, for not all reacted in the same way; some Urdu papers wrote against the prosecution of *Angare*. For example, in *Sarguzashat*

---

76. The *Hindustan Times* on 21 February 1933 in Mahmud, "Angāre," 448.

77. Ali and Rashed, "Progressive Writers' Movement," 91–92.

78. "In Defence of Angare, Shall We Submit to Gagging?" written by Muhammad uz-Zafar and Ahmad Ali, published on 5 April 1933 in *The Leader*, Journal of Allahabad India. Patel, *Lyrical Movements, Historical Hauntings*, 93–94.

79. Patel, *Lyrical Movements, Historical Hauntings*, 93–94.

The Issue of Offensive Writing and Publication and Amendments

in February 1933, though accepting that some themes in *Angare* were offensive, the reaction to the issue was criticized and the accusers of *Angare* were asked ". . . to set a correct example of Islam; because Islam is a light which is an enemy of darkness."[80] *Payam*, published on 5 March 1933 in Aligarh, wrote that:

> . . . Condemnation, proscription and legal action are no answer to blasphemy and atheism. How ironic that the very people who claim the right of free speech from the Government are not willing to concede the same right to their countrymen. The result of this is that fire keeps kindling unnoticed and burst into flames when it gets a chance . . . Such anger and rage can silence criticism for some time but the question still remains. The progress of the human mind cannot depart from the path of research.[81]

The statements and thoughts published in the *Hindustan Times* against the authors, and the statements mentioned above in *Sarguzashat* and *Payam*, show the different understandings of Muslims who did not consider that the accusation of the authors of *Angare* was reasonable nor their work truly offensive. Others wished to take serious legal steps and actions to punish them. The British authorities could have pointed to some support for publication from others within the Muslim community if they had wanted. Calm discussion of Islam or any other religion, indeed religious discussion in general between and within religious communities, was still legal under section 298 of Offences Relating to Religion, as discussed in the first chapter. However, the prosecution of *Angare* suggests that the British authorities and the Islamic religious clerics formed an alliance to ban the book under section 295-A. This not only raises questions about the decision, but also why and how Muslim clerics had such influence over the Muslim community and why the British authorities followed the clerics' lead to ban the book.

First, the short stories in *Angare* were in Urdu and its stories were written in a literary form that challenged established norms of Urdu language and literature. The language used could be prosecuted under section 295-A to

---

80. Mahmud, "Angāre," 449.
81. *Payam,* translated and quoted by Mahmud, "Angāre," 449.

enforce revision but only to clarify an "intention" that was outrageous as well as malicious, the defining criteria used for publications offensive to a religious community. Why were these changed forms of the Urdu language considered offensive? Historically, the Urdu language gained wide recognition and status because its script and style had become identified with Islam, indeed it became a symbol of Islamic ideology linked, therefore, with the language of the Qur'an.[82] Geeta Patel makes clear in her historical appraisal of the Urdu language that since the eighteenth century, forms of Urdu prose had formal guidelines for judging the correctness and aesthetic status of the language. By the mid-nineteenth century, the area of form and its failures, *islah*, had moved into a different realm organized around the "intent of writing to reform the populace at large and Muslim communities in particular."[83] Such a religious mandate was then used to assess literary works against that fixed yard-stick in the nineteenth century, which was preserved and intensified in the twentieth, entering a period which became "synonymous with punishments and exiles."[84] Discussing all legal issues of the writing and publishing of Urdu literature is beyond this research but it is important to discuss what was found offensive in the literature of *Angare* in a legal and religious perspective.

In the British era, one of the offensive styles of writing in the case of *Angare* came from Western literature's impact on the Urdu language and literature. Here it is important to note that English had long been imposed as a language of study and by the 1830s was declared the official language with the major aim to "form . . . a class of persons Indian in blood and colour but English in taste, in opinions, in morals and in intellect."[85] The previously important languages such as Hindi, Urdu, Bengali, Persian, Arabic and many others were marginalized.[86] Introducing a western slant in Urdu literature through *Angare* was simply offensive, for the authors intended

---

82. Sufia M. Uddin, *Constructing Bangladesh: Religion, Ethnicity, and Language in an Islamic Nation* (Delhi: Vistaar, 2006), 4; Tazeen M. Murshid, *The Sacred and Secular: Bengal Muslim Discourses, 1871-1971* (Calcutta: Oxford University Press, 1995), 287–296.

83. Patel, *Lyrical Movements, Historical Hauntings*, 88–89.

84. Patel, 88–89.

85. It was suggested by Thomas B. Macaulay to reform the language replacing with English Language. See Jalal and Bose, *Modern South Asia*, 67.

86. Zaman, *Ulama in Contemporary Islam*, 64.

to break established norms of the language and introduce a more liberal style with a direct impact on the social problems of the Indian society, as Mahmud notes:

> *Angare* came as an act of defiance against all traditional norms. It deliberately jettisoned much of the traditional language of Urdu literature and introduced new style. Drawing inspiration from the writing of James Joyce, Virginia Woolf and D. H. Lawrence, and in some cases Marxist writings, the young writers experimented with new techniques in writing which aimed at a more direct impact in its stark and unvarnished portrayal of human existence.[87]

This assessment of the western style of writing as offensive was often based on the assumption that linguistic modernity and change would cause the decline of established Urdu writing and its often religious gate-keepers. It is also significant to note that the response of the authors to religion in the *Angare* text was regarded and formulated as the "new secularism" which generally implies the notion of rejection of or insult to religion.[88] Though the authors, in publishing *Angare*, "dreamt of winning for Urdu language"[89] their dreams were undermined by the critics' view that it was "not a great piece of literature."[90] Nevertheless, their intention of publishing modern Urdu literature did not stop. After the ban on the publication of *Angare*, the writers issued their statement of defence and plans for future publications from Delhi, drafted by Mahmuduzzafar and published in *The Leader* Allahabad in April 1933:

> ... the book [*Angare*] at once raised a storm in Muslim circles. It was said to be . . . [an] attack on Islam and everything decent in the society . . . The authors of this book do not wish to make any apology for it. They leave it to float or sink of itself. They

---

87. Sajjad Zaheer and Mahmuduzzafar, the writers of *Anagre,* studied in London and gradually drifted towards socialism. Mahmud, "Angāre," 447.

88. Patel, *Lyrical Movements, Historical Hauntings*, 98.

89. Ali and Rashed, "Progressive Writers' Movement" quoted by Mahmud, "Angāre," 448.

90. Carlo Coppola, "The Angare Group: The *Enfants Terribles* of Urdu Literature," quoted by Patel, *Lyrical Movements, Historical Hauntings*, 92.

are not afraid of the consequences of having launched it. They only wish to defend "the right of launching" it and all other vessels like it . . . They stand for the free criticism and free expression in all matters of the highest importance to the human race in general and the Indian people in particular . . . Our practical proposal is the formation immediately of a League of Progressive Authors, which should bring forth similar collections from time to time, both in English and the various vernaculars of our country[91]

It was a call for claiming the "right of free expression" and, despite the court case, this style became a significant marker of progressive writing in the history of Urdu literature, the Progressive Writing Movement, launched in 1936, citing the writers of *Angare* as leading figures in the history of Urdu literature.[92] One of the future objectives of the progressive association was "to secure literature and other arts from the conservative classes in whose hands they have been degenerating so long."[93]

Apart from the issue of Urdu literature as a religious sentinel, the second probable and major reason for banning *Angare* was "the moral language and themes" of its authors. Ahmad Ali, one of the authors of *Angare,* insisted the text and indeed the genre were influenced by social conditions of India.[94] In the stories of Zaheer and Rashid Jahan, the writers attempted to raise some traditional, social and religious themes and issues they saw in middle class conservative Muslim families, culture and behaviour in a male-dominated society. Among many perceived causes for grievance among those who claimed that religion was insulted was the portrayal of sex and sexuality, described in Zaheer's story *Janat Ki Basarat* (the vision of Paradise), a story which portrays a sanctimonious cleric fondling a copy of the Qur'an in his sleep as he dreams of nubile *houris* in heaven. However, the intention of Zaheer as expressed in the statement of defence was rather different:

---

91. *The Leader*, Allahabad "In Defence of Angare, Shall We Submit to Gagging?" quoted in Ali and Rashed, "Progressive Writers' Movement," 91–97; Patel, *Lyrical Movements, Historical Hauntings*, 93–94.

92. Mahmud, "Angāre," 454.

93. Ali and Rashed, "Progressive Writers' Movement," 94–95.

94. Mahmud, "Angāre," 451–452.

> Sajjad Zaheer . . . is concerned chiefly with a criticism and satire of the current Muslim conceptions, life and practices. His attack is directly primarily against the intolerable theological burden that is imposed from childhood upon the average Muslim in this country—a burden that leads to a contortion and a cramping, an internal torture of the inquisitive or speculative mind and the vital vigorous body, of both man and woman.[95]

Zaheer's stories may have expressed a few such themes. However, it was the stories of Rashid Jahan, the female doctor, which were regarded as particularly offensive and threatening. Generally in her stories Jahan presented women's experiences of social isolation and concealment under the veil, as well as mistreatment by the husband even if he is western-educated. Historically, in the late nineteenth century, some prominent Islamic male scholars also dealt with the issue of woman's oppression in education, her legal marriage status, the issue of *parda* (veil), as well as her lower status than a man, which was described as common social practice in British India.[96] The question arises why such conditions and issues, acceptable to discuss in the nineteenth century, were regarded as offensive in the stories written by Jahan in *Angare*. Malik argues that *Angare* was an internal critique of patriarchal practices within the Muslim society and social life.[97] One of the commonly accepted ideas was the supremacy of man, who in Jahan's stories had clear authority to suppress women at home. Such supremacy

---

95. Statement of defence "In Defence of Angare, Shall We Submit to Gagging?" quoted in Patel, *Lyrical Movements, Historical Hauntings*, 94.

96. Muslim reformers such as Syed Ahmad Khan from Aligarh (1817–1898), Maulana Ashraf Ali Thanvi of Deoband (1864–1943) and Mumtaz Ali from Lahore (1860–1935) evolved a critique of a contemporary Muslim religious social life and British colonial rule. Thanvi devotes a lot of space in *Behishti Zever*, (Ornaments of Paradise) published in Lahore, to attacking and rooting out false custom and woman's ignorance as a problem of the society. Likewise, Ahmad Khan dealt with such issues particularly woman's education and veil in *Tahzib un-Niswan* (women's civilisation) and Ali defended Woman's Rights in *Huquqs un-Niswan* (women's Rights) published to answer the criticism by missionaries in Lahore that woman's oppression is a part of Islamic faith. See Gail Minault, "Women, Legal Reform and Muslim Identity," in *Islam, Communities and the Nation: Muslim Identities in South Asia and Beyond*, ed. Mushirul Hasan (Delhi: Manohar, 1998), 139–158.

97. Maleiha Malik, "Angare, the 'Burning Embers' of Muslim Political Resistance: Colonial and Post-Colonial Regulation of Islam in Britain," in *Colonial and Post Colonial Governance of Islam: Continuities and Ruptures*, eds. Marcel Maussen, Veit Bader and Annelies Moors (Amsterdam: Amsterdam University Press, 2011), 203.

goes beyond what the new social awareness and modernity, implied in the stories, was willing to accept in silence, and shocked the readers of that time, particularly Urdu speaking Muslims. *Angare*'s treatment of sexuality and mistreatment by husbands, women's health and pregnancies was offensive for traditionalists, a view which later spread across other parts of India.[98] By raising such issues, Jahan tried to suggest birth control methods, an unacceptable issue for many conservative families who were key advocates for the family in the nineteenth century, as well as in Indian Urdu literature.[99] Probably the most offensive aspect of Jahan's stories was to take such issues "out of house" particularly in the play *Behind the Veil*, where she broke the rules by "open[ing] up a peephole into the sacred space of the house hold, the space that was hidden from the gaze of the outside, a bedroom in the women's quarter, the *zanana*,"[100] (a place of women).[101] Rashid, mediating as a doctor between the *zanana* and the rest of Indian society, plays a similar role in her writing that exposes the poor medical conditions and isolation of a woman who has never been out of the *zanana*, never met the doctor or lawyer as such transactions are *parda nashin*, conducted through male mediators.[102] Coppola and Zubair note that Rashid was qualified to raise family issues through her medical profession and knowledge and to write on the subject for the people relying on old beliefs and methods. He insists that:

> Rashid Jahan thus covers the spectrum of her experiences and her socio-political beliefs in her writings. She intended her short stories to be educational and followed the progressive line in her choice of subject matter. As a woman, a Muslim and a doctor, she utilized those areas to provide her material and to direct her attention back to correcting and readjusting the values and inequities that she saw there . . . [as] a most influential person

---

98. Susie Tharu and K. Lalita, eds., *Women Writing in India: 600 BC to the Present*, vol. 1 (London: Rivers Oram Press, 1993), 83, 117; Gopal, *Literary Radicalism in India*, 68.

99. Coppola and Zubair, "Rashid Jahan," 173.

100. Patel, *Lyrical Movements, Historical Hauntings*, 108.

101. "Zanana" women's place, from the Persian word "zan," a woman, and "ana," place. It is the part of the house of native women, entirely separated from that occupied by men. Mary Weitbrecht, *The Women of India and Christian Work in the Zenana* (London: James Nisbet, 1875), 94.

102. Patel, *Lyrical Movements, Historical Hauntings*, 120.

of her class. The complete immersion in radical politics, medicine and literature side by side is clear evidence of the goals that she set for herself.[103]

Rashid's offence was also to have had the courage to break tradition and start a career as a woman. Coppola and Zubai notes that Rashid Jahan "became a symbol of emancipated woman; in conservative homes an example of all the worst that can occur if a woman is educated, not kept in *purdah* [veil], and allowed to pursue a career."[104]

All thoughts about this aspect of the *Angare* publication, discussed above, can be summed up in the conclusion that breaking traditional rules in such a male-dominated society was simply a religious offence, a blasphemy, which offended some Muslims of Aligarh and Lukhnow. The secular tension challenged the self-image of those orthodox Muslims who idealized *ashraf*, noble ethics, values and language coming from the Middle East Islamic world, values which they considered threatened by the new reformation and western values.[105] The nature of the set rules and orthodoxy as the power to protect tradition clashed with other views from the wider community which may have had doubts about certain practices and beliefs.[106] Malik suggests that the *ulama* became the gatekeepers of a particular Islamic scholarly tradition, which they saw as being the guardian of the Muslim identity and presence of Islam in British India, a tradition which they felt was threatened by the modern writers of *Angare*.[107] Not all Muslims of British India accepted their views.

Such social and traditional reasons, however, would not have been strong enough to ban the publication under section 295-A, had it been treated on its merits alone, especially given that the stories of the first volume of *Angare* were not written "intentionally" to insult the Prophet Muhammad within the meaning of that section. And if there was any offensive theme in a few

---

103. Coppola and Zubair, "Rashid Jahan," 181.
104. Coppola and Zubair, 166–183; Gopal, *Literary Radicalism in India*, 68.
105. Murshid, *Sacred and the Secular*, 286.
106. Talal Asad, *The Idea of an Anthropology of Islam* (Washington: Centre for Contemporary Arab Studies, Georgetown University, 1986), 15.
107. Saira Malik, "The Social Transformation of the 'Ulama' in British India During the 19th Century," *Journal of Islamic Law and Culture*, 12, no. 1 (2010): 56.

stories, there was room under section 295-A to demand corrections, *islah*, certain changes in words and lines in the text in contention: this was not done in the case of *Angare*. After reviewing and analyzing reasons for accusation from the literature and moral language of *Angare*, it is now important to discuss the political manoeuvrings which underlay the banning of the book which also was considered offensive by the British government.

The publication of the stories in *Angare* also showed negative aspects of British colonial rule. Mahmood notes that a few stories of *Angare*, those written by Sajjad Zaheer and Ahmed Ali, were intended to critique social and religious practices based on ignorance. However, they were also written in protest against what they felt was a disgraceful acquiescence in foreign rule and inequalities in British-Indian society.[108] The contemporary political circumstances of the 1920s and 1930s were a serious threat to British colonial rule. Throughout the 1920s, as discussed above, the British confronted critical social disorder and threats to Hindu-Muslim relations based on religious issues and publications. However later in the 1930s, the situation dramatically changed when the British "government feared a confrontation with anti-British forces more strongly than a continuation of Hindu-Muslim violence."[109] Most of the publications in 1930s were inspired by the freedom movement which played an important role to encourage people to fight for freedom from colonial rule.[110] By the 1930s the colonial authorities were interacting with the religious leaders, *ulama* and clerics, as the representatives of the Muslims of British India.[111] *Angare* was published in the era of this freedom movement and was inspired by it, and this was a key reason for banning it, religion being a useful hook to use. Under such circumstances, the British were able to suppress dissent within the communities over which they exercised colonial rule, particularly the educated liberal voices that were starting to organize anti-colonial and nationalist political organization.[112] It is clear how religious issues were handled by the

---

108. Mahmud, "Angāre," 447.

109. Barrier, *Banned*, 98.

110. In 1930 a Muslim movement influenced by socialist ideas was started up in North West Frontier Province which announced in 1931 they would "win the freedom for the country." Mahmud, "Angāre," 455.

111. Malik, "Social Transformation of the 'Ulama," 56.

112. Malik, "Angare, the 'Burning Embers,'" 202–203.

authorities especially where policy-makers could use policies for their own political advantages, and where:

> ... Obedience of the people to the decisions of the power command becomes habitual ... In some cases the method may include isolation from all sources of support ... These individuals are the silent group. The voice of the professional ... may have something to say about policy, but it usually goes unheeded.[113]

This brief reference to some political reasons behind the ban on *Angare* make it reasonable to suggest that the written matter in *Angare* was treated as a religious insult punishable under section 295-A of the IPC, because the government could use this law both to placate some Muslim leaders and quell dissent against their own rule. However, banning the book did not stop the authors from publishing on colonial matters as they later became more concerned to write on colonial power. One of the aims of the Association of *Angare* was "to produce and translate literature of a progressive nature, to fight for cultural reaction, and in this way to further the cause of Indian Freedom and social generation ... To fight for the right of free expression of thought and opinion."[114]

2.5. Conclusion

The revision of the religious offences law from the 1920s to 1947 was a response to some important incidents which left deep marks that remained into the post-colonial period. Bringing the first amendments was a significant step by the British government. The application of the addition to Chapter XV not only shows that the demands of Muslims to amend the law were accepted but that after revision resulting from some cases it was declared that the issue of offensive writing was indeed and perhaps primarily a malicious intention to wound Muslims. It can be assumed that a really malicious insult would cause a government to protect people and beliefs through the rule of law. However, the case of *Angare* presented a totally different picture, showing how socio-political influences and anxieties can

---

113. F. Hunter, *Community Power Structure: A Study of Decision Makers*, quoted in Steven Lukes, *Power: A Radical View*, 2nd ed. (Basingstoke: Palgrave Macmillan, 2004), 3.
114. Ali and Rashed, "Progressive Writers' Movement," 94–95.

affect the law-makers with the power to use religion to strengthen its position. This is yet one more legacy from the colonial era which has continued until the present. The fight for freedom from colonial rule continued until the British left South Asia in 1947. In an independent political arena, it was important to establish and enable social, economic and political dynamics in the component states of the newly divided subcontinent – India, Pakistan and subsequently Bangladesh. However, as the next chapter will show, concern about the destabilising effect of religious hatred as expressed in the legislation on religious offences would remain an important element in the post-colonial period.

Part II

Implications of Offences Relating to Religion from Post-1947 in the Independent Subcontinent (India and Pakistan)

CHAPTER 3

The Legacy of British Law in Independent India and Pakistan

The Indian subcontinent was one of the most religiously diverse regions in South Asia. Religion played a significant role in the independence movement and was one of the powerful tools both driving for independence in the British colonial era and directing the post-independence division of South Asia into Hindu and Muslim countries[1] on the basis that Hindus and Muslims, from two different religions, could not live together.[2] Before handing over power to the Indian subcontinent, it was declared by the British government that "India is hopelessly . . . split by racial and religious division which we cannot bridge and which became more and more acute as any real transfer of power by us draws near."[3] That division led to two nations in which Christians as a minority in each sought protection under the Muslim and Hindu majority nations of Pakistan and India. The focus of this chapter is how two and then three countries dealt with the Offences

---

1. James, *Rise and Fall of the British Empire*, 412.
2. In the Two Nation Theory it was declared that "They [Hindus and Muslims] are not religions in the strict sense of the word, but are, in fact, quite different and distinct social orders and it is a dream that the Hindus and Muslims can ever evolve a common nationality. This misconception of one Indian nation has gone far beyond the limits and is the cause of most of our troubles and will lead India to destruction if we fail to revise our notions in time . . . To yoke together two such nations under a single State, one as a numerical minority and the other as a majority, must lead to growing discontent and final destruction of any fabric that may be so built up for the government of such a state." Mohammad Ali Jinnah in M. H. Saiyid, *Mohammad Ali Jinnah (A Political Study)*, 2nd ed. (Lahore: Shaikh Mohammad Ashraf, 1953), 432.
3. The statement was delivered by Winston Churchill and quoted in Michael Fry, *The Scottish Empire* (Berlin: Tuckwell, 2001), 437.

Relating to Religion legislation and fulfilled the law's spirit to protect religious communities.

Though British rule ended in the subcontinent in 1947, it left its legacy such as law and order that is still in practice. After 1947 (the partition of India and Pakistan), the title of the Indian Penal Code remained for independent India but was changed to that of the Pakistan Penal Code for that country. Similarly, after 1971 the Pakistan Penal Code came to be known simply as the "Penal Code" in independent Bangladesh. Thus, except for changes in the title, the Penal Code of 1860 remained largely unchanged with only minor modifications in a divided South Asia. The new countries, just as the British did in writing and applying the law, claimed that under it every person would be liable to punishment without distinction of rank and faith provided the offence with which anyone is charged had been committed in India and Pakistan.

The application of the law, Chapter XV: Of Offences Relating to Religion of 1860 was expected to play a key role in encouraging and bringing toleration in religious issues to all religious communities badly scarred by the communal violence following the Partition of India and Pakistan. The main objective of this law, as discussed in the first part of the thesis was, and still is, to protect religious communities from having their place of worship intentionally injured or defiled (section 295), their religious communities outraged through offensive writing and speech (Section 295-A), their religious assembly disturbed (section 296), their place of worship trespassed upon (section 297) and their religious feelings wounded by words (section 298).

It has been shown in Part 1 how the law regarding Offences Relating to Religion was applied, criticized and amended in British India. Major criticism occurred on the issue of offensive writing and speech, particularly in the 1920s that brought amendments in Chapter XV as already discussed. Part 2 will examine how the aim of the Offences Relating to Religion laws, to preserve religious tolerance and avoid intolerance, fared over the years in the two and then three countries. Of particular interest will be the fact that the legislation concerning offensive writing and speech under section 295-A and section 295, defiling a sacred place and object, have been used more than any of the other legislation concerning religious crimes described in

Chapter XV: Of Offences Relating to Religion law, sections 296, 297 and 298 rarely being prosecuted in India and Pakistan.

Apart from protecting religious communities under the legislation on religious offences, India and Pakistan each decided to declare it a fundamental right to provide religious freedom to religious communities in 1948. The Constitution of India declared India a secular state, and in section 25 (1) provides that all citizens are "equally entitled to freedom of conscience and the right freely to profess, practise and propagate religion."[4] According to section 19, all Indian citizens have the right to freedom of speech and expression and are subject to reasonable restrictions for preserving *inter alia*, public order, decency or morality.[5] Likewise, Pakistan adopted fundamental rights that give the same religious freedom to all religious communities.[6] Under these provisions both countries claimed and reiterated their democratic values and secularism. Secularism may denote a notion of a separation of religion and state, or it may guarantee freedom of religion to all religious communities, and equality of citizens for equal opportunities without any discrimination on religious grounds, or it may be used to denote opposition to religion and its influence. It has a multi-dimensional meaning in the South Asian context. India is a secular state: Pakistan was initially. Nandy discusses secularism as a western concept which, he asserts, plays an important part in religious intolerance and violence among different religious classes in India.[7] For Madan, it is used when religion persists as a powerful element in personal identity, claiming religion as a "constitutive of society."[8] In Pakistan's general socio-cultural context, secularism has been used to mean Islamic democracy and has been regarded as reflecting

---

4. Fundamental rights quoted in Gour, *Indian Penal Code*, 413–414.

5. K. N. Chaturvedi, *The Constitution of India* (Delhi: Government of India, Ministry of law and Justice, 2007); Government of India, Law Commission of India, "Report on Conversion/Reconversion to Another Religion – Mode of Proof," Report no. 235, December 2010, available online http://lawcommissionofindia.nic.in/reports/report235.pdf.

6. M. Zafrullah Khan, *Islam and Human Rights*, 5th ed. (Islamabad: Islam International Publication, 1999), 1–9; Martin Lau, *The Role of Islam in the Legal System of Pakistan* (Leiden: Martinus Nijhoff, 2006), 95–106.

7. The point is discussed in detail in Ashis Nandy, "The Politics of Secularism and the Recovery of Religious Tolerance," in *Secularism and its Critics*, ed. R. Bhargava (New Delhi: Oxford University Press, 1998), 321–344.

8. T. N. Madan, "Secularism in Its Place," *Journal of Asian Studies* 46, no. 4 (1987): 748.

the "insignificance of religious thinking."[9] In short it can be said that in the post-colonial period in India and Pakistan religious interests arose, which gradually limited the full freedom of religious expression, whether in writing and speaking, evangelism, or other religious practices. Before discussing the evolution and even transformation brought about by this growing erosion of the secular principle, it is necessary to consider how religious communities and political power initially regarded religious issues and how Chapter XV: Of Offences Relating to Religion, the main discussion point of the chapter, was used in India and Pakistan from 1947.

3.1 The Application of Chapter XV of Religious Offences in India post-1947

It has been argued that such laws, for the protection of religion, reveal the secular democratic values on which India bases its secularism. There is no state religion in India but all religious communities such as Hindus, Muslims, Sikhs and Christians are protected by the law particularly as constituted in Chapter XV: Of Offences Relating to Religion in the 1860 IPC. In the main, Indian courts and the judicial system applied Chapter XV without any major contradictions or critical consequences, passing adequate judgements to maintain religious harmony from 1947 until the 1970s. Significantly, in terms of providing religious protection, the courts and the judicial system were prepared to be very circumspect in considering religious issues and to "pay due regard to the feelings and religious emotions of different classes of persons with different beliefs irrespective of the consideration whether or not they share those beliefs, or whether they are rational or otherwise, in the opinion of the Court."[10]

---

9. Muhammad Imtiaz Zafar, "Can Pakistan be a Secular State?" *Research Journal of South Asian Studies* 28, no. 1 (January–June 2013): 165–185; Ishtiaq Ahmad, "The Pakistan Islamic State Project: A Secular Critique," in *The State and Secularism: Perspective from Asia*, eds. Michael Heng Siam-Heng, Ten Chin Liew (Singapore: World Scientific Publication, 2010), 185–210.

10. From a judgement in 1958 when the accused, Veerabadran Chettiar, protesting against idol worship, broke an image of the god Ganesh in public and said publically that he intended to insult the feelings of the Hindu community as part of his campaign against idol worship. This act was considered offensive and liable under section 295 for defiling the sacred object of Hindu worship. Veerabadran Chettiar v. E. V. Rama Swami Naiker, AIR (1958) SC 1032-5; Gour, *Penal Law of India*, 2182.

In India the most common religious offence has been writing and speaking outrageously and maliciously on a religious matter, which is prosecuted under section 295-A of IPC, all the ingredients and objectives of which were discussed in the second chapter. The most important legal aspect of this section is to note the critical circumstances in which prosecutions had occurred under the British when offensive books and pamphlets, particularly about the life of the Prophet Muhammad, were published in the 1920s in British India, which as we saw led to major changes in the legal history of Offences Relating to Religion. It is interesting to note both continuation and change in post-colonial publications, particularly those targeting the sacred personages of Muslims or other religions, and indeed such publications continued in independent India. Such events brought one change or amendment in section 295-A of the Indian Penal Code, increasing the punishment from two years to three years in 1961,[11] although it seems the circumstances surrounding the various cases reported under section 295-A in India post-1947 were not as critical as in British India.

The Indian courts followed and declared the same objective of section 295-A while passing judgment on cases brought for offensive writing and speech whether the case fell under section 295-A, deciding whether an act was done with malicious intention to hurt the feelings of the other religious community, or not.[12] For example, in the cases of *Baba Khalil Ahamad v. State*, six books were considered offensive which had received protests from a number of persons in the Muslim community whose religious feelings had been injured. According to the case, "Abu Malik represented Muawiya

---

11. Amended by Act 41 of 1961, Gour, *Indian Penal Code*, 418; Another change was made in the procedure of section 298. An offence under section 298 originally was non-cognizable in British India, which means that a police officer shall not arrest an accused without warrant, but now it is "cognizable" which gives power to a police officer for arresting anyone without a warrant, although this in the state of Andhra Pradesh only.

12. Various religious cases have been recorded in ILR (Indian Law Reports), AIR (All India Reports) and Cr. LJ (Criminal Law Journals) which mostly have been successfully constituted in India within the meaning of the Law of Religious Offences particularly section 295-A for protecting malicious writing and speech. Shiv Ram Das v. The Punjab State, AIR (1955) 28; 1955 Cr. LJ 337. 1957 CRS 860, AIT (1960) Madras 258, AIR (1971) Bombay, 1971 Cr. LJ 1773, (1980) Cr. LJ 448, (1983) 1446, (1985) Cr. LJ 797, (1995) SEC 214, (1995) Cr. LJ 1316.

as a pious person and applicant represented him as a mean character."[13] In November 1952, a handbill was published in Benares describing Yazid, son of Muawiya, as one entitled to be admitted to heaven, whereas in other pamphlets Muawiya was praised and represented as a leader of Hanafi Muslims. The applicant was a Sunni who considered it his duty to dispel doubts and misunderstandings about the position of Yazid and Muawiya in Islamic history. With this object, the defendant wrote six books in reply to one written by someone professing another religion who had attacked his religious views. The court decided when anyone chooses to write such books, particular care in the language and manner of writing is necessary. In the court's opinion, the six books contained matter and language offensive and considered punishable under Section 295-A of IPC. The Uttar Pradesh State Government was, therefore, justified in passing the order for their forfeiture.[14]

Yet protection for hurt feelings related to religion was not uncontested, for controlling such speech in India was felt to violate the constitution which declares freedom of religious expression under Article 25 and 26 of the Indian Constitution.[15] However, it has been argued that "Chapter XV which deals with the offences relating to religion is not affected by the operation of Article 25 of the constitution."[16] For example, in 1969 in the case of Sant Das Maheswari, the contradiction between the limited freedom of writing and expression under section 295-A and religious freedom of expression under Article 25 and 26 was raised. It was held that section 295-A does not prohibit or make punishable anything which is mere profession, practice or propagation of a religion within the meaning of Article 25 but what is made punishable is a deliberate and malicious intention of outraging the religious feelings of any class.[17] The Madras court laid down the following law while discussing Section 295-A:

---

13. For more detail see Baba Khalil Ahamad v. The State, AIR (1960) All 715; 1960 Cr. LJ 1528; Sheikh Abdillahi Nassir, "Yazid was never Amirul Muminin," *Al-Islam.org*. The six books were written due to a dispute about the succession (*Imamate*) in the leadership of Sunnis and Shias. To Sunnis, Abu Baker, Umar and Usman were the first *Khilifas* (successors) and Ali was the fourth. However, Ali was also the first *Khilifa* to Shia.

14. Baba Khalil Ahamad v. The State of UP, AIR (1960) All 715; (1960) Cr. LJ 1528.

15. Ramji Lal Modi v. The State of UP, AIR (1957) SC 623.

16. Gour, *Indian Penal Code*, 414.

17. Sant Das Maheswari v. Babu Ram Jodoun, AIR (1969) Allahabad 436; the similar judgment was passed in Siva Ram Das v. The State of Punjab, AIR (1955) Punjab 28; *Baba*

The right of freedom of speech and expression guaranteed under Article 19 (1) (a) of the Constitution will no doubt enable a citizen to criticise the religion and the religious beliefs of a class of persons. Article 25 of the Constitution confers a right on all persons to freedom of conscience and a right freely to profess, practice, propagate religion subject to certain conditions and a person is entitled to express and propagate his views so long as he does not affect the public order, morality and health or offend any of the provisions of the Constitution or laws of the land.[18]

The statement makes clear that though religious communities have religious freedom, the expression of that freedom cannot affect the public peace. It is similar to the comment of Naguib Mahfouz that "we need to differentiate between speech and disrespect for religious symbols. Every man has a right to stretch his arms, for example, but not to the extent that he hits the face of the [next] person."[19]

Though the application of Chapter XV: Of Offences Relating to Religion remained largely unedited in the IPC, the application of the anti-conversion laws (or Freedom of Religion Acts) has challenged the freedom of expression as briefly indicated below. A detailed review of the Indian conversion acts being inappropriate here other than noting its application, importance and meaning particularly with the reference to the social and historical context of legislation on religious offences as affected by the anti-conversion laws.

3.1.1 The Impact of Conversion Acts on Chapter XV: Of Offences Relating to Religion

Conversion is a broad term referring to a highly variable and potentially syncretistic process in which social identities and cultural styles, frequently but not exclusively linked to religion, are transformed.[20] It is clear that people may convert for religious reasons as well as social ones. Though,

---

Khalil Ahmad v. The State of UP, AIR (1960) All 715 and *Ramji Lal Modi v. The State of UP*.

18. Public Prosecutor v. P. Ramaswami, AIR (1964) Madras 258.

19. Naguib Mahfouz in Mahmudul Hasan, "Free Speech, Ban and 'Fatwa': A Study of Taslima Nasrin Affair," *Journal of Post Colonial Writing* 46, no. 5 (December 2010): 549.

20. Andrew Buckser and Stephen D. Glazier, *The Anthropology of Religious Conversion* (New York: Rowman & Littlefield, 2003), 17.

the material interests tied to converting, such as access to education and employment, were frequently associated with a certain social and ethnic identity. It was especially in these cases that people who had not converted, as well as believers of the faith of the convert, might question the validity of the conversion. In that case the convert was marginalized in a way that could not be protected under the law. Under colonial governance, all religious communities could use freedom of religious discussion to enable conversion, though the government itself did not encourage conversion to Christianity in the mid-nineteenth century. This was a period when their control was uncertain, and religious change could tip the balance. Thus while the convert's social position had to be negotiated within their family of origin as well as in the church of their reception, their legal position was not helped by British law.[21]

Though the application of Chapter XV rarely caused great turmoil in India, the role and meaning of the original law, to encourage religious discussion and toleration without religious antagonism in the context of a genuine exchange of ideas not excluding the possibility of conversion, has been radically affected by anti-conversion laws in some Indian states. The conversion acts promulgated in the 1950s and 1960s in India have arguably also affected the fundamental human rights for religious freedom of conscience, which is shown in various case studies, and will be reviewed later in this chapter. In order to maintain religious freedom, the Indian Parliament initially rejected the Indian Converts Bill in 1955 after members of the legislature, such as A. M. Thomas and Prime Minister J. Nehru, warned of the potential for harassment of a large number of people.[22] However, the desire to regulate conversion gained the support of state government officials by 1956 and since 1968 offenders can be legally prosecuted in some states of India.[23] It

---

21. The point is discussed in detail by Gauri Viswanathan, "Coping with Death: The Christian Convert's Rights of Passage in Colonial India," in *After Colonialism: Imperial Histories and Postcolonial Displacements*, ed. Gyan Prakash (Princeton: Princeton University Press, 1995), 183–210; Gauri Viswanathan, *Outside the Fold*, xvii.

22. Julian Saldanha, *Conversion and Indian Civil Law* (Bangalore: Theological Publications in India, 1981), 145.

23. The Bharatiya Janata Party (BJP) is the main driving force behind anti-conversion legislation. Currently, anti-conversion laws are in force in five states: Orissa, Madhya Pradesh, Chhattisgarh, Himachal Pradesh, and Gujarat. In Arunachal Pradesh and Rajasthan, the laws have been passed but not yet implemented. The acts are: Orissa Freedom of Religion Act,

is necessary to comment on the place of the anti-conversion laws in the legal history of India, as it affected the application of Offences Relating to Religion of the Indian Penal Code and Human Rights from the 1970s.

Generally the anit-conversion laws deal with religious conversion particularly from Hinduism to another religion. Anti-conversion laws do not prescribe harsh punishments such as the death sentence or life imprisonment, but imprisonment for a maximum of one or two years. It has been argued that such laws are mainly applied to preserve the Hindu caste system by preventing castes, such as Dalits (untouchables), from converting from Hinduism,[24] lest conversion from Hinduism eventually decreased the Hindu population.[25] Mass conversion had already been criticized by Hindus in the first half of the twentieth century, such as the several thousand lower caste people who converted to Christianity in the 1920s and 1930s in Orissa and the eastern region of Chhattisgarh. The Arya Samaj (Aryan Society), which had earlier been active in protecting Hindu practices, including the cow-slaughter issue later, started protesting conversions in this period, as well as arranging reconversion ceremonies to protect Hindus.[26] Gandhi was also one of those who opposed mission work, especially that leading to the conversion of Hindus, in the 1930s and 1940s.[27]

While conversion may be for religious reasons, frequently conversion to Christianity was associated with a certain social and ethnic identity. Although it was not the only way to acquire a new identity, some lower-caste Indians integrated themselves into the colonial system by joining the army or by

---

No. 21 of 1968; Madhaya Pradesh Freedom of Religion Act, No. 27 of 1968; The Himachal Pradesh Freedom of Religion Bill, No. 31 of 2006. Saldanha, *Conversion and Indian Civil Law*, 160.

24. James Andrew Huff, "Religious Freedom in India and Analysis of the Constitutionality of Anti-Conversion Laws," *Rutgers Journal of Law & Religion* 10, no. 2 (2009): 1–36, available at https://lawandreligion.com/sites/law-religion/files/Religious-Freedom-Huff.pdf; Arpita Anant, "Anti-conversion Laws," *The Hindu*, 17 December 2002, available at http://www.hinduonnet.com/thehindu/op/2002/12/17/stories/2002121700110200.htm.

25. Sumit Sarkar, "Christian Conversions, Hindutva, and Secularism," in *The Crisis of Secularism in India*, eds. Anuradha Dingwaney Needham and Rajeswari Sunder Rajan (Durham, NC: Duke University Press, 2007), 356–367.

26. J. E. Llewellyn, *The Arya Samaj as a Fundamentalist Movement: A Study in Comparative Fundamentalism* (New Delhi: Manohar, 1993), 99–103.

27. Susan Billington Harper, *In the Shadow of the Mahatma: Bishop V. S. Azariah and the Travails of Christianity in British India* (Grand Rapids: Eerdmans, 2000), 292–345.

serving as indentured labourers in British colonies. All the same, many consciously saw the social reform movements within Christianity as an opportunity for upward mobility, educational and political advancement.[28] Thus missionaries' attitude towards the lower castes, even to colonialism which they by no means blindly supported, enabled many converts to search for a new means of protest and liberation from their lower status and caste.

From 1947, in independent India, the anit-conversion laws were recommended to be enforced in Madhya Pradesh by the Christian Missionary Activities Enquiry Committee, which objected to conversion to Christianity by enticement with promises of employment, education, or social and health services.[29] Voluntary converts cannot be prosecuted under the conversion acts, but after 1950, any person could be punished for attempting to convert another from one religious faith to another by the use of force, inducement, allurement, or any fraudulent means or aiding any person in such conversion.[30]

Historically, the "intention to convert" is also linked with the British Offences Relating to Religion especially section 296, which as we have seen allowed "voluntary" religious discussions in religious assemblies, and section 298 which declared religious discussions which might lead to conversion legal for all communities. Likewise neither an "intention" to convert nor converting was a crime liable to prosecution under section 298.

After independence, new political powers, particularly the Hindu Nationalist Party, strongly opposed conversion from Hindu traditions.[31] Arguments in favour of the application of conversion acts are often contested as being contradictory. First, preventing conversion contradicts the fundamental right to freedom of conscience enshrined in the Indian Constitution's assurance of the freedom of conscience and the right freely

---

28. George Oommen, "The Emerging Dalit Theology: A Historical Appraisal," *Indian Church History Review* 34, no. 1 (June 2000): 19–37.

29. Saldanha, *Conversion and Indian Civil Law*, 145–146; Chad M. Bauman, "Postcolonial Anxiety and Anti-Conversion Sentiment in the Report of the 'Christian Missionary Activities Enquiry Committee,'" *International Journal of Hindu Studies* 12, no. 2 (2008): 181–213.

30. American Centre for Law and Justice, "'Religious Freedom Acts': Anti-Conversion Laws in India," 26 June 2009, http://media.aclj.org/pdf/freedom_of_religion_acts.pdf.

31. Smita Narula, "Overlooked Danger: The Security and Rights Implications of Hindu Nationalism in India," *Harvard Human Rights Journal* 16 (Spring 2003): 41–68.

to profess "practice and propagate religion."[32] According to P. V. Reddi, in viewing fundamental rights, "it is well-settled that the freedom of conscience and the right to profess a religion implies freedom to change the religion as well."[33]

Second, though illegal means of conversion can be prosecuted, voluntary conversion should not be so treated. The distinction is in practice largely irrelevant, given that courts have sentenced priests for converting people even after converts provided statements that they converted voluntarily,[34] assuming that converts, especially if low-caste, lacked independent judgment and their conversion was thus illegitimate.[35] The outcome of such legal changes could be disastrous, such as when state governments required those wanting to convert to notify their "clear intentions" to convert to government officials in advance in eastern Madhya Pradesh and Chhattisgarh in 2006. The result in Chhattisgarh was that conversion to Christianity brought violence and isolation and made Christians more vulnerable to accusation at the hands of local communities.[36] The anti-conversion laws have been misused by religious communities, particularly when the law has been taken into hands of local communities to punish converts and to harass minorities in India.[37]

Such applications of anti-conversion laws affected the security of religious communities in India today. Religious communities were not as vulnerable

---

32. Huff, "Religious Freedom in India," 12.

33. Justice P. V. Reddi, in Government of India, Law Commission of India, "Report on Conversion/Reconversion," 7.

34. Laura Dudley Jenkins, "Legal Limits on Religious Conversion in India," *Law & Contemporary Problems* 71, no. 2 (Spring 2008): 109–116, available at: http://scholarship.law.duke.edu/lcp/vol71/iss2/9

35. *Times of India* in 2002 noted: "Twenty-two persons, including seven women belonging to Satnami community [a Scheduled Caste], converted to Christianity at Mirigunda village, in Raigarh district . . . The converted families have sent written communication to the district magistrate, SDM and the SO [police] claiming they changed their religion voluntarily and without any allurement, in the presence of two priests who had come from Delhi on August 10. They claimed they had changed their religion after reading the Bible and there was no pressure on them." Kumar Mishra, "22 Convert to Christianity," in *Times of India*, 23 August 2002, quoted in Jenkins, "Legal Limits of Religious Conversion," 116.

36. Bauman, "Postcolonial Anxiety," 181–213.

37. Similar incidents and critical riots occurred in Gujarat persecuting Christians in 2002 and violence in Himachal Pradesh in 2006 to persecute Christians. See P. Augustine Kanjamala, "Orissa: killing Christians to Stop Tribals and Dalits from developing and achieving dignity in Religious Freedom Acts" in Jenkins, "Legal Limits of Religious Conversion."

to accusation or punishments until the increasingly firm application of anti-conversion laws with no effective redress when local communities took the law in their hands to punish a person accused of conversion. The major problem is that the "intention" to allow religious discussions and conversion, explained in section 296 and 298, can still be used to discuss religious matters freely but can nevertheless breach the peace of religious communities, which Chapter XV sought to avoid. Having glanced at India it is now important to see how Pakistan protected religious communities and how Chapter XV: Of Offences Relating to Religion was applied to religious issues.

3.2 The Application of Chapter XV: Of Offences Relating to Religion in East Pakistan post-1947

Like India, Pakistan inherited Offences Relating to Religion contained in Britain's Penal Code. The legislature, in adopting this law, aimed to maintain religious tolerance among religious communities in Pakistan, which was based on the notion that all Muslims in British India formed a nation, and should have their own state where their political rights can be protected.[38] Though Pakistan had been an Islamic country of South Asia since its inception in 1947, it claimed and intended to make the country secular, with religion a personal matter and all citizens of the then East and West Pakistan protected equally by the law, with no division on racial or religious grounds.[39]

The vision of Pakistan (East and West) expressed by the early founders was that there should be equality between Muslims and minorities, such as Christians and Hindus. Pakistan's founder and first leader, Mohammed Ali Jinnah, dreamed of a progressive Pakistan based on the rule of law.[40] In his Presidential address to the first constituent Assembly of Pakistan on 11 August 1947, Jinnah said: "the first duty of the Government is to maintain law and order, so that life, property and religious beliefs of its subjects are fully protected by the state."[41] Addressing the Pakistani religious communities

---

38. Murshid, *Sacred and the Secular*, 170.
39. Nizami, *Supplement to Commentary*, 215.
40. Stephen Philip Cohen, *The Idea of Pakistan* (Washington, DC: Brooking Institution, 2004), 161.
41. Jinnah's Presidential address, quoted in Pirzada, *Fundamental Rights*, 85; Saleena Karim, *Secular Jinnah & Pakistan: What The Nation Doesn't Know* (Belcara, ROI: CheckPoint,

he said: "We are starting with this fundamental principle that we all are citizens and equal citizens of the one state. You may belong to any religion or caste or creed that has nothing to do with business of the state."[42] In his speeches, equal citizenship beyond religion, caste or creed was expressed. Ayesha Jalal comments that "neither the speech, nor the legacy of which it is a part, has mattered very much in filling the deep crevices that constitute the contested narratives of Pakistani history."[43]

It has been a crucial continuing concern and question ever since 1947 in Pakistan whether Jinnah used religion to create a Muslim state or a modern democratic country. Bose and Jalal note an important historical fact that though religion and culture have been important elements in the identity of Indian Muslims there was no agreement on religion as political ideology. However, the local and regional politically-motivated Muslim League, which was initially not sufficiently established to develop its framework, eventually rustled up the semblance of mass support which could be won by a precise political program to claim a separate Muslim part of India. In this context, from 1947 ". . . the partition of India is celebrated as the ultimate victory of Islam in the subcontinent."[44] Therefore throughout the history of Pakistan, the question of Islamizing Pakistan remained critical and unclear. The main reason for discussing the initial foundation and potential sources of conflict in such detail is to show how Pakistan's initial steps to change its constitution not only threatened the unity of the whole but also gradually brought major changes in religious, legal and constitutional history in post-1971 Pakistan.

Pakistan officials did not change Chapter XV of 1860 after independence other than trivial amendments relating to "citizens of Pakistan" in section 295-A of the Pakistan Penal Code (PPC), for example, the words "His Majesty's subjects" were deleted and replaced with "the citizens of Pakistan."[45] Initially, both the East and West wings of Pakistan practised the law without

---

2010), 152.

42. Muhammad Ali Jinnah, Speech 11 August 1947 in Chunakara, *Blasphemy Law*, 9.

43. Ayesha Jalal, "Conjuring Pakistan: History as Official Imagining," *International Journal of Middle East Studies* 27, no. 1 (1995): 76.

44. Jalal and Bose, *Modern South Asia*, 192–194; The political struggle of Jinnah is discussed in detail in Ayesha Jalal, *The Sole Spokesman: Jinnah, the Muslim League and the Demand for Pakistan* (Cambridge: Cambridge University Press, 1985).

45. Chunakara, *Blasphemy Law*, 9.

any major change. However, a gradual change occurred concerning arguments between East and West Pakistan over the secular or religious nature of the state. It was not only an issue of religious ideology for the country but also an issue of "ethnic pluralism and its lack of recognition that has always posed the most serious threat and challenge to Pakistan's heavily centralized system."[46] Such issues led Pakistan to continuing ethnic and religious strategies, experienced as oppressive by minorities, differentiating religious classes and sects, and their norms and beliefs, in East and West Pakistan.

West Pakistan had a dominant ruling class based on Punjabi political leadership that believed in a strong central government, with the Urdu language as a symbol of unity and Islamic ideology for both wings of Pakistan.[47] These values were not acceptable to East Pakistan and could not unite Pakistan. The reasons for the Punjabi insistence over what appeared to East Pakistan Bengalis as oppression are complex. Historically, though the supremacy of the English language over local languages was introduced in the 1830s in British India, according to Bose and Jalal, the Bengali and Urdu languages continued to be important at the lower level of the administrative and judicial system in eastern and northern India. They further note that it was in Punjab where British officials used English and adopted Urdu as the language of government.[48] This legacy remained in Punjab, West Pakistan, where Urdu became the national language and English was acceptable for educational purposes: accepting Bengali language became a serious issue.

Apart from the politics of language, it has been argued that distinct social and ethnic statuses are evaluated differently in these two Muslim communities, East and West Pakistan. One is *ashraf*, meaning noble born, mostly from Arab backgrounds, Persia and the Mughals as well as converts from the high castes of Hindus. *Ajlaf*, also known as *atraf*, denotes those people who

---

46. Iftikhar H. Malik, "The State and Civil Society in Pakistan: From Crisis to Crisis," *Asian Survey* 36, no. 7 (July 1996): 677.

47. Though the issue of state language started in 1947, it became critical in 1952 when lives were sacrificed in a movement demanding the Bengali language for East Pakistan. In 1961, 98 percent of Bengali population spoke Bengali, 4 percent English and only 1 percent Urdu. See Robert D. Campbell, *Pakistan: An Emerging Democracy* (Princeton, NJ: Van Nostrand, 1963), 226. It was also argued that Urdu language was considered an Islamic language which given that shared faith could (or should be used to) keep the bond of East and West Pakistan. Murshid, *Sacred and the Secular*, 296–320; Uddin, *Constructing Bangladesh*, 4.

48. Jalal and Bose, *Modern South Asia*, 84.

are lower than noble, belonging to occupational groups and crafts such as fishing, trading and weaving.[49] There is also a third group, *arzul*, the lowest class of all and a class of Hindu defined untouchables, all which are part of the Islamic structures of South Asia.[50] The Urdu language alone simply became the "preeminent symbol of Muslim Identity" and of *ashraf*, the Urdu-speaking *atraf* in the west, being in effect bundled together with all other non-*ashraf*, in both parts using local languages such as Mandal, Sarkar and Bengali as people of lesser socio-religious status.[51] One of the slogans of eastern students clearly showed the conflict: "[we] refuse to believe that any language under heaven can be Islamic or Christian or heathen."[52] Accepting the Bengali language for the Bengal province of East Pakistan became for Punjabis a dilemma of choosing between "religious" and secular language as well as a status matter for Punjabis.[53] The *ashraf* intelligentsia held to the historical prejudice against Bengali Muslims, their language, culture and occupations, considering Bengali as poor and uncultured.[54] It seemed that adopting a language other than Urdu became almost a religious offence for elite West Pakistanis, who saw themselves as the protector of a united Pakistan through Islamic *ashraf* norms.

Apart from this basic cultural issue, East Pakistan also had another reason to object to the supremacy and constitution designed by West Pakistan. The background of the religious communities of the then East Pakistan, its social and economic, as well as judicial level, and circumstances, also lies behind the refusal to accept the first efforts of West Pakistan toward making the constitution accord with the general principles of an Islamic state, including the exclusion of non-Muslims as head of the state.[55] The first demand made

---

49. Discussed by A. K. Nizamul Karim, *Changing Society in India and Pakistan* (Dhaka: Oxford University Press, 1956), 12; Imtiaz Ahmad, "The Ashraf-Ajlaf Dictionary in Muslim Social Structure in India," *Indian Economic and Social History Review* 3 (1966): 268–274; Levy, *Social Structure of Islam*, 73.
50. Karim, *Changing Society in India*, 120–122.
51. Metcalf, *Islamic Revival in British India*, 210.
52. Pakistan student rally, draft constitution, Umar Dalil in Murshid, *Sacred and Secular*, 303.
53. Murshir, *Sacred and the Secular*, 334.
54. Rao Farman Ali, "Bhuto, Shekh Mujeeb, Bangladesh," in Murshid, 332–333.
55. Hasan Zaheer, *The Separation of East Pakistan: The Rise and Realization of Bengali Muslim Nationalism* (Oxford: Oxford University Press, 1994), 28–48.

by East Pakistan was to revive the early promise that the country would not be theocratic. Due to the facts of economic life in East Pakistan, Bengali Hindus were never excluded from the main stream of social and political life, for they were the backbone of the Bengali economy.[56] The basis for the East Pakistan argument also relied on the generally good relationship between Hindus and Muslims that encouraged the Muslims of Bengal to give equal rights to the Hindu minority. Hasan Zaheer notes that there was no Islamic extremism in East Pakistan to divide and detract the people from the real issues. He further comments that:

> By and large, the Muslim middle classes had a love-hate feeling towards the corresponding Hindu classes; there was a deep cultural affinity between them. Having achieved state power to redress the economic and other imbalances, the Muslims had no difficulty in co-operating with the Hindu minority in the political, social, and cultural fields.[57]

There was another very important factor that "East Pakistan had a Hindu minority which was twenty-five percent of its population, and this kind of parochialism injected rigidity into national politics which did not help the integration of the two wings."[58] Rehman Sobhan observes that at partition in 1947 there "was not a single large scale industrial enterprise in East Bengal controlled by Bengali Muslims."[59] In short it can be said that for East Pakistan to have oppressed Hindus in those early decades would have been economic suicide. It can also be seen that compared with West Pakistan, the minorities of East Pakistan, especially Hindus, were strong enough to lend effective support to that government's refusal to change the common constitution to one which did not support minorities in the mainstream of political and social life. Historically, the issue of being a minority had a significant impact on Muslims of India, for they claimed during the independence movement that their rights were threatened by the Hindu

---

56. Minutes of the meeting held on 26 May at President of West Pakistan in 1971 quoted in Zaheer, *Separation of East Pakistan*, 329, 467–471.

57. Zaheer, 15.

58. Zaheer, 15; Murshid, *Sacred and the Secular*, 235–269.

59. Rehman Sobhan, "Growth and Contradictions within the Bangladesh Bourgeoisie," *Journal of Social Studies* 9 (July 1980): 3.

majority.⁶⁰ In the post-colonial era it was claimed that minority issues in Pakistan would be resolved by Muslims but on the question of giving equal rights to minorities, West Pakistan was suspicious of the Hindu minority and wished to minimize their influence in the political life of Pakistan as a whole.⁶¹ This was not a good sign for minorities.

Apart from economic and political controversies between East and West Pakistan, the judicial and legal system remained both effective and independent particularly in protecting religious minorities under the law, Chapter XV: Of Offences Relating to Religion. For example, the Hindus of Bengal were effectively protected in one case, *Okil Ali v. Behari Lal*, when the Muslim defendants, Okil Ali and others, were sentenced under section 295 for hurting the feelings of the Hindu community of Akilpur, Dacca, (Dhaka after 1982) and the capital of the then East Pakistan, in 1962.⁶² The prosecution's case was that the Hindus of Akilpur had a place of worship known as *Krishnatala* in the same village where they offered *puja* worship each year. The area of the place was fenced off and there was a *Kadam* tree in it with an altar around the tree. On 16 November 1959, the defendants Okil Ali and others came along variously armed and cut down the *Kadam* tree, destroying the altar. As a result, the feelings of the Hindus of that village had been wounded. The court of Dacca reviewed the religious issue, including the social circumstances as well as (remaining true to the original law) the intention behind the incident. The defence's case was that the disputed land belonged to the petitioner, Okil Ali, by purchase from Ahmad Ullah which formerly belonged to Jahur Ali. Having failed to purchase it from Ahmad Ullah, the complainant had filed the case falsely.

It was declared by advocate A. W. Chowdhury that section 295 of PPC 1860 did not require investigation into possession or ownership of the land. It was also observed that in the settlement agreement the disputed land was not recorded as a place of worship and that there was uncertainty with regard to the land itself. The advocate also cited the decision that was taken in *Bechan Jha v. Emperor* (1941) in British India that unconsecrated

---

60. Declared in the speech of Suhrawardy at the Constituent Assembly of Pakistan, CAP Debates, 6 March 1948, quoted in Murshid, *Sacred and The Secular*, 336.
61. Murshid, 340–341.
62. Okil Ali v. Behari Lal Paul, PLD (1962) Dacca 487.

places cannot be considered mosques and thus cannot be the basis of cases under section 295. It was accepted that the place in the case of Okil Ali in Dacca of East Pakistan was not consecrated. However, it was also, and importantly for our purposes, accepted that the *Krishnatala* was known to all religious communities of that region, including the petitioners, as sacred and attacking it was an act which they must have known would have been likely to wound the feelings of Hindus. The advocate handed down a lesser sentence of rigorous imprisonment for two months to Okil Ali and others for hurting the feelings of the Hindu community, though not for blasphemy, for which the sentence would be rigorous imprisonment for six months and a fine of Rs 200.[63] It is significant to note that even though the charge of religious offence was not fully proved by the court the judgement was still made for hurting the religious feelings of the Hindu minority of Dhaka of East Pakistan under the 1860 law.[64]

Considering the early years of Pakistan's history, it can be seen that the religious, social and constitutional development of East Pakistan was different from West Pakistan. Keeping the idea of secularism, East Pakistan did not accept the constitutional changes to make Pakistan an Islamic country. So a conflict, which escalated into the war of 1971, was fought particularly to prevent Bengalis from demanding the maintenance of a secular state. East Pakistan separated after the war, becoming Bangladesh, another Muslim-majority country in South Asia. After the partition of Pakistan into its East and West wings, Bangladesh later had the religious and political freedom to make an independent constitution. It is therefore necessary briefly to consider how the application of the law of Chapter XV: Of Offences Relating to Religion, intended to protect religious communities, has fared in Bangladesh.

---

63. *Okil Ali v. Behari Lal Paul.*

64. After much searching, this is one religious case in East Pakistan which has come to light that gave protection to the Hindu community under the law of Offences Relating to Religion, there may be more.

3.3 Chapter XV in Bangladesh

Initially the constitution of Bangladesh, adopted in 1972, incorporated fundamental principles of state policy, socialism, democracy and secularism.[65] Article 9 of the constitution stated:

> The unity and solidarity of the Bengali nation, which deriving its identity from its language and culture attained sovereign and independent Bangladesh through a united and determined struggle in the war of independence shall be the basis of Bengali nationalism.[66]

The political history of Bangladesh post-partition is replete with questions, arguments and clashes between the religious and secular ideologies and political parties. The separation of Pakistan and Bangladesh shows that Bangladesh is associated with secularism, most clearly revealed in the Sheikh Mujib period, whereas Pakistan is usually equated with Islamic ideology. Like India and Pakistan, Bangladesh generally accepted and declared the fundamental freedom of religion in the law which was another step to securing Bangladesh as a secular country. The 1860 British Law became known as the Bangladesh Penal Code, including the legislation on Offences Relating to Religion.

Initially the government of Bangladesh decide to ban Islamic parties in 1971, preferring those based on nationalism and liberalism. Through the exercise of political power, the Jamaat-e-Islami[67] party had constantly discouraged the secular system of law and encouraged developing Islamic

---

65. Report on the Inquiry Committee, appointed by AIML, 1938 in Murshir, *Sacred and the Secular*, 133.

66. Article 9 of the 1972 Constitution of Bangladesh, quoted by M. Anisuzzaman, "The Identity Question and Politics," in *Bangladesh: Promise and Performance*, ed. Rounaq Jahan (Dhaka: The University Press Limited, 2000), 56.

67. *Jamaat-e-Islami* is a religious political party founded by Maulana Abul A'la Maududi in August 1941 in Lahore. This party has never been a popular political party in the subcontinent even in early Pakistan but now it is actively struggling to establish Islamic law there. See John L. Esposito, *Islam and Politics* (Syracuse: Syracuse University Press, 1984), 90–144; Bill Musk, *Passionate Believing* (Tunbridge Wells: Monarch, 1992), 70; Anthony Hyman, Muhammad Ghayur and Naresh Kaushik, *Pakistan: Zia and After* (London: Asia Publishing, 1988), 22.

jurisprudence in Islamic countries such as Pakistan and Bangladesh.[68] The main reason for banning it in Bangladesh was its declaring of the independence struggle and war as un-Islamic and supporting West Pakistan's oppression of Bengal.[69] In the 1950s, most members of Jamaat were in West Pakistan, with few in the East, and though it only polled 4.5 percent in the 1970 elections, Jamaat was the second most popular Islamic party in East Pakistan.[70]

It was a significant responsibility and challenge for an independent Bangladesh to control or stop the move from secularism to having a state religion. Most scholars argue that the notion of nationalism and secularism was associated with the idea of Mujibur Rehman, the founder of Bangladesh, who was assassinated in 1975. After that first period, the survival of secularism in Bangladesh was in some doubt, and indeed the next President, who imposed martial law, Sadat Muhammad Sayem, amended Article 38 and declared Bangladesh an Islamic state as well as lifting bans on the Islamic political parties. That historic change meant that Bangladeshi nationalism reverted to "a traditional, conservative, and largely Islamic society,"[71] with Islamic parties successfully empowered to take part in politics in Bangladesh. Whether the nation would change the laws, including those on religious offences, became a critical issue. Over time, the government was pressured to change the law and make it Islamic, Jammat-e-Islami pressing hard to restore the Islamic ideals of the united Pakistan period in an Islamic state.[72]

Even though the government of Bangladesh was requested by such Islamic parties to make changes in the law, it did not attempt to change the Penal Code of Bangladesh (BPC) particularly Chapter XV: Of Offences

---

68. Abul A'la Maududi, *The Islamic Law and Constitution*, 7th ed., trans. Khurshid Ahmad (Lahore: Islamic Publications, 1980), 276; Esposito, *Islam and Politics*, 163, 188–189.

69. Arshi Saleem Hashmi, "Bangladesh Ban on Religious-Based Politics: Reviving the Secular Character of the Constitution," *Spotlight on Regional Affairs*, electronic journal (12 February 2011), available at http://www.ssrn.com

70. Freeland Abbot, "The Jama'at-i-Islami of Pakistan," *The Middle East Journal* 11, no. 1 (1957): 45–47.

71. John Cleland, *The Determinants of Reproductive Change in Bangladesh, Success in a Challenging Environment* (Washington, DC: World Bank, 1994), 123; the point also has been argued by Abu Abdullah, "Social Change and Modernisation," in *Bangladesh: Promise and Performance*, ed. Rounaq Jahan (Dhaka: University Press, 2000), 147.

72. Hashmi, "Bangladesh Ban," 62.

Relating to Religion. In 1993, Islamic political parties started proposing changes to Chapter XV particularly wishing to add new sections to punish severely those who defile the name of the Prophet Muhammad and defile copies of the Qur'an. However, the government rejected such pressure, declaring that punishment for hurting religious sentiments was already present in the legislation on Offences Relating to Religion of the BPC and that the government had the power and authority to confiscate or ban offensive published material which offends religious communities.[73] The government of Bangladesh clearly felt that the law of religious offences covered in Chapter XV was enough to control religiously motivated issues. However, there were demands, particularly from Jamaat-e-Islami, to declare the Ahmadiyya sect as non-Muslims and some attacks have been perpetrated on its centres, mosques and homes. It also demanded that Shias be declared non-Muslim, but they have not yet come under physical attack.[74] The government did not declare either Ahmadis nor Shias as non-Muslim, but did ban all Ahmadi Muslim publications on 9 January 2004.[75]

In short, it can be concluded that granting equal religious freedom and rights to non-Muslims was an issue in the initial history of India and Pakistan. Though Bangladesh experienced Islamic pressure in terms of religious rights for those judged to be minorities, it did not make any changes in Chapter XV, unlike some Indian states whose anti-conversion laws opposed the spirit of certain chapters. Whether Islamic parties in Bangladesh will achieve their aims is beyond the scope of this thesis, which will now turn to the central issue of how West Pakistan dealt with religious offences.

---

73. In 1993, Motiur Rahman Nizami, Secretary General of the Jamaat-e-Islami – the largest Bangladeshi Islamic party, tabled in Parliament a "blasphemy bill" which was not accepted. Ali Riaz, *God Willing: The Politics of Islamism in Bangladesh* (Lanham, MD: Rowman & Littlefield, 2004), 102–103.

74. Hashmi, "Bangladesh Ban," 62.

75. Fundamentalists are also relentlessly threatening to annihilate those who speak in favour of the Ahmadiyya sect. The Jamaat-e-Islami lawmaker Delwar Hossain Sayeedi called the allies of Kadianis the "enemy of Islam." See Riaz, *God Willing*, 102–103; Shahriar Kabir, "Multidimensional Communal Repression and Proposed Blasphemy Law," 6 February 2012, http://www.secularvoiceofbangladesh.org.

CHAPTER 4

The Application of Chapter XV: Of Offences Relating to Religion in West Pakistan from 1947 to 1979

While Pakistan took significant steps to bring changes in the constitution, it did not declare a full *Shariat* or Islamic law in the country, nor was there significant change in the legislation (other than as a result of losing part of the country) until 1979. One of the major aims of this chapter, therefore, is to review the incidence and implications of religious offences from 1947 till 1979, which in the light of post-1979 Pakistan was a period of struggle to avoid or mitigate violence through toleration. One of the major factors behind this effort was that the majority of politicians and leaders who ruled Pakistan between 1947 and 1979 tried to hold on to Jinnah's dream of Pakistan who assured the people that the country would not become a theocratic state. Despite the years of struggle for independence, there were still unresolved constitutional and political issues affecting the initial post-1947 years, one of which was the nature of the country: could Pakistan be fully theocratic or was it firmly secular?

It was a period in which some politicians brought Islamic elements into the constitution which others revoked to keep the balance. For example, Ayub Khan (1907–1974), president of Pakistan from 1958–1969, argued that there was a universal agreement that Pakistan had a democratic constitution that would enable it to organize itself according to the principles of Islam, but in which all communities of non-Muslims would be free to adopt their own religious principles. The rights of all Pakistani communities as a whole, he insisted, should pervade, allowing them to organize and to

123

run their affairs without compromise or oppression.[1] As the president of the martial law regime from 1962–1969, he revised the constitution in 1962 to re-balance religion and polity. The objective of this change was to declare Pakistan no longer an Islamic republic but just the Republic of Pakistan and it was declared that the legal system of Pakistan would not be Islamized.[2] Ayub's opposition, based on religious ideas then current in Pakistan, led him to ban the Jamaat-e-Islami party in 1964 for its questioning of his refusal to Islamize Pakistan.[3] However, Ayub then championed Islam during the presidential campaign of 1964, promising to ensure an "Islamic way of life" in the country, if elected.[4] It can be said that although he himself was secular, by appealing to religious sentiments he also attempted to use religion for political advantage.

On the one hand it was a struggle to keep the country secular and on the other, Islamic parties such as Jamaat-e-Islami, though remaining active in their hope of achieving theocracy in Pakistan, have "never been able to establish any government" but continued its agitation to "implement *Sharia* in the country."[5] The constitutional processes indicated an uneasy blend of politics and religion, which remained significant in Pakistan.[6] Such conflict did not only affect the unity of the East and West wings of Pakistan but also brought major changes in the legal history in West Pakistan, discussed in the next chapter. Having looked at the post-1947 experience of India and Bangladesh, in this chapter we shall examine how West Pakistan dealt with religious issues and religious communities in terms of providing religious

---

1. Muhammad Ayub Khan, *Friends Not Masters: A Political Autobiography* (London: Oxford University Press, 1967), 194–205.

2. Lau, *Role of Islam*, 5–6.

3. Murshid, *Sacred and The Secular*, 348.

4. Ayub set adversary body and an Islamic Research Institute to search legal elements of Islamic principles. It was said in his speech on 14 December 1964. Murshid, *Sacred and The Secular*, 352.

5. Malik, "State and Civil Society," 677.

6. That procedure can be seen in various constitutions where major religious interests and amendments have been introduced, such as 1956, despite some religious concerns. The Constitution of 1962 reverted back to secularism, a move which ended with Ayub's political demise in 1969, the constitution of 1973 again taking religious steps. The major changes in the legal history of Pakistan started from 1979, affecting all minority communities. John, *Religion, State and Intolerance*, 24–27; David F. Forte, "Apostasy and Blasphemy in Pakistan," *Connecticut Journal of International Law* 10, no. 1 (Fall 1994): 30.

protection under Offences Relating to Religion in the Pakistan Penal Code (PPC). It is therefore necessary to assess the religious communities and controversies in Pakistan which changed the legal history of Pakistan.

Historically, the core objective for changes in the law, particularly Chapter XV on religious offences, related to religious controversies within and between communities and the political advantage to the law-makers. It has been noted in the first part of this thesis that the extent of Hindu-Muslim controversies amid the pre-Independence tensions and anxieties led British officials to make major changes in the legislation concerning religious offences to protect the sanctity of the Prophet Muhammad from offensive publications and speeches in the 1920s, and maintain their rule. From 1947 in Pakistan, the gradual rise of the Ahmadi-Muslim controversies, especially those regarding Ahmadis' controversial beliefs about the Prophet Muhammad, encouraged the Muslim community of Punjab to mobilize and agitate with all the legal and political power it could muster to introduce further additions to Chapter XV: Of Offences Relating to Religion of PPC. Before reviewing this, it is important to note how Ahmadi-Muslim tension rose up in the Punjab and how political, judicial and Muslim power in the Punjab dealt with religious controversies and offences which later critically affected the legal system and all religious communities particularly minorities of Pakistan.

4.1 Religious Communities of West Pakistan

Pakistan is a largely Sunni Muslim country, around 75 percent being of that group, with between 15 and 20 percent Shia and, according to Iftikhar Malik, 8 percent being other minorities: Christians, Hindus, Ahmadis, Baha'is, Buddhists, Jains, Kalasha (of Chitral), Parsis and Sikhs.[7] This chapter discusses just the Ahmadis (declared as non-Muslims in 1974), Christians and Hindus, as their presence arouses more resentment in social and religious

---

7. There are different estimates of the size of the minorities of Pakistan. For example, according to the census of 1990, minorities were 3.1 percent of the total population but later the census of 1998 showed the minorities nearing 11–13 million. Malik suggests that the reason for these uncertain estimates is that some communities may not have chosen to declare their ethnic and religious background. Iftikhar H. Malik, *Religious Minorities in Pakistan* (London: Minority Rights Group International, 2002), 10–12.

life, as well as in the arena of religious offences. It is significant to note that most of these communities are in the Punjab province and, historically, most legal and religious controversies between Hindu-Muslim communities occurred in the North-West Punjab province of what was British India. However, the nature of the religious offences has changed and religious controversies now usually occur between Muslims and Christians, Ahmadis and Muslims and among Muslim sects.

Historically, in the Indian subcontinent, some of the available evidence points to the establishment of Christianity in the North-West region as early as the coming to India of the apostle Thomas in the first century. There are some indications that he visited the Indo-Parthian kingdom of King Gondoforos whose capital was in Texila, in modern day Pakistan. Though Christianity may have been established, it did not survive.[8] Neither the Syrian Orthodox nor the Jesuits had any influence in this region. In Pakistan today, Christians, mostly converted from lower castes in the second half of the nineteenth century in Punjab, are the largest minority group predominantly living in Punjab Pakistan;[9] groups of Megs, Chuhras, and Dalits, doing menial jobs, and farmers converted to Christianity. Chuhras were considered lower-class sweepers and cleaners, which became a derogatory word used to insult Christians, and today even though not all are poor, this term is commonly used as a title to describe Christians.[10] This historical legacy remains even in contemporary Pakistan where they can be harassed and accused of their lower caste status, as discussed later. Though ethnically Christians were long marginalized in social life they and Hindus, mostly located in Sindh province, were by and large protected from major religious controversies and violence in West Pakistan. This will be demonstrated later in this chapter by discussing some religious cases, particularly Christian and

---

8. John Rooney, *Shadows in the Dark: A History of Christianity in Pakistan up to Tenth Century* (Rawalpindi: Christian Study Centre, 1984), 9–12; Neill, *History of Christianity*, 26–30, 166–190.

9. Frederick Stock and Margaret Stock, *People Movements in the Punjab* (Bombay: Gospel Literature Service, 1975), 69; Fry, *Scottish Empire*, 185; Pieter Streefland, *The Sweepers of Slaughterhouse, Conflict and Survival in a Karachi Neighbourhood* (Assen: Van Gorcum, 1979), 7.

10. Stock, *People Movements in the Punjab*, 15–16, 69; Taylor, *Land of the Five Rivers*, 2.

Muslim accusations brought under Chapter XV: Of Offences Relating to Religion, in the Punjab province.

After 1947, the legislation on religious offences was not applied to protect the Ahmadiyya sect started by Mirza Ghulam Ahmad (1817–1898) in Punjab who constantly faced severe criticism in offensive speeches and publications for their controversial beliefs about the Prophet Muhammad.[11] This procedure raises various questions regarding Ahmadis' religious and social status in Pakistan and their protection proclaimed by political and judicial authority. Most importantly it also reveals the limited application and scope of the legislation on religious offences even in early Pakistan, as it had been applied in British India to protect all religious communities. Before examining this, therefore, it is necessary to review Ahmadis' historical existence and religious issues in Pakistan.

It is not relevant to discuss the whole history of the Ahmadiyya movement but it is important to discuss their growth as Muslims in British India and how their beliefs were unacceptable to the majority of Muslims of Pakistan, some of whom agitated for their punishment. Historically, the Ahmadiyya Movement was started by Mirza Ghulam Ahmad in Qadian, Punjab when he claimed his spiritual standing by introducing his book *Barahin-e-Ahmadiyya* (The truth of Islam), in the early 1880s and later formally established a new Islamic sect, or community, in 1889.[12] Some of his controversial claims were his declaration that Allah appointed him as the renewer (*mujadded*) of Islam and the Messiah, being a second appearance of Jesus Christ (*Masih-e-Mawud*). The Ahmadis' view about *Jihad* (holy war) conducted through the pen, argument and proof rather than warfare was also suspicious to orthodox Muslims.[13] Furthermore, Ahmad's most controversial claims were that he was the *Mahdi,* the new incarnation of the Prophet Muhammad and that "I

---

11. Wilfred Cantwell Smith, *Modern Islam in India: A Social Analysis* (Lahore: Minerva Book Shop, 1943), 298–320; Malik, *Religious Minorities in Pakistan*, 10.

12. Several periodicals to propose Ahmadi Islam were published in Qadian, Punjab. Among those writings were *The Review of Religions*, published in English in 1902 and *Badr* and *al-Hakam* in Urdu language. Yohanan Friedmann, *Prophecy Continues: Aspects of Ahmadi Religious Thought and Its Medieval Background* (Berkeley: University of California Press 1989), 1–13.

13. Sadia Saeed, "Political Fields and Religious Movements: The Exclusion of the Ahmaddiyya Community in Pakistan," in *Political Power and Social Theory*, vol. 23, ed. Julian Go, (Bingley, UK: Emerald Group, 2012), 189–223.

am a prophet of God. Every Muslim must obey me in religious manners."[14] It was a critical challenge to the core belief of Islam that declares Prophet Muhammad as the "seal" and the last of the Prophets, so that after him no more messengers of Allah will be sent to the world.[15]

The Ahmadiyya movement was a supporter of British rule because it allowed all religious communities to profess and propagate their beliefs. Such loyalty of the Ahmadiyya, especially the Qadiani branch, towards the British remained after the death of Ahmad in 1909.[16] During the 1930s and 1940s, during the struggle for independence from the British, Ahmadis were unsure whether to live in India or Pakistan. However, it was declared by Mahmud Ahmad, the son of Ghulam Ahmad and successor of Ahmadiyya, that they would support Pakistan in 1942.[17] Ahmadis did not support the Congress, a Hindu political party, due to Gandhi's unwillingness to commit himself to allow missionary activities and conversion in an independent India.[18] It can be said that initially Ahmadis were more concerned about religious freedom and later assumed that it would be secured in Pakistan.

From 1947 Qadian, the birthplace of the Ahmadi sect, became a part of India and Ahmadis moved their headquarters to Pakistan, to the piece of land called Rabwa which was bought to build a new town and office for it. In the newly born Pakistan there was rarely any resentment between Sunni Muslims and Ahmadis at a social level. Generally, Ahmadis enjoyed well-being as they were economically strong, serving in the important offices in Pakistan. For example, Zaferullah Khan was the first foreign minister of

---

14. Friedmann, *Prophecy Continues*, 133: another Mahdi also appeared in Sudan at the same period.

15. Mahmoud M. Ayoub, *Islam: Faith and History* (Oxford: Oneworld, 2005), 31–40; Arent Jan Wensinck, *The Muslim Creed: Its Genesis and Historical Development* (London: Frank Cass, 1965), 17; Douglas Pratt, *The Challenge of Islam: Encounters in Interfaith Dialogue* (Aldershot: Ashgate, 2005), 80.

16. From 1909, after the death of Ghulam Ahmad, the Ahmadiyya movement was run by his successors, later splitting in two groups called Qadiani and Lahori. The main disagreement between two groups is based on the claims of Ahmad as Prophet. The Qadiani stressed Ghulam Ahmad's claim as Prophet and Lahori held that Ahmad never claimed to be more than a *mujaddid*, re-appearance of Prophet Muhammad. Friedmann, "Ahmadiyya."

17. Mahmud Ahmad, "The Nehru Report and Muslim Rights, Calcutta 1930," in Friedman, "Ahmadiyya."

18. Mahmud Ahmad, "The Cabinet Mission and the Duty of Indian Leaders," (1946) in Friedman, "Ahmadiyya."

Pakistan, appointed by Muhammad Ali Jinnah, the founder of Pakistan.[19] It was noted in the third chapter that though West Pakistan objected to Hindus in East Pakistan serving in government offices, they initially allowed Ahmadis, to demonstrate their commitment to the rights of religious communities in the constitution.

However, any Ahmadi-Muslim peace ended in the Punjab province as encounters with Sunni and Shia Muslims gradually became critical on religious, social and political levels, bringing major changes to Chapter XV: Of Offences Relating to Religion of the Pakistan Penal Code. The Ahmadi-Muslim issues and beliefs were used to provoke people's sentiments through offensive speeches and publications, particularly to mobilize Muslims of Punjab, not only to judge Ahmadis but also to change the constitution of Pakistan. Notably the "Report of the Court Inquiry Constituted under Punjab Act 11 of 1954 to Enquire into the Punjab Disturbances of 1953" delivered by Justice Mohammad Munir and Justice M. R. Kayani of Lahore High Court (known as the Munir Report) is an important historical source through which we can see the major violent incidents, religious offences and judicial power, as well as how religious and political leaders dealt with religious controversies and cases. It will be helpful to set this out in more detail.

4.2 Ahmadi-Muslim Controversies and Religious Offences from 1947–1954

In 1949, the Ahrar Movement or Majlis-e-Islam (Society of Free Men of Islam),[20] an Islamic party, first started public meetings and agitations to have Ahmadis declared non-Muslims as well as to exclude them from political office.[21] Another prominent association, Majalis Tahafuz Khatam-e-Nubuwwat

---

19. Saeed, "Political Fields and Religious Movements," 196, 199.

20. Ahrar Movement was a small Islamic movement founded in 1931 in British Punjab which actually started campaigns to declare Ahmadis non-Muslims in 1930s which was not accepted. This party was not in favour of the creation of Pakistan but later most of the members settled in Punjab Pakistan and established the party in 1949. Lahore High Court, *Report of the Court of Inquiry Constituted Under Punjab Act II of 1954 to Enquire into the Punjab Disturbances of 1953* (Lahore: Government Printing, Punjab, 1954), available online, http://www.thepersecution.org/dl/report_1953.pdf, 10–13.

21. Saeed, "Political Fields and Religious Movements," 202–203; Friedmann, *Prophecy Continues*, 37–39.

MTKN (Association of Protection of the Finality of the Prophethood) was created by the members of Ahrar to protect the sanctity of the Prophet in 1949.[22] Like the 1920s circumstances occurring in British Punjab to protect the Prophet Muhammad from offensive publications in Punjab, discussed in the second chapter, once again the issue of protecting the Prophet occurred in West Pakistan but this time with a more powerful and sensitive argument to preserve the finality of the Prophet which, according to Ahrar, was violated by Ahmad's claim to regard himself as the last prophet of Islam. Religious sentiments were incited and this movement succeeded in attracting large audiences at meetings, some political leaders speaking against Ahmadis, dealt with below. In December 1949 it was recommended by a police investigator, Anwar Ali, that certain Ahrar leaders be prosecuted under section 153-A of PPC for creating animosity between religious classes or the Punjab Public Safety Act but this was rejected by the politician, Malik Muhammad Anwar, who said: "the Muslims are very touchy on the point of Ahmadism and to prosecute the Ahrar for their vituperations against the Ahmadis would give them an air of martyrdom in the eyes of the public which they do not deserve."[23] This is one of the early examples where the law on religious insult was disregarded, not only section 153-A for creating animosity between classes, but also 295-A of Chapter XV for outraging the feelings of any religious class by speech and publication. Though the government claimed to protect Ahmadis by refusing to accept the religious demands of declaring them non-Muslims, Ahrar and other agitators were "left free to carry on their propaganda . . . to any extent."[24]

Between 1950 and 1953, the agitation of Ahrar along with other Islamic parties, such as Jamaat-e-Islami, increasingly demanded that the state declare Ahmadis non-Muslims. The *ulama* and Jamaat-e-Islami not only agitated to declare Ahmadis non-Muslims but also started campaigns to change the direction of Pakistan by arguing that the government should avoid having any traces of western nationalism, but should follow the principal objective

---

22. Jamal Malik, "Ahrar Movement," in *Encyclopaedia of Islam*, 3rd ed., eds. Kate Fleet, Gurden Kramer, Denis Matringe, John Nawas, and Everett Rowson, Brill Online, 4 December 2012, http://referenceworks.brilonline.com/entries/encyclopedia-of-islam-3ahrar-movement-COM_23398.

23. Lahore High Court, *Report of the Court of Inquiry*, 278.

24. Lahore High Court, 256–259, 278–279, especially 279.

of establishing an Islamic Pakistan.[25] Jamaat-e-Isalmi under Maududi attempted to articulate the anti-Ahmadi demands as a constitutional issue. This agitation, using political and social levers, laid the groundwork to change the application of religious offences.

According to the Inquiry Report of the Lahore High Court, the method of agitation chosen by Islamic parties was organising large-scale meetings to deliver disruptive speeches and producing offensive publications to incite violence against Ahmadis which spread across Punjab.[26] Let us examine some of the religious publications and their impact on Muslims in Punjab. In 1952 some publications and newspapers such as *Azad* (which means free), published articles with offensive themes and words which described Ahmad as an adulterer, drunkard, knave, slanderer, liar and many other names regarded as offensive. In December 1952 the Home Secretary was approached to take action by arguing that warnings in the past had no effect on the publishers as this newspaper "had continued to indulge in publishing matter which definitely outraged the religious susceptibilities of a class of people in, Pakistan." In December 1952, the Inquiry Report recorded that defamatory articles of *Azad* against Ahmadis were punishable under section 295-A for outraging the religious feelings of any religious community and section 153 for creating animosity between Muslims and Ahmadis but that the central government did not give any guidance on how to tackle these publications.[27]

Mazdoor (laborer), another Urdu newspaper published in Multan, Punjab, by Sayyad Abuzar Bukhari, threw itself into the controversy and consistently carried on the campaigns against the founder of Ahmadism, Ahmadi leaders, and their beliefs as well as the official leader, Zaferullah Khan. One of the issues, of 13 June 1952, gave a vulgar description about the head of the Ahmadi community which the Inquiry Report did not detail. However, the Inquiry Report declared that "if those words have been uttered in the presence of the member of the Ahmadiyya community . . .

---

25. Lahore High Court, 134, 152; Maududi, *Islamic Law and Constitution*, 276.

26. The more influential and major cities of Punjab where public meetings were held against Ahmadis were: Lyallpur known as Faisalabad today, Sargodha, Sialkot, Rawalpindi, Gujranwala, Montgomery known as Sahiwal today, Multan, Muzaffargargh and Okara. Lahore High Court, *Report of the Court of Inquiry*, 53.

27. Lahore High Court, 101–103, 335–336, especially 103.

the result would have been a broken skull."[28] The article was examined by the Director of Public Relations but a mere warning was given to publishers without taking any legal action.

Some books and pamphlets were also regarded as offensive, such as the pamphlet, *Marziyon ke Napak Azaim* (Impure Aims of Marzayis), Ahmadis, noted by the Criminal Investigation Departmenton on 4 August 1952. It was regarded as offensive as it attacked Ahmadi beliefs, regarding their existence in Pakistan as traitors and as unfaithful to Pakistan's creation. According to the Lahore High Court, the pamphlet roused bitter feelings between Muslims and Ahmadis but again no legal action was taken.[29]

Some publications declared that Ahmadis should be executed, such as the pamphlet, *Ash-Shahab* written by Maulana Shabir Ahmad Usmani who constantly published *fatwa* declaring that the Ahmadis were apostates (*murtadds*) and that the appropriate penalty in Islam for apostasy (*irtidad*) is death. The pamphlet cited the execution of two Ahmadis: Rahman Khan who was executed and Abdul Latif who was stoned to death, in Afghanistan in 1903. In March 1950, it was reported to Anwar Ali, who drew government attention to take possible steps to deal with this publication that was inciting the Muslim community of Punjab to kill Ahmadis. Some thought the pamphlet should be banned but others that a "strong warning would be sufficient" to control the issue.[30]

Abul A'la Maududi (1903–1979) was arrested for writing the pamphlet, *Qadiani Masala* (Qadiani problem) published in March 1953. In the pamphlet, he quoted from Ahmadi literature challenging the Ahmadi faith and prophethood, arguing that "Pakistan had ... to excise a cancer (Ahmadiyyat) from Muslim society."[31] Maududi was sentenced to death for his anti-Ahmadi agitation and publication when finally martial law was applied in Punjab in 1953. However, later his punishment was commuted to two years imprisonment.[32]

---

28. Lahore High Court, 87.
29. Lahore High Court, 327.
30. Lahore High Court, 18.
31. Lahore High Court, 250.
32. Leonard Binder, *Religion and Politics in Pakistan* (Berkley, CA: University of California Press, 1961), 83, 261–296; C. J. Adams, "The Ideology of Mawlana Mawdudi,"

After this short review of some publications, mentioned above, it cannot be denied the nature of some publications was written intentionally to insult Ahmadis, and thus fell under 295-A. However, the procedure for dealing with such writing and publication was significantly different and controversial. Before analyzing the application and the role of politics and the judiciary in dealing with offences in West Pakistan, let us examine some speeches delivered against Ahmadis in Punjab.

In the Inquiry Report, various speeches are recorded which were delivered between 1950 and 1953. It is not relevant to discuss all events where speeches were delivered in meetings, processions and mosques but just those where religious speech not only became a threat to maintain law and order but also caused riots as well as the loss of life and property of Ahmadis. The protest, through speeches and meetings, was based on the beliefs and claims of Ahmadis, particularly the prophethood of Ahmad which caused agitation to declare them non-Muslim. Therefore according to the Lahore High Court, various speeches were delivered in different cities of Punjab by using derogatory remarks and abusive words and language for Ahmadis and Zaferullah Khan such as *waladuzzina, waladul-haram* (bastard), *khanzir* (swine), harlots, whores, bitches, drunkard, fornicator, adulterer, cheat, *goonda*, bloody, immoral, shameless, a juggler, a wretched person, nonsense and many other vulgar words.[33] Some speeches marked Ahmadis as the lowest religious class of Pakistan. For example, at an Ahrar meeting on the 25 August 1952 in Montgomery (known as Sahiwal today), it was said by Muhammad Ali Jullundri that Ahmadis "were worse than sweepers or cobblers, [they] should not be allowed water from water taps or to sit with you in the same tonga."[34] Clearly Ahmadis were regarded as lower than sweepers, the term historically used for indigenous Christian citizens of Pakistan, and Ahmadis were rejected both from orthodox Muslim social circles and even Muslim graveyards.[35]

---

in *South Asian Politics and Religion*, ed. D. E. Smith (Princeton: Princeton University Press, 1966), 379–380.

33. Lahore High Court, *Report of the Court of Inquiry*, 195–196.

34. Lahore High Court, 328, 331.

35. Disrespect to the dead of any religious class was liable to be taken under Section 297 of Chapter XV which examines the intention of insult, ignoring religious sentiment, in respect of the dead and sepulchres but it was not applied.

Various speeches not only socially marginalized Ahmadis but also incited Muslims to break the law in taking action to judge Ahmadis. For example, Sadia Saeed checked one of the speeches of Ata Ulla Shah Bukhari, one of the Ahrar leaders, who often stated that if Ghulam Ahmad had claimed prophethood in his lifetime, he would have killed him with his own hands: such statements provoked the killing of Ahmadis.[36] In various speeches, for example in 1952, a speech was delivered in meetings held in Rawalpindi that "Mirzais were *zindeeq* [unbeliever and an apostate] and punishable with death. Every Muslim should add the word *kazzab* (liar) to the name of Mirza Ghulam Ahmad. Whoever kills a pretender gets the reward of a hundred martyrs."[37] One such listener, Muhammad Ashraf, a nineteen-year-old man, murdered Ghulam Muhammad, an Ahmadi school teacher in Okara, Punjab in 1950. He confessed that he "killed a *kafir* (unbeliever)," after hearing a speech in Okara where the name of Illam Din Ghazi, who killed Rajpal for publishing the offensive book in 1920s as discussed in the second chapter, was mentioned which provoked him to take the decision to kill an Ahmadi.[38] The main cause of all this religious violence in Punjab was anti-Ahmadi speeches and writings. One of the reports given by Anwar Ali will suffice to show the consequences of speeches particularly delivered by Ahrar:

> The Ahrar have exceeded the bounds of decency and have been making sacrilegious attacks against Ahmadis. They have even been responsible for provoking violence against the Ahmadis. . . . At a village near Okara, Ahmadi preachers were waylaid and their faces blackened. At Rawalpindi, an Ahmadi was killed, although it could not be clearly established that the murder was communal. At Samundri, an Ahmadi mosque was set fire to and reduced to ashes [and] . . . a young . . . doctor, who was an Ahmadi, was attacked at Quetta and stoned to death.[39]

---

36. Saeed, *Political Fields and Religious Movements*, 202.
37. Lahore High Court, *Report of the Court of Inquiry*, 331, 39–40.
38. Lahore High Court, 24–25.
39. Though various reports are recorded which reveals similar consequences but this was reported on 1 October 1951 to the central government. Lahore High Court, 34.

This report not only shows the critical consequences of speeches but also the various kinds of religious offences which could be prosecuted under the legislation on religious offences (Chapter XV) within its meaning: but the actual nature of the religious controversies and their proper application is unclear. For example, burning Ahmadis' places of worship could be prosecuted under section 295, which protects places of worship as well as protects objects of any religious class from damage and defilement as discussed in the first chapter. Moreover, the report clearly shows that Ahmadi preachers and their religious assemblies or worship were disturbed on various occasions. For example, on 16 and 17 February 1952, one of the meetings organized by Ahmadis in Sialkot included their *Tabligh* Conference (Conference for Propagating). Despite being protected by police, it was disturbed with shouting and offensive slogans such as *kufr ka jalsa band karo* (stop assemblies of the unfaithful).

Ahmadis reported these disturbances on many occasions and claimed that protecting religious faith, its propagation and practice should be "an absolutely clear policy" of the government.[40] Section 296 of Chapter XV of PPC could have been applied to protect religious assemblies and processions of any class from aggressive disturbances and interruptions as has been discussed in the first chapter. Failing to support Ahmadis, or any other religious class, ignored section 298 of Chapter XV which allows all religious communities to discuss their religious views and propagate their faith without aggressive and abusive action and language. It can be argued that not only section 295-A, dealing with offensive publications and speeches, as Lahore High Court mentioned in the Report, but the entirety of Chapter XV: Of Offences Relating to Religion of the Pakistan Penal Code, could have been used to deal with anti-Ahmadi controversies. However, the Lahore High Court declared that there was a complete breakdown of law and order concerning religious issues and analyzed the historical application of religious controversies and cases, especially the British way of dealing with religious offences:

---

40. Among some incidents are: meetings that were disturbed and interrupted which were held on the life of the Prophet on the occasion of *Seerat-ul-Nabi* held by Bashir Ahmad, the successor of Ahmadis in Lahore on 22 November 1951 and in Lyallpur (Faisalabad) on 18 November 1951. Lahore High Court, *Report of the Court of Inquiry*, 36, 35–39.

> ... Dissension had admirably suited the British who wanted the people over whom they were ruling to be engrossed in religious differences, as long as such controversies did not amount to a threat to law and order ... the British looked upon such disputatious with complete equanimity, perhaps with satisfaction.[41]

According to this statement, Justice Munir seemed to have wanted to avoid fanning religious dissension by controlling conflicts between Muslims and Ahmadis, although ignoring the evident conflict did precisely that, increased the problem, against the intention of the religious offences in British India Act. It was also observed on some occasions that the anger of Muslims was more aroused when Ahmadi leaders made comparison between the religious intolerance prevailing in Muslim countries and the liberal religious policy followed by the British.[42]

The government had ultimate power to deal with religious issues. Between 1950 and 1953, it was constantly informed that religious publications and speeches were a threat to "the stability of the state" and such "aggressive sectarianism should, in the opinion of the Central Government, be suppressed with a heavy hand."[43] According to the Lahore High Court, several prosecutions under section 153-A and section 295-A of the Pakistan Penal Code were recommended for publishing matter, speeches and slogans against Ahmadis but "under these two sections ... no prosecution was ever ordered or launched."[44] However, it was admitted in the Lahore High Court Report that "if the Punjab Government had made judicious use of sections 153-A and 295-A of the Penal Code, the situation would not have deteriorated to the extent."[45] The question arises why section 295-A was not used and whether its application could have controlled the issue of offensive writing and speech.

Historically, section 295-A was applied in 1927 though the demand of judicial, religious, political leaders and Muslims especially in Punjab

---

41. Lahore High Court, 196.
42. Lahore High Court.
43. Lahore High Court, 33–35, 302, 332–333.
44. Lahore High Court, 279.
45. Lahore High Court, 291.

to protect the Prophet Muhammad from the offensive publications and speeches written by the Arya Samaj to insult Muslims.[46] The aims of section 295-A have been reiterated by various lawyers and legal experts such as Shaukat Mahmood, a Lahore High Court advocate, who noted that in terms of religious writing and a speech, the inquiry has to be confined to the question of "malicious intention to outrage the religious feelings of a class of citizens. Even a true statement may outrage religious feelings."[47] The same presumption can be applied when any argument in favour of one religion reached the level of abuse of another.[48] However, such application of section 295-A was not used for anti-Ahmadi publication and speech. It can be assumed that section 295-A as originally applied to protect the Prophet Muhammad and subsequently holy personages of other religions could have been used to declare Ahmad and his successors persons to be protected by the law within the meaning of the section. However, the declared prophethood of Ahmad was so unacceptable for non-Ahmadi Muslims that the laws relating to religious order were not applied. The main concern here is to what extent religious communities can profess their faith and have freedom of expression.

According to the Inquiry Report, the judges clearly expressed the view that all religious communities of Pakistan should enjoy equal rights. The report regarded sectarian agitation as a threat to the religious freedom of all who have the right to proclaim from the pulpit whatever they believe even if it is unacceptable or offensive. For example, what Christians teach regarding Christ as the son of God is unacceptable and offensive in Islam, but they have a right to practise this faith as it is their basic belief. According to the Inquiry Report by agitating against Christians, Shia Muslims and Ahmadis: "Is it the intention to make this country [Pakistan] a battle field for warring groups and religions with the ultimate object that the vanquished will either perish or be converted?"[49] It was also a question whether law and

---

46. It is discussed in detail in chapter 2, 82–97.
47. Mahmood, *Pakistan Penal Code*, 784.
48. Kazir Abdul Hamid, ed., *The All Pakistan Legal Decisions*, vol. 12 (Lahore: PLD, 1962), 629; Malik Mir Muhammad, ed., *The All Pakistan Legal Decisions* (Lahore: PLD, 1962), 850.
49. Lahore High Court, *Report of the Court of Inquiry*, 71, 203.

order could be prioritized over religious beliefs and communities to control controversies. If not, then religious attack could indeed critically wound the religious feelings of any class without effective penalty as it was declared that:

> Faith is a matter for the individual and however false, dishonest or ridiculous it may appear to be to another, it may still be held sincerely and honestly by the person who professes it, and we have not the slightest reason to doubt that the Ahmadis hold the founder of their community and its subsequent leaders including the present head in deep reverence. Any attack on these personalities must, therefore, have deeply wounded the religious susceptibilities of the Ahmadis.[50]

Though no one should suffer on the basis of personal beliefs, the historical review of all incidents discussed above suggest that religion, particularly Islam, did indeed become superior to law and judicial rules and other religious beliefs were critically marginalized and were unprotected. Section 295-A, which was successfully applied to protect Prophet Muhammad from offensive publications and speeches in British Punjab, was also marginalized over other statutes to deal with anti-Ahmadi publications. For example, though religious writings and speeches, mentioned above, were declared to be actionable under section 295-A, the actual legal procedure was different. Some cases were tried under the Punjab Public Safety Act or section 144 of the Code of Criminal Procedure, which empowers the government to issue orders to control processions and assemblies, the most common method was to warn agitators and leave them without any legal trial.

According to Lahore High Court report, one of the meetings in Sargodha Punjab held by Ahrar was banned under section 144 in June 1952. Later, it was decided by Ahrar that meetings could be organized in the mosques which was still a contravention of the order of section 144 which applied to meetings in the mosque. Various leaders such as Master Taj-ud-Din Ansari, Sheikh Husam-ud-Din and Muhammad Abdullah were prosecuted under section 144 and received sentence of six months rigorous imprisonment. However, on 16 July 1952, when the cases came up for hearing, it was declared by the District Magistrate that prayers and religious freedom

---

50. Lahore High Court, 279.

were allowed in the mosque and the accused were acquitted the same day.[51] Notably, it was observed that there was a difficulty over the religious issue: mosques were used to deliver speeches about the finality of the Prophet Muhammad (*Khatam-e-Nubuwwat*), which is indeed a sacred, respectable and foundational right and faith of Islam, but according to the report it was mostly done to protest against Ahmadis.[52] The government, as mediator, had the power to control the proper use of mosques, loud speakers and speeches but it remained inactive. Therefore, on many occasions speakers were merely warned, which according to the Inquiry Report did not stop religious parties making provocative speeches. It is now crucial to see how and why religious issues were dealt with in such a manner.

Khwaja Nazim-ud-Din, the prime minister of Pakistan (October 1951 to April 1953), did not wish to accept religious pressure to declare Ahmadis non-Muslims, for he held that religious freedom of expression should be equal for all communities. However, according to the Lahore High Court, he did not take firm action to control the violence and religious offences motivated by the Ahmadi-Muslim controversies even when such violence went beyond limits. He supported the religious expression of Ahmadis by arguing that:

> Fatwas or *kufr* have been quite a feature of Islam since the Four Caliphs, but they have never resulted in the denial of civic rights to the individuals or classes against whom the decree was made. . . . But . . . liberty of expression did not mean licence . . . going beyond the limits.[53]

It is essential to mention that the root cause of the trouble was the government officials and politicians themselves who had "made religion their source of slogans and strength" for anti-Ahmadi demands. For example, in many cities of Punjab, the members of the Muslim League, a political party, began to associate themselves with the association for protecting the Prophet Muhammad, Tahaffuz-e-Nubuwwat, taking part in agitation. Apart from those who supported Islamic parties, the Inquiry Report particularly

---

51. Lahore High Court, 62.
52. Lahore High Court, 91.
53. Nizam-ud-Din in Lahore High Court, 291–292.

criticized the Chief Minister of Punjab, Mumtaz Daultana who used Ahmadi controversies and agitation for his own political advantages.[54] According to the Lahore Court Daultana, as a minister in charge of law and order, was responsible for religious crimes and cases, but either left them without legal trial or gave publishers, writers and speakers mere warnings. Regarding such controversial application, the Lahore High Court declared that the opinions of the law were rejected and the religious controversies were treated as a "peaceful theatrical performance where processions [were] stage-managed and slogans raised for the benefit of a contented audience."[55] The report concludes that civil and political authorities, who were supposed to be responsible for the maintenance of law and order, had become helpless and lost both the power and the ability to cope with religious offences, which caused major riots and the declaration of martial law in Punjab in March 1953.

The Lahore High Court's Inquiry Report clearly shows that law and order broke down, which not only caused the riots but also the removal of the political authorities who were regarded as responsible for the critical circumstances and religious controversies. Political figures such as Iskander Mirza (1956–1958) and Ayub Khan (1958–1969) continually faced religious pressure, but Ahmadis were not declared non-Muslims until 1974, when circumstances had radically changed. Such a move was rejected in 1953. Before discussing these changed circumstances, it is important to note a few religious cases tried under Chapter XV: Of Offences Relating to Religion, between 1956 and 1979, to show how the judicial system of Pakistan, even though under political control, remained neutral and impartial in religious cases, especially regarding the protection of Muslims, Muslim sects and

---

54. The most known leaders were Mian Abdul Bari was the President of the Provincial Muslim League from 16 April 1949 to 20 August 1950, Sufi Abdul Hamid from 20 August 1950 to 28 October 1951 and Mumtaz Daultana from 1951. Daultana was the most important government official who supported Ahrar and delivered in one of his speeches on 30 August 1952 that "to-day Pakistani . . . seeks to claim Islamic government. . . . those who do not believe the Holy Prophet to be the last of the prophets are outside the pale of Islam." (Lahore High Court, 97). He also openly gave patronage to the publication of newspapers particularly *Zamindar* (started 1903 in Lahore and banned on 2 March 1953) which continually published inflammatory matter against Ahmadis. Lahore High Court, *Report of the Court of Inquiry*, 50, 96–97, 135, 161, 192, 294–295, 386.

55. Lahore High Court, 386.

Christians. We shall also see whether Chapter XV: Of Offences Relating to Religion could have provided legal aid to Ahmadis.

4.3 The Application of Chapter XV from 1956 to 1979

It is clear that the application of the religious offence laws (Chapter XV) was limited in West Pakistan's history but the most used clauses of Offences Relating to Religion were section 295, to protect sacred places of worship and objects, and section 295-A, to protect against maliciously motivated writings and speeches.

4.3.1 Protection of Sacred Places of Different Classes under Section 295

Section 295 of PPC protects all sacred places and objects from any damage, whether those of Muslims or those of all religious minorities in Pakistan. The section has been discussed in detail in the first chapter, but here it is important to note that cases brought under section 295 were clearly judged on the base of "intention to insult." Following the same objectives as applied in British India, religious communities of Pakistan could bring any case under section 295 as long as that included evidence that a certain place of worship was consecrated for religious practice. For example, Noor Muhammad, petitioner, built a *tharra*, a terrace in Khasra No. 1270/492, evacuee land, in 1954 from subscriptions of some residents of Mohalla, Islamabad, and it was used as a mosque by members of the Shia sect. It was demolished on 17 November 1967 with the permission and consent of the respondent and a new mosque near the same site built for the members of the Sunni sect.[56] The court reviewed the religious tension between Sunni and Shia to decide if there was evidence to make an accusation of offence. However, the evidence did not support the accusation and the court dismissed the case. According to the evidence on the file, the 1954-built mosque was on common ground rather than *waqf* legally allotted property for religious worship, which could be considered as a sacred place of worship. The Lahore High Court of Pakistan especially relied on the judgement passed in *Bechan Jha*

---

56. Noor Muhammad v. Fiaz Ahmad, PLD (1960, West Pakistan) Lahore 567.

v. Emperor in declaring that the hut could not be considered a mosque or sacred place of worship and thus did not fall within the meaning of section 295.[57] It was accepted that the same rule applies to Islamic, Christian and Hindu places of worship in Pakistan. The *Noor Muhammad v. Fiaz Ahmad* case ended with the decision that the *tharra* in dispute could not be regarded as a mosque and therefore the person who demolishes such a structure could not be convicted under section 295 of PPC.[58]

In the second case it can be seen that the mere suspicion that a damaged place or object might be seen as sacred is not grounds for offence. For example, the accused in Sharaqpur, Punjab, was charged on 4 June 1976 with removing the inscriptions (*kataba jat*) *Ya Sheikh Abdul Qadir Jilani Rehmat Ullah Elaheh* "May God have mercy on Sheikh Abdulqadir Jilani" from the arches and outer gate of a mosque. It was alleged that in so doing, the accused injured the religious feelings of the Sunni Muslims.[59] The High Court made some cautious observations about the requirements of section 295 PPC lest they prejudice the proceedings before the magistrate. The petition was dismissed and it was held that inscriptions are not sacred objects nor could the petitioners be said to have offended or insulted the religion of any class as inscriptions are not a part of the religion of any Muslim.

The cases discussed above clearly show that the legal system and courts in Pakistan successfully declared the context and meaning of section 295 to protect Muslim sects in dispute over what constitutes defilement of mosques in Punjab. Judgements make clear the danger of people being, or being made to be, roused to anger on religious grounds or by appeal to their sentiments.

The following important examples discuss how in Punjab, Christian and Muslim beliefs were discussed comparatively in a broad way as part of maintaining the notion of religious freedom of expression through speech or publication. They also show how these communities were protected when "insults or attempts to insult the religion or the religious beliefs" were upheld in cases taken under section 295-A of PPC.

---

57. The trial magistrate, before passing judgement, discussed a similar case *Bechan Jha v. Emperor*, of the British Colonial Era where a few Muslims of Kujra in North India used a hut as a place of worship in 1941. For details see chapter 1, section 295, 42–48.

58. *Noor Muhammad v. Fiaz Ahmad*.

59. Shafiqur-Rehman v. The State, (1976) P. Cr. LJ 1456, Lahore.

4.3.2 Protection of Christian Community from Offensive Publications under Section 295-A

In 1952, an advocate of the Lahore High Court, Khawaja Nazir Ahmad, published a book called *Jesus in Heaven on Earth*.[60] According to the Punjab Government, the book was offensive on the grounds that it was an attack on four fundamental Christian beliefs. According to the book, Jesus was born of the matrimony of Mary and Joseph and he did not die on the cross but was removed from the cross while still alive. After his wounds had healed, Jesus and his mother went to Murree and her grave is said to be found there.[61] Justice M. R. Kiayani, a Judge of Lahore High Court, found the contents of the book clearly fell under section 295-A. He described the author, Nazir Ahmad, as full of "religious fervor, touching occasionally the high-water mark of fanaticism, so essential for a missionary."[62] On 16 April 1953, the Governor of Punjab forfeited all copies of this book to the government of Pakistan by declaring that it was written intentionally "to insult the religious beliefs of one of the classes [Christians] of subjects of Pakistan."[63] Justice Kiayani also had some advice for the government, which had taken two years to take action against the book, adding by way of warning against the misuse of the laws that:

> Although the religious beliefs of the Christians have been insulted by this book, it will not be easy to presume on the strength of the words used, that the author had "deliberate

---

60. *"Jesus in Heaven on Earth" v. The Crown.*

61. Murree is a popular mountainous city in the province of Punjab, Pakistan. Although there is a popular belief that Murree was named after the Virgin Mary, mother of Jesus, it derived from *"marhi"* which means a high place. Murree was founded in 1851 by the Governor of Punjab, Henry Lawrence, and was originally established for British troops. After partition it became a popular city for tourists for its cool environment. See "Murree," in *Concise Dictionary of World Place-Names*, ed., John Everett-Heath (Oxford: Oxford University Press, 2005).

62. *Jesus in Heaven on Earth* was first published by the Woking Muslim Mission & Literary Trust, Woking, England in April 1952 then reprinted in 1952, 1956, 1972 and 1988, being re-published in the USA in 1998.

63. *"Jesus in Heaven on Earth" v. The Crown*; Even though the book was banned, nevertheless new editions in English and Urdu translations were published in 1998 by Ahmadiyya Anjuman Isha'at Islam Lahore Inc., Columbus, Ohio, USA, and available online. See the official website of The Lahore Ahmadiyya Islamic Movement www.ahmadiyya.org/bookspdf/jihoe/main.htm

and malicious intention of outraging" their religious feelings. The intention is burdened by so many heavy adjectives that attack [sic] be very clearly abusive, obscene or vulgar before it can cause mischief of s. 295-A, or to Christians, or indeed to any religious body.[64]

It should be noted the book *Jesus in Heaven on Earth* was not written by a Sunni or Shia Muslim but an Ahmadi. At the time of the *Jesus in Heaven on Earth* case in 1952–1954 the Ahmadi community, though called Muslim, was constantly facing criticism through offensive publications and speeches in Punjab as discussed above. This case does not mention the Ahmadi background of the author and it cannot be said that the judgment was based on religious or sectarian difference. The judge not only passed judgment on the above case on the publication of *Jesus in Heaven on Earth* but also gave orders that the defenders control their social and religious protest. Justice Kiayani declared of two Christians, Mr C. E. Gibbon and Mr S. P. Singha, both representatives of the Legislative Assembly, who sought to be made party to this case, or for that matter anyone who sought to bring a private prosecution for religious offence, that:

> It was unnecessary for Mr. Gibbon to file an affidavit, and it was futile to argue that Mr. Gibbon alone was offended. We do not expect Mr. Gibbon to arm himself . . . and preach violence from the steps of the Assembly building to a very peaceful community. But if we look for resolutions and protests meetings, and processions carrying blackened faces on donkeys and fireworks and tear-gas before we take action, then we foster cold contempt and hatred and sap the foundations of the State.[65]

Justice Kiayani was concerned and personally felt that the matter was between the government and the publishers. Though the judiciary used their power to dissuade the Christian community from protesting, particularly if that would criticize government officials, the judge ruled in a neutral manner making clear Muslims were, by and large, to be discouraged from wounding the feelings of Christians.

---

64. *"Jesus in Heaven on Earth" v. The Crown.*
65. *"Jesus in Heaven on Earth" v. The Crown.*

Continuing the discussion of section 295-A in West Pakistan, it is also interesting to see other religious cases regarding tolerance for religious discussion and speech, especially where Islamic faith was evaluated in Christian publications. Such publications were brought under section 295-A on the bases of wounding the religious feelings of Muslims. The following cases indicate to what extent religious communities could be allowed to evaluate each other and what kind of judgments protected Islam from assault under section 295-A.

4.3.3 Protection and Discussion of Islamic Publications and Faith under Section 295-A

A Christian book published in British India was considered offensive and a case was brought under section 295-A of PPC. According to Pakistan Legal Decisions (PLD) in *Punjab Religious Book Society v. The State*, the book *Mizan ul-Haqq* (Balance of Truth) was considered offensive under the section 295-A in 1959.[66] The book was written about a hundred years before by a German Christian missionary, C. G. Pfander (1803–1865).[67] He was initially affiliated with the Basel Mission and was appointed a missionary in Shusha, Azerbaijan from where he also visited and did some missionary work in Persia, Baghdad, and Teheran. He was expelled from the Persian borderland by the Russian authorities because Christian-Muslim controversies were linked to his missionary activity. He was later appointed by the Church Missionary Society (CMS) in Agra and Peshawar, India from 1837 to 1857 and his focus was to address the *ashraf*, the noble class in general and Muslim *ulama* in particular, in the hope that through them the Christian message would filter down to other Muslims of British India.[68]

Pfander was known for writing apologetic literature for Muslims[69] and was involved in proselytization to defend the Christian dogma and Biblical

---

66. *Punjab Religious Book Society v. The State.*
67. Carl Gottlieb Pfander, *Mizan-ul Haqq or the Balance of Truth* (London: Church Missionary House, 1867).
68. Avril Ann Powell, *Muslims and Missionaries in Pre-Mutiny India* (London: Routledge, 2003), 153–157; Church Missionary Society, "Register of Missionaries," cited in Jeffery Cox, *Imperial Fault Lines: Christianity and Colonial Power in India 1818-1940* (Stanford: Stanford University Press, 2002), 59.
69. Gerald H. Anderson, ed., *Biographical Dictionary of Christian Missions* (New York: Macmillan Reference, 1998), 532.

text.⁷⁰ His most important apologetic work was *Mizan ul-Haqq*, originally written in German entitled *Waage der Wahrheit*, (Balance of Truth) translated into Armenian and first published in Moscow in 1831. It was later translated into Persian as *Mizan ul-Haqq* that established "the evolution of controversy between Christianity and Islam" which particularly displeased the *ulama* of northern British India.⁷¹ One of the reasons for regarding this offensive was that it was written to defend biblical scripture and revelation which according to the Islamic view was corrupted.⁷² William Muir notes that Pfander's whole argument was based on the gospel being preached to the entire world "preparatory to the glorious advent of Christ; and with a solemn parting admonition to the Moslem [Muslim] reader."⁷³ Avril Powell notes that in his "Address to Muslims," Pfander expressed his ideas in an ingratiating tone, for his words were not written "in order to revile Muhammad."⁷⁴ Pfander even quotes various Qur'anic references to prove that the Qur'an itself testifies to the reliability of the Christian scriptures and Christ.⁷⁵ However, it was also observed that Pfander "sowed the seeds of enmity and hatred in the hearts of Indian Muslims [who] started to suspect the missionary efforts as a plot to destroy Islam."⁷⁶

Despite all these controversies, *Mizan ul-Haqq* was used by generations of Christian missionaries and Christians as an apologetic tool to defend Christianity. It was translated into various languages such as English, Arabic and Urdu, and reprinted many times in the colonial and post-colonial

---

70. Pfander preached and distributed books on several occasions and conducted *Munazra*, an open religious discussions with Muslim *ulama* of Agra not only to defend Christianity but also to invite people to convert to it. See Cox, *Imperial Fault Lines*, 58–59. The point is discussed in detail in Avril Ann Powell, "New Focus on Islam: The Reverend Carl Pfander and the *Mizan Al-Haqq*," in *Muslims and Missionaries in Pre-Mutiny India*, 132–157, see also 163–171.

71. Pfander to Venn, 4 January 1856 in Cox, *Imperial Fault Lines*, 137–139.

72. Pfander, *Mizan ul-Haqq*, part 1 and 2.

73. William Muir, *The Mohammedan Controversy: Biographies of Mohammed, Sprenger on Tradition, the Indian Liturgy, and the Psalter* (Edinburgh: T & T Clark, 1897), 22–24; Pfander, by using various Qur'anic references, argued that the Qur'an itself testifies to the reliability of the Christian scriptures and Christ. See Pfander, *Mizan ul-Haqq*, 398–399.

74. Powell, *Muslims and Missionaries*, 145, 151.

75. Powell, 398–389.

76. As argued by Christian Troll, quoted in Gerald H. Anderson, ed., *Mission Legacies: Biographical Studies of Leaders of the Modern Missionary Movement* (Maryknoll: Orbis Books, 1994), 268.

periods.⁷⁷ In Pakistan, the Punjab Religious Book Society (PRBS), Lahore, had published the Urdu translation of *Mizan ul-Haqq* in 1891 and had been selling it since that time in British India. The fifth edition published in Lahore, West Pakistan, in 1953, the sixth year of Pakistan's independence, was the one particularly considered offensive to Muslims of West Pakistan. The issue started when, according to the *Gazette of West Pakistan* on 27 April 1959, an order appeared on the issue of offensive writing. It was said in the order that:

> The book entitled *Mizan ul-Haq* published by the Punjab Religious Book Society (PRBS), Lahore, and printed in its Pakistan printing works, Lahore, contains matter which is calculated to outrage the religious feelings of the Muslims of Pakistan, publication which is punishable under section 295-A of the Pakistan Penal Code (XLV of 1860).⁷⁸

Upon this complaint the government of West Pakistan exercised its power conferred by section 99-A of the Code of Criminal Procedure, 1898, to "declare forfeit every copy of the book wherever found of the aforesaid book or its Urdu translation."⁷⁹

On 22 June 1959, PRBS submitted an application under section 99-B of the Code of Criminal Procedure to have the above order set aside. F. M. Najmud Din in an affidavit said that "the deponent had been in the service of the PRBS since February 1920, that the book entitled *Mizan ul-Haqq* was being sold by PRBS, Lahore when he joined services, that all through his service the book had been sold and that so far as he knew no one had objected to any portion of the book in question."⁸⁰ Noting the history of the book, he asked how it was that only now should the book be regarded as an outrage to the religious feelings of Muslims of West Pakistan.

A significant reason for questioning the application was that no indication was given about which passages of the book were said to be malicious. Aftab

---

77. Muir, *Mohammedan Controversy*, 20; Lyle Vander Werff, *Christian Mission to Muslims, the Record: Anglican and Reformed Approaches in India and the Near East, 1800-1938* (Pasadena, CA: William Carey Library, 1977), 42–43.

78. *Punjab Religious Book Society v. The State*.

79. *Punjab Religious Book Society v. The State*; Nelson, *Pakistan Penal Code*, vol. 3, 1304.

80. *Punjab Religious Book Society v. The State*.

Husain, advocate, brought some offensive passages from *Mizan-ul Haqq* to court and read those which he believed could be said to be offensive and thus fall within the section 295-A of PPC.[81] When the passages were read out it was clear to the Bench of the Lahore High Court that though they could not be said to be entirely inoffensive, most of the passages did not appear to fall within section 295-A of PPC. Advocate Aftab Husain proposed that according to section 99-D of the Code of Criminal Procedure, it is clear that:

> If the law relied upon by the provisional Government for passing an order under section 99-A of the code of criminal procedure of 1898 is applicable even to some of those portions of the forfeited writing which were considered objectionable by the provisional Government, an order passed under section 99-A of the Code of Criminal Procedure could not be set aside.[82]

Mr Jeremy, the counsel for the application, argued that no order under section 99-A had been passed earlier and that the book, circulating for a century, contained no objectionable matter. He argued that even if action had been considered necessary, section 99-A could not have been invoked before 1922.[83] Jeremy presented another fact when arguing against the accusation that *Mizan ul-Haqq* was considered malicious and hurtful for many Muslims of West Pakistan. He said:

> Before the coming into being of Pakistan in 1947 real power with regards to matter of this kind was in the hands of persons a vast majority of whom were non-Muslims and even if action was not taken by them deliberately, their inaction cannot be a conclusive circumstance . . . This contention would have had quite some force if there had been evidence either to the effect that the book had been read by a number of Muslims and they had declared that book to be open to no objection or to the effect that the contents of the book had been given

---

81. The following pages of the book *Mizan ul-Haq* were objected to: 103–104; 129–130; 147; 273–274; 341; 376; 379; 475. See, *Punjab Religious Book Society v. The State*.

82. *Punjab Religious Book Society v. The State*.

83. Sections 99-A, 99-B to 99-G were inserted in 1922 by Press Laws Amendment Act (Act KIV of 1922). *Punjab Religious Book Society v. The State*.

so much publicity that it could be presumed that its contents were known to everyone and yet no Muslim had raised a protest against the book.[84]

Jeremy argued that the book in question had been published earlier and no objection had been raised and the applicant believed that the book did not contain offensive matter. Although the Lahore High Court in dealing with this case was sympathetic to the possibility that the book in question could outrage the religious feelings of the Muslims of Pakistan, the court agreed that the publisher of this book did not violate section 295-A of the Pakistan Penal Code because the requirement of "intention" had not been satisfied. It was held that though the book was "not entirely inoffensive in tone so far as liability under 295-A, P. P. C was concerned—the order of forfeit was set aside on counsel's assurance that offensive passages would be deleted from the next edition and the present edition would not be circulated."[85] The court also ordered that the Provisional Government should pay the applicant's cost of this application and Rs 300 for the opposing party's legal costs because the government was judged at fault in bringing the case.

The first significant point in the above case is that the court, by and large, emphasized that the Pakistan judiciary must consider religious disputes, written or spoken, under section 295-A from the objective viewpoint of normal susceptibility and not from an oversensitive perspective. Second, to pass any judgement or to convict any book as offensive, the issue must be fundamentally "intentional and malicious" within the meaning of section 295-A of the Pakistan Penal Code, to avoid an individual, whether Muslim or non-Muslim, from turning innocent comment into offensive attack. The third significant point in the above case makes clear that the Pakistan court allowed vigorous religious discussion to clarify the case, which significantly preserved freedom of expression. In judgements of this nature, the Lahore High Court recognized that when evaluating alleged violations of section 295-A, the court must put itself in the place of a "neutral person," that is a party with no religious bias, in order to discuss the issue impartially.[86] In

---

84. *Punjab Religious Book Society v. The State.*
85. *Punjab Religious Book Society v. The State.*
86. *Punjab Religious Book Society v. The State.*

reviewing this case, it can also be argued that the judicial system seemed, by and large, committed to protect *all* religious communities and also to give room to the expression of religious views. However it can also be seen that the court, despite holding to a secular system of neutral judgement, did not feel free to leave the controversial texts or books in their original form, which may indicate concern for restoring community peace. Despite much of the text in question being declared inoffensive, the whole was nevertheless ordered to be edited.

The most important point of the above case is that Pakistan, having a majority of Muslims, appears increasingly to have had to deal with religious issues even if those issues had not been previously considered offensive for a particular religious class in British India. Let us look at another case where a book was considered offensive, outraging the Muslim community, brought under section 295-A. The core of this particular case was an assault on the most sacred values and beliefs of Muslims who declare the Prophet Muhammad as the "seal" (i.e. the last) of the prophets of Allah. Yet the case also demonstrates that though opinions about the Prophet were a sensitive matter, religious freedom was still given to review, discuss and analyze the offensive writing.

The case was brought under section 295-A on 4 October 1960 against the book entitled *Development of Muslim Theology, Jurisprudence and Constitutional Theory*, which was regarded as offensive to the Muslims of West Pakistan.[87] This book was originally written by a Scottish-born Christian author, Duncan Black Macdonald (1863–1943) and published in America in 1903.[88] Macdonald later became a professor at Hartford Seminary, USA, and was known as a scholar in the field of Christian approaches to Islam.[89] Unlike Pfander, he did not serve as a missionary in any Islamic country but

---

87. *Muhammad Khalil v. The State*.

88. Duncan B. Macdonald, *Development of Muslim Theology, Jurisprudence and Constitutional Theory* (New York: Scribner's Sons, 1903).

89. Macdonald's efforts led Hartford Seminary to create a study center known as the Duncan Black Macdonald Center for the Study of Islam and Christian-Muslim Relations, which is still used for communities to discuss their religious views. See http://www.hartsem.edu/macdonald.

his aim was to establish the field to prepare missionaries to serve in Muslim countries and to introduce the study of Arabic and Islam to United States.[90]

His *Development of Muslim Theology* discussed the historical development of the Muslim state in Arabia, in which the legal ideas and schools of law were developed and the theology of Islam was established and embodied in a form that has endured until now.[91] He discusses the Prophet Mohammed's life and contribution to the legal system of Islam. According to Temple Gairdner, Macdonald's interest was less in Christianizing Muslims than in understanding Islam.[92] Bodine argues that Macdonald, in his writing, approached Muslims as individuals, as human beings who have values of religion which should be understood before any effort was made to present Christianity.[93]

His book was published and used by missionaries and Muslims alike in British India until the post-colonial era, being published in Pakistan in 1960 and recommended by Punjab University, Lahore, as a text in political science for the degree of Master of Arts.[94] However, in the court case of 1960, the defendant, Sheikh Muhammad Khalil, proprietor of the Premier Book House, Lahore, was accused on the grounds that it was a malicious publication. The prosecution alleged that the book: (a) is offensive in terms of promoting feelings of enmity between different sects of Muslims of Pakistan, and (b) is written with the deliberate and malicious intention of outraging the religious feelings of Muslims.[95] It was also asserted that the book had been written as an attempt to insult the religious feelings of different sects of Muslims of Pakistan and Muslims in general. If proved, the publication would be punishable under both section 153-A for creating enmity between

---

90. Macdonald in J. Jermaine Bodine, "Duncan Black Macdonald, 1863–1943: Preparing Missionaries for the Muslim World," in *Mission Legacies: Biographical Studies of Leaders of the Modern Missionary Movement*, ed. G. H. Anderson (Maryknoll, NY: Orbis Books, 1994), 469–474.

91. Macdonald, *Development of Muslim Theology*, 6–8.

92. W. H. T. Gairdner in Anderson, *Mission Legacies*, 469.

93. Bodine, "Duncan Black Macdonald.".

94. *Muhammad Khalil v. The State*.

95. *Muhammad Khalil v. The State*.

Islamic sects and section 295-A for insulting the religious feeling of these sects.[96]

The case raised several questions particularly regarding its publication in the Pakistani context. During the trial, the first point taken into consideration was whether section 153-A, texts creating enmity between sects through malicious writing, is applicable. It was observed that section 153-A was intended to cover a case where a Shia, for instance, hurt the feelings of Sunnis, or Muslims hurt feelings of Hindus or another minority group and created enmity between them. The court clearly observed that there was no intention in the book to set one Islamic sect against another. It was further held that section 153-A could not be applied to D. B. Macdonald who wrote a book in 1903 containing opinions which subsequently displeased Muslims in Pakistan in 1960. Considering this context, it was held that generally the book did not fall within the section 153-A as it did not intend to cause any enmity among Islamic sects or classes of Pakistan.

The second point taken into consideration was whether the case falls under section 295-A for outraging the feelings of Muslims. Section 295-A clearly shows that to be found guilty there must be a deliberate and malicious "intention" to outrage the religious feeling of a class in Pakistan. It was held that section 295-A could not be applied as there was no deliberate intention, either from the original author or from the publisher in Pakistan, to hurt the feelings of Muslims of Pakistan. However, the court declared that in its opinion some passages are offensive and the defendant, Sheikh Muhammad, who did not want the book banned, offered to edit some passages of the book to mitigate the problem. In doing so the court took those passages into its consideration, deciding whether they should be removed or left unedited as in the original text.[97]

Most of the problematic pages talk about the life of the Prophet Muhammad as a legislator, but the court firmly declared that it did not find any objection to those passages nor did it agree that those passages were written with the intention of wounding Muslims. However, some pages

---

96. *Muhammad Khalil v. The State.*

97. The discussed passages of the book *Development of Muslim Theology, Jurisprudence and Constitutional Theory* were: 10, 21, 56, 69, 70, 121–122, 127–128, 145, 150 and 178–179. See *Muhammad Khalil v. The State.*

were edited and the court proposed some revision. For example, one such passage, page 59, brought to the court, deals with the Prophet as a legislator:

> Till his death, ten years later, he ruled his community as an absolute monarch, as a prophet on his own right. He sat in the gate and judged the people. He had no need of a code, for his own will was enough. He followed the customary law of the town, as it has been described above, when it suited him, and when he judged that it was best. If not, he left it and there was a revelation. So the legislative part of the Quran grew out of such scraps [sic] sent down out of heaven to meet the needs of the squabbles and questions of the townsfolk of al-Madina. The system was one of pure opportunism; but of what body of legislation can that not be said. Of course, on the one hand, not all decisions were backed by a revelation, and Muhammad seems, on the other, to have made a few attempts to deal systematically with certain standing and constantly recurring problems—such, for example, as the conflicting claims of heirs in an estate, and the whole complicated questions of divorce—but in general, the position holds that Muhammad as a lawyer lived from hand to mouth.[98]

The words objected to in the paragraph were: "absolute monarch" and "opportunism." After reviewing the whole paragraph, the court declared that nothing has been found objectionable in the words of "absolute monarch." The word "opportunism," although derived from opportunity is used to imply a sacrifice of principle and is, therefore, repugnant. The reference to revelation is clearly sarcastic. The court therefore proposed to reshape only two lines of the passage: "He followed the customary law of the town, as it has been described above . . . when he judged that it was best. If not . . . there was a revelation." So in the proposed edited version only "when it suited him," and "he left it" were deleted and the rest of the passage remained as it was in the original text.[99] Another objectionable paragraph,

---

98. *Muhammad Khalil v. The State.* Macdonald, *Development of Muslim Theology*, 59.
99. *Muhammad Khalil v. The State.*

on page 70 of the book, was considered offensive, discussing revelation to the Prophet Muhammad:

> From time to time he got into difficulties. A revelation proved too wide or too narrow, or left out some important possibility. Then there came another to supplement or correct, or even to set the first quite aside—Muhammad had no scruples about progressive revelation as applied to himself. Thus through these interpretive acts, as we may call them, many flat contradictions have come into the Qur'an and have proved the delight of generations of Muslim Jurisprudence.[100]

In this passage only two lines "From time to time he got into difficulties," and "Muhammad had no scruples about progressive revelation as applied to himself" were considered offensive. Accepting this, the court proposed the passage be reshaped thus:

> . . . A revelation proved too wide or too narrow, or left out some important possibility. Then there came another to supplement or correct, or even to set the first quite aside . . . Thus through these interpretive acts, as we may call them, many flat contradictions have come into the Qur'an and have proved the delight of generations of Muslim Jurisprudence.[101]

It is also important to note that while some paragraphs were edited by the court others, which were subject to objection such as this paragraph on pages 121–122, remained unaltered:

> Traditions, too, which have reached us, even show him setting his face against all discussions of dogma and repeating again and again, in answer to metaphysical and theological questions, the crude anthropomorphisms of the Qur'an. But these questions and answers are probably forgeries of the later traditional school, shadows of future warfare thrown back upon the screen of the patriarchal age.[102]

---

100. Macdonald, *Development of Muslim Theology*, 70.
101. *Muhammad Khalil v. The State*.
102. Macdonald, *Development of Muslim Theology*, 121–122.

After reviewing this passage, the court declared that apart from the fact that the second sentence qualifies the author's opinion (in so far as it finds expression in the word "crude") there is no doubt that a section of Muslims are themselves guilty of ascribing a human form to the deity. They lose sight of the figurative meaning which is intended to be conveyed by the use of the terms "seeing" and "hearing" in relation to God. The court therefore did not find any harm in the use of the word "crude" particularly when used by a non-Muslim, American author who will no doubt read first the plain meaning of the Qur'an.[103] So the passage, in the opinion of the court, was not offensive at all and was allowed to remain as it was in the book.

On the whole, after reviewing all paragraphs, the court declared that "we do not think that the description [of the book] is incorrect or insulting" as outrageous and malicious intention is not involved to write as well as publish the book.[104] The court also set aside the order of forfeiting and directed that all forfeited copies be restored to the applicant to make minor modifications as agreed. Significantly, the "research purpose," declared by Macdonald for analyzing and evaluating religious discussion was one of the main reasons for passing such judgment, as the court noted that "in English, German or French there is no book to which a teacher may send his pupils for brief guidance on the development of these institutions."[105] At this point, addressing the students of Pakistan, the Court declared that:

> The research value of the book has to be preserved and that certain passages even though somewhat offensive, should be left intact in order to give an idea to the research students of the personal opinion which the author held about Muslim Theology.[106]

The declaration given above in terms of protecting the opinion about the Prophet under section 295-A of PPC demonstrates that the law as constituted in Punjab, Pakistan before the 1980s, provided religious freedom of expression to a very considerable extent in Pakistan's legal and judicial

---

103. Macdonald was not American by birth, though the court may have thought that he was. *Muhammad Khalil v. The State.*
104. *Muhammad Khalil v. The State.*
105. Macdonald, *Development of Muslim Theology*, vii.
106. *Muhammad Khalil v. The State.*

history, even allowing reflective and critical discussion of the life of the Prophet Muhammad and his teaching as questioned in the *Development of Muslim Theology, Jurisprudence and Constitutional Theory*. After viewing these passages of the book it can be argued that this is one of the most famous cases of an alleged insult to the Prophet Muhammad registered under section 295-A in Lahore prior to the introduction of section 295-C known as the Blasphemy Law, for which the penalty was death.

Significantly this case was dismissed by the Sessions Court following its withdrawal by the government. It is also important to note that after this case in which, according to the appellants, the Prophet's life was disgraced, there was no chaos, critical protest or violence such as occurred in anti-Ahmadi agitation as discussed above and indeed currently in Pakistan. The hypothetical question arises whether if this book were to be accused under section 295-A today in Pakistan, it could be discussed at all, setting aside the fact, which will be discussed in the next chapter, that a new section, 295-C, prescribes the death sentence for committing blasphemy against the Prophet Muhammad. In 1960, the whole issue was discussed calmly: even if it could be discussed today, would the same calm reign? Section 295-A still stands in Chapter XV: Of Offences Relating to Religion of Pakistan Penal Code to protect against malicious writing, but it has little or no power today to deal with cases like this which will be discussed in the following chapter, Section 295-C having virtually nullified it.

Returning to the pre-1979 position, and regarding the application of section 295-A particularly dealing with the crime of offending Islamic faith, Pakistani courts continued to dismiss prosecutions where the act was not done with malicious intention.[107] It is also important to note that people were accused not only over writing or publications but also speeches, and in dealing with the issue of offensive speech, section 295-A relied on what has been said intentionally to offend. The following case showed that accusations based on any personal reason were not deemed to be liable under section 295-A. One example will suffice. Major-General Fazal-i-Raziq, the Chairman of WAPDA (Water and Power Development Authority), Lahore

---

107. Qaisar Raza v. The State, (1979) P. Cr. LJ 758 (Khairpur, Sindh) when in Karachi, Sindh Province, a fifteen-year-old Qaisar Raza, was accused of writing the names of the first three Caliphs on the "palms" [sic] of his feet. The case was dismissed.

gave a speech to the officers of WAPDA on 18 June 1977. He impressed upon the officers the importance of *huqooq-al-abad* (rights of people), the need to earn an honest livelihood and to complete Tarbela Dam in Punjab Province as early as possible in order to rebuild the economy of the country. A few months later, Riaz Ahmad, the office superintendent in WAPDA House, filed a complaint against Fazal-i-Raziq, under section 295-A of the PPC on the grounds that the speech was a deliberate and malicious attempts to outrage the religious feelings of the Muslims.[108] The complaint was quashed on technical grounds, with the Lahore High Court holding that prosecutions under section 295-A, as the Code of Criminal Procedure, 1898, were to be taken up only on the authority of the Federal or Provincial Governments, and not by way of private complaint. The court also reviewed the use of the law for private issues or feuds. Riaz Ahmad allegedly misused the law as he was the office superintendent in WAPDA House, and had been removed from his post on 5 July 1977. It might be worth noting that other sub-sections of section 295-A of the Pakistan Penal Code do not have such safety provision, rendering the legislation susceptible to abuse by private individuals for reason other than faith.

The case also demonstrates that before passing judgement the court was aware of the accuser's personal beliefs, situation and religious zeal. The decision in this case clearly demonstrates that to convict anyone under section 295-A in Pakistan, the determining factor was whether the speaker or writer had the deliberate and malicious intent to incite religious hatred by an intentionally offensive speech.[109] Considering this case it can be said that people tried to misuse the law to settle private matters, Riaz Ahmad filing his complaint in his private capacity, but this was not accepted by the court.

All cases occurring between 1956 and 1979 clearly reveal that the judiciary had the capacity and generally the will to protect religious communities, Muslims and Christians, from any social or personal matter passing for religious hurt. It can also be argued that the judiciary could have dealt with religious controversies of Ahmadis but anti-Ahmadi speeches and writings were not prosecuted under section 295-A. Before going into the details, it is

---

108. Major General Fazal-i-Raziq, Chairman WAPDA v. Ch. Riaz Ahmad, PLD (1978) Lahore 1082.

109. Abdul Karim v. The State PLD (1963) Karachi 669.

important to see how circumstances dramatically turned violent in Punjab following the anti-Ahmadi controversies and riots of 1974, with similar religious agitation, protest through publications and speeches as occurred in 1953. Let us examine how the social and religious controversies brought amendments in the constitution of Pakistan as well as the definition of religious status of Muslims and non-Muslim minorities.

4.4 The Anti-Ahmadi Riots and Religious Offences from 1974

The decade of the 1970s brought major changes in the political and religious life of Pakistan, the separation of East Pakistan in 1971 also seeing major changes in religion and politics. Islamic norms were further empowered in what had been West Pakistan after the loss and separation of the Bengal Province which had put pressure to maintain secularism as discussed in the previous chapter. The issue of publication and speech against Ahmadis remained but major events took place, particularly anti-Ahmadi agitation in 1974.[110] As discussed earlier in the chapter, numerous religious cases against Ahmadis were not prosecuted under the legislation on religious offences law from 1949 till 1974. However, one incident, a fight between Ahmadi and non-Ahmadi students, was regarded as a religious insult which revived anti-Ahmadi agitation and became a major force leading the government to accept the religious demands to change the constitution of Pakistan and declare Ahmadis a non-Muslim minority.

According to the case, discussed by Sadia Saeed, a group of non-Ahmadi Muslim students of Nishter Medical College, Multan, were attacked by Ahmadis at the train station of Rabwa on 30 July 1974.[111] People took the incident seriously before any explanation, legal opinion and reason of the fight was declared. According to Saeed the protest resulted in a social

---

110. Before 1974, a member of the association to protect the finality of the prophethood *Tahaffuz-e-Nubuwwat*, Agha Shorash propagated the same agitation through publishing weekly magazines *Chattan* to revive the anti-Ahmadi agitation which was latter banned by the Punjab government in 1968. Abdul Karim Sharish Kashmiri v. The State of West Pakistan, PLD (1969) Lahore 289 in Sadia Saeed, "Politics of Exclusion: Muslim Nationalism, State Formation and Legal Representations of the Ahmadiyya Community in Pakistan," (PhD thesis, University of Michigan, 2010).

111. Saeed, "Politics of Exclusion," 210; Faruqi, *Question of Faith*, 25.

boycott of Ahmadis which later caused violence against Ahmadis, including throwing Ahmadi students from hostel rooms, stoning and burning Ahmadi shops and factories as well as beating Ahmadis.[112] Saeed notes that there was a wide emotional coverage given to the event by newspapers which later became a pretext for religious groups and parties to re-launch a social movement demanding Ahmadis be declared non-Muslims.[113] Various religious announcements, publications and speeches were produced to incite Muslims against Ahmadis. For example, on 16 June 1974, the front page of the National Newspaper, *Nawa-e-Waqt* wrote that:

> It is the Religious Duty of all Muslims that the deniers of the Finality of the Prophethood of Prophet Muhammad (PUBH), the Qadianis, be completely boycotted. That they [the Muslims] maintain no relationships with them [the Qadianis] and do not buy and sell products made by them. . . . and on the Day of Judgment, with the *Shafa'at* [intercessions] of the Last of the Prophet PBUH earn a high place in Heaven.[114]

One of the major causes that shook Pakistan was a "nationwide" protest led by major Muslim parties. This was including students and trade unions, members of the union parties in the national and provincial assemblies and local clerics and mosques who supported the movement to protect the finality of the Prophet Muhammad (*Khatam-e-Nubuwwat*). They demanded Ahmadis to be declared non-Muslims minority and removed from key jobs.[115] Such critical circumstances led the government to investigate the case.

According to Saeed, the government appointed a High Court Judge, K. M. A. Samdani, to investigate the incident in Rabwah. The Ahmadi students maintained that they had been provoked into the fight with the Nishtar

---

112. *Dawn*, Karachi, 23 June 1974 in Saeed, "Political Fields and Religious Movements," 211–212.

113. Saeed, "Politics of Exclusion," 200–201.

114. *Nawa-e-Waqt*, Lahore, 16 June 1974, translated and quoted by Saeed, "Political Fields and Religious Movements," 212.

115. Saeed, "Political Fields and Religious Movement," 210–211; In 1970s main Islamic parties were: Jamaat-e-Islami and its student wing, Islami Jamaat-e-Tulbah IJT (Islamic student Movement), Jamaat-e-Ulama-e-Pakistan JUP (Society of Ulama of Pakistan) and Jamaat-e-Ulama-e-Islam JUI (Society of Ulama of Islam). Sayyed Vali Reza Nasr, *Islamic Leviathan: Islam and the Making of State Power* (Oxford: Oxford University Press, 2001), 93.

Medical College students who had shouted offensive slogans at Ahmadi students in addition to verbally harassing a group of girls at Rabwah station. The non-Ahmadi students of Nishtar Medical College denied the charges and claimed that they were provoked by Ahmadi students shouting blasphemous slogans and distributing offensive Ahmadi literature to the Nishtar Medical students. Saeed further notes that Justice Samdani saw the fact that the Ahmadi community was a distinct and separate sect was relevant to the case, although the lawyer acting for the Ahmadiyya community of Rabwah protested that Ahmadiyya religious beliefs were irrelevant.[116]

According to the statements, it can be assumed the issue was based on allegedly offensive speech, slogans or distributed religious publications. Once again, section 295-A would be applicable if the case was based on a genuine religious insult.[117] However the application of Chapter XV: Of Offences Relating to Religion of the Pakistan Penal Code had already sealed the outcome. The ambivalence in the case is shown in the comment of the High Court Judge, Samdani, that the claims of violent beatings of non-Ahmadi students were widely and inaccurately exaggerated.[118]

Though there was no final judgment which declared whether the case was based on a religious quarrel or not, throughout the inquiry the non-Ahmadis' position remained strong, for they insisted that the attack was pre-planned and was authorized by the "Ahmadi administration of Rabwah, as part of their strategy to overturn Islam and institute the Ahmadiyya religion in Pakistan."[119] According to Saeed "the exact status of the Ahmadi community was not discussed but the 'heretical' and 'blasphemous' practices of the community were neatly threaded in with discussions about the organization of the Ahmadi *Jamaat* in, and their administration of, Rabwah."[120]

---

116. Saeed, "Politics of Exclusion," 210.

117. Mahmood, *Pakistan Penal Code*, 784.

118. K. M. A. Samdani, interviewed and quoted by Saeed, "Political Fields and Religious Movements," 210.

119. Saeed, "Politics of Exclusion," 211.

120. Saeed, "Politics of Exclusion," 217; In 1999, the name Rabwah, Ahmadis' headquarter was also changed and is known as Chanab Nagar today. See "Changing Name of Rabwah," *The Persecution of Ahmadis*, 31 December 2010, available on http://www.persecutionofahmadis.org/change-of-name-of-rabwah/.

It can also be seen that the judicial system was not seen as crucial to the religious issue, as Zulfiqar Ali Bhutto (Pakistan People's Party [PPP] prime minister from 1971–1977) declared in a speech on 13 June 1974 that the Ahmadi issue would be resolved in a Special Committee of the National Assembly, who would debate whether Ahmadis were Muslims or not. Bhutto himself was not present in the Assembly meeting when various Ahmadi leaders were invited to the assembly to discuss their religious views and to answer questions about their faith. The discussion was mainly about the Ahmadis' political history and their association with the British, regarded as a threat to Muslim unity, Ahmadis' beliefs about Jihad and beliefs as a threat to Islam and Ahmadis' social and political endeavours as a threat to the state. Most importantly discussion on the finality of Prophet Muhammad, *Khatam-e-Nubuwwat*, successfully resulted in declaring Ahmadis a non-Muslim minority on 7 September 1974.[121] To rephrase the definition of a Muslim, the National Assembly adopted the Constitution Amendment Act which added Ahmadis to the list of minorities and made changes in the Article 260 (3) of 1973 of the constitution which took Ahmadis out of the definition of a Muslim which defined a Muslim who believes:

> In the absolute and unqualified finality of the Prophethood of Muhammad (peace be upon him), the last of the prophets, and does not believe in, or recognize as a prophet or religious reformers, any person who claims to be a prophet, in any sense of word and any description whatsoever, after Muhammad (peace be upon him)

And non-Muslim means:

> A person who is not a Muslim and includes a person belonging to the *Christian*, *Hindu*, *Sikh*, *Buddhist* or *Parsi* community, a person of the *Qadiani* Group or the Lahori Group who call

---

121. The discussion on Ahmadi in the National Assembly was later published. Mufti Taqi Usmani and Moulana Sami-ul-Haq, *Qadianism on Trial: The Case of the Muslim Ummah against Qadianis Presented Before the National Assembly of Pakistan* (Karachi: Idaratul-Ma'arif, 2005).

themselves Ahmadis or any other name of a *Bahai*, and a person belonging to any of the Scheduled Castes.¹²²

The statement given above clearly differentiates minorities on the basis of their religion without mentioning their citizenship or religious rights. Malik notes that historically "a regime, through Parliament, assumed the role of arbiter on faith."¹²³ Jalal notes that "defining a Muslim from a non-Muslim was a particularly explosive device in a context where the state's Islamic posturing was already at odds with the basic principles of a nation-state."¹²⁴ However, it was done to declare Ahmadis as non-Muslims and to expel them from the Muslim community. The constitution of Pakistan as an Islamic country asserted that only Muslims could hold government office by declaring their faith in the finality of the Prophet Muhammad which simply excluded Ahmadis from such office. The non-Muslim status of Ahmadis also caused their social and economical decline as it threatened their admission to government jobs, educational institutions and provincial legislatures on the basis of their minority status, determined by quotas reserved for other minority groups such as Christians and Hindus of Pakistan.¹²⁵

It can clearly be seen that a long awaited declaration about Ahmadi religious status and Muslim definition was a significant step in changing the direction of Pakistan towards theocracy as intended by Islamic parties who initially "opposed Jinnah and League's movement for Pakistan."¹²⁶ Such demands can be heard by Islamic parties speaking in the National Assembly rephrasing the status of Pakistan and its citizens. As reviewed by Saeed:

> Anti-Ahmadiya demands were couched within public narratives about the state, its functions, its ideology, its responsibility to

---

122. (Constitution of Pakistan 1974); Paul A. Marshal and Nina Shea, *Silenced: How Apostasy and Blasphemy Codes are Choking Freedom Worldwide* (Oxford: Oxford University Press, 2011), 89; Theodore Gabriel, *Christian Citizens in an Islamic State: the Pakistan Experience* (Aldershot: Ashgate, 2007), 60–61.

123. Malik, "State and Civil Society," 684.

124. Ayesha Jalal, "Ideology and the Struggle for Democratic Institutions," in *Old Roads, New Highways: Fifty Years of Pakistan*, ed. Victoria Schofield (Karachi: Oxford University Press, 1997), available online on page 8, https://ajalal01.pages.tufts.edu/Articles/schofield.pdf.

125. The point is discussed in detail in Saeed, "Political Fields and Religious Movements," 213–218.

126. Jalal, "Conjuring Pakistan," 73–89.

the majority of Pakistanis, its relationship to Islam [because] the basis of the origins of Pakistan were founded on Islam and that Islam alone provided justification for the existence of an independent Pakistan.[127]

From 1974, another major concern was whether Ahmadis could practise and propagate their faith as a non-Muslim minority or not. After declaring Ahmadis non-Muslims, the initial report written for Bhutto declared that the "permanent solution" of the Punjab disturbances and religious agitation had been found, and declared Ahmadis a "minority living in the Islamic Republic of Pakistan, their rights and privileges to be protected."[128] Such claim can be seen in one of the cases *Abdur Rahman Mobashir v. Amir Ali Shah* in 1978, when the Lahore Court, on the question whether the Ahmadi community after being declared non-Muslims are prohibited from using mosques, held that "there is no positive law investing the plaintiffs with any such right to debar the defendants [the Ahmadiyya community] from freedom of conscience."[129] Significantly, Justice Hussain of the Lahore High Court, following the *Sunna*, tradition of the Prophet and the Qur'an, declared that the religious rights of non-Muslims must be respected like those of Muslims; therefore Ahmadis cannot be prohibited from calling *azan* or building mosques as it is a duty of Muslims to protect non-Muslim subjects.[130] Interestingly sections 295, 296 and 298 of Chapter XV: Of Offences Relating Religion, relating to religious freedom and protection of sacred places and worship given under the law were never applied or declared, but in this case article 20 of the 1973 Constitution was invoked, granting fundamental rights to all minority citizens of Pakistan.

A crucial issue is whether Chapter XV of PPC, rarely used in practice, could be fully used to protect all religious minorities, including Ahmadis, and for how long. Though Ahmadis were non-Muslims by definition, they could still practise their faith as a minority under section 298 of Chapter XV: Of Offences Relating to Religion, which allows all religious communities to profess, as well as discuss, religious faith. Generally, their places of

---

127. Saeed, "Politics of Exclusion," 214–215.
128. Usmani and Sami-ul-Haq, *Qadianism on Trial*, 3, 208–209.
129. Abdur Rahman Mobashir v. Amir Ali Shah, PLD (1978) Lahore 133.
130. *Abdur Rahman Mobashir v. Amir Ali Shah*.

worship, objects, rights of religious funeral services and burial grounds with Christians, Hindus and other religious communities, as discussed in the previous chapters, were protected under the legislation on religious offences. However, the initial support for their rights did not last long.

4.5 Conclusion

It cannot be denied that the somewhat unclear balance between the religious and the secular in Pakistan's constitution, referred to at the beginning of this chapter, evolved into a real source of difficulty for minority communities and eventually affected judicial approaches to religious offences in Pakistan. The changed political context and anti-Ahmadi controversies affected various areas in the legal history and perception of the law producing perhaps the most critical impact on the definition and implication of Offences Relating to Religion in the Pakistan Penal Code, in Pakistan's history. This procedure reveals two aspects: the continuing maintenance of communal violence and the political and judicial ability to incite communal agitation as well as to protect and maintain the law and order.

Communal violence was not new to Punjab Province but goes back to Hindu-Muslim violence based on the same issue of insulting Islam through offensive writing and speech. However, the nature of re-created communal and mob violence and agitation in the Ahmadi-Muslim encounter seemed more critical in Pakistan. Such conflicts also reveal that there is no clear record of cases formally tried under the legislation on relgious offences, as various religious issues, though noticed, were not prosecuted in the early history of Pakistan. A critical approach has been to see how governing authorities used agitation for their own political advantages. The British had used the law for their political advantages, as has been discussed in the case of *Angare*, but the political advantages accruing to the governing authorities of Pakistan led to some extraordinary and indeed unprecedented applications of law and order.

From 1947 to 1979, the law from Chapter XV: Of Offences Relating to Religion was not used to protect the Ahmadis from religious controversies and violence, although it still remained an important piece of legislation without any change or amendment in accordance with the original meaning, procedure and intention to protect religious communities in Pakistan. There was a successful attempt by governing officials to change, or at least control, the former law and its proper procedure to deal with anti-Ahmadi controversies and cases. The judiciary and courts also clearly tried to maintain a degree of independence to give full freedom to discuss religious contradictions that may have been considered offensive, as occurred in publications discussed above in Pakistan. However, in 1974, the procedure of Islamization was officially begun by governing legislation and constitutional change. One of the main concerns of this thesis is how this procedure critically affected judicial decisions and procedures of the legislation on religious offences (Chapter XV) and made its future use controversial if not ineffective in terms of the original intention. In 1979, Chapter XV was amended to allow Ahmadis to be prosecuted for performing their own religious practices, and after the early 1980s the religious clashes and controversies affected religious freedom, the law on religious offences and the use of the category "blasphemy," with severe punishments, which is the main discussion of the following chapter.

Part III

Implications of Offences Relating to Religion from Post-1947 in the Independent Subcontinent (India and Pakistan)

CHAPTER 5

The Legislation on Offences Relating to Religion and Islamization of Pakistan (1979–1988)

Historically, the law has been challenged and amended to preserve certain beliefs when people felt threatened and wounded, or governments needed support from a particular constituency. For example, Chapter XV: Of Offences Relating to Religion of the Indian Penal Code was significantly amended in the 1920s particularly after the protest of the mob and judiciary to protect the Prophet Muhammad from offensive publications in the British Punjab. After independence, this pattern also affected the application of Chapter XV of the Pakistan Penal Code especially regarding the extent to which it can be used to maintain religious peace in the society and how the ruling powers and judiciary regard it. The particular issue concerning the finality of the Prophet Muhammad underlay all the Ahmadi-Muslim arguments which later led to changes in Chapter XV.

In the process of amendment after the Ahmadi disaffiliation, it may be suggested that sectarianism was intensified as Chapter XV changed from its original meaning, procedure and intention. The original maximum sentence for committing a religious offence in Chapter XV was two years with a fine, which was also successfully applied in Pakistan, as the last chapter clearly demonstrated. However, between 1979 and 1986, the question of religious offences became critical, indeed a matter of life and death amid sectarian Pakistan as the Offences Relating to Religion law changed in its application, especially but not only for minority religious communities. The outcome was that both the intentions of Chapter XV of PPC and its penalties were drastically altered, the new rules altering the intention and outcome of the legal history of the legislation on religious offences in Pakistan.[1]

Before analyzing the results, it is helpful to note the source and aim of these changes, both of which were based on popular religious demands and political interests in Pakistan during the 1970s. First, we shall examine how this related to political interests especially under Zia-ul-Haq's regime (1977–1988) and the demand by Muslims and Muslim religious parties to protect Islamic beliefs. Second, we shall see if and how judicial power was able to deal with religious issues independently from the 1980s onwards.

5.1 The Political Power of Zia-ul-Haq and Religious Offences

After taking power from Bhutto, Zia-ul-Haq was aware of the religious demands for theocracy as well as the religious-based criticism aimed at Bhutto: by following these demands and using Islamic norms, this military leader would be able to stabilize his political position.[2] According to Sayyed Vali Reza Nasr, Zia was inspired by reading Islamic books written by Maulana Abul A'la Maududi of Jamaat-e-Islami who had placed significant emphasis on applying theocracy in Pakistan.[3] The process started in 1977 when Maududi and his party Jamaat-e-Islami put forward their proposal for a more Islamic Pakistan to Zia-ul-Haq, in the year he became president. Maududi claimed that under Islamic law Pakistan, an independent Islamic political state, would not only restore Islam but that Islamic law would equally protect non-Muslims and their rights.[4] This last claim regarding minorities and freedom of expression will be examined later in this chapter.

The Islamization of Pakistan was largely motivated by Sunni militancy. Historically, we have seen how major ethnic and religious issues and

---

[1]. Cris E. Toffolo and Charles Amjad-Ali, "Christians in Pakistan Confront Charges of Blasphemy," *The Christian Century* 115, no. 21 (July 1998): 716.

[2]. Mumtaz Ahmad, "The Crescent and the Sword: Islam, the Military, and Political Legitimacy in Pakistan: 1977-1985," *The Middle East Journal* 50, no. 3 (Summer 1996): 374.

[3]. Nasr, *Islamic Leviathan*, 136–138.

[4]. Esposito, *Islam and Politics*, 90–144; Musk, *Passionate Believing*, 70; Sayyed Vali Reza Nasr, *Mawdudi and the Making of Islamic Revivalism* (New York: Oxford University Press, 1996), 80–106.

sectarianism had already separated East and West Pakistan and expelled Ahmadis from the Islamic community. Furthermore, such sectarianism, according to Nasr, controlled the Islamic discourse of Pakistan and brought another sectarian division that viewed Shia Islam as a threat, quite apart from the threat the new Sunni militancy would pose for powerless minorities.[5] According to Malik, the Sunni-Shia conflict took place when a group such as the Anjuman-e-Sipah-e-Sahaba (the Army of the Friends of the Prophet) from Jhang, Punjab demanded that "Pakistan should be declared a Sunni state."[6] Most of the Shias living in the Kurram Agency, surrounded by Sunni tribes, were inspired by the Iranian Revolution, angering those around them. Sectarian clashes took place when one of the Shia from Kurram, Maulana Mausavi, was murdered, bringing sectarian agitation and killing in Jhang, Karachi, Lahore and Peshawar. Tehreek-e-Fiqh-e-Jafria was established to push for the Shia version of Sharia which further caused Sunni-Shia agitation and specific assassinations and murders.[7] Sunnis and Shias saw Pakistan's reformation through their own sectarian visions, although as has been noted, Shias are targets of Sunni power and feared they would face the same fate as Ahmadis.[8] However, one of the most important consequences of this conflict is to note that such sectarianism later defiled mosques, damaging them with bomb blasts and not only assassinating worshippers but also causing serious disturbances to religious assemblies, which again violated the laws on Offences Relating to Religion.

Zia-ul-Haq, with his religious interests, aimed to bring *Nazame-e-Mustafa*, the Islamic Order of God, and proclaimed his vision that, "Pakistan was created in the name of Islam, [and] will continue to survive only if it sticks to Islam. That is why I consider the introduction of the Islamic system an essential pre-requisite for the country."[9] The number of *ulama* (Islamic

---

5. S. V. R. Nasr, "The Rise of Sunni Militancy in Pakistan: The Changing Role of Islamism and the Ulama in Society and Politics," *Modern Asian Studies* 34, no. 1 (January 2000): 139–180; Zaman, *The Ulama in Contemporary Islam*, 114.

6. Malik, *Religious Minorities in Pakistan*, 13.

7. Malik, *Religious Minorities in Pakistan*, 12–13.

8. Ali Riaz, *Faithful Education: Madrasas in South Asia* (New Brunswick: Rutgers University Press, 2008), 109.

9. Hamid Khan, *Constitutional and Political History of Pakistan*, 2nd ed. (Karachi: Oxford University Press, 2001), 579.

scholars on the council of Islamic ideology) was increased[10] to promote and implement a thorough-going program of Islamization, determined to see Pakistan reach this goal of becoming an Islamic state.[11] It is important to note that through the Islamization procedure, Zia did not aim to bring full *Sharia* Law but to strengthen the Islamic system by establishing and imposing some Islamic Penal Codes between 1979 and 1986[12] which created a division between secular and Islamic laws.[13] Before viewing this change, it is necessary to note how such legislation was brought and maintained by refashioning the judicial system of Pakistan.

5.2 Islamization, Law and Order and the Creation of Federal *Shariat* Court

The judiciary was affected by political control in the 1980s as indeed in earlier periods, although under Zia a more direct confrontation was essential for him to ensure the passage of his ideas. The legislation dealing with religious offences was clearly controlled by Zia through reforming the judicial structure of Pakistan, not just Chapter XV but also the basis of the judicial system inherited from the British. From 1980, first, Zia wished to bring the existing laws of Pakistan into conformity with *Shariat* Islamic law and therefore second, created a Federal *Shariat* Court (FSC) and *Shariat* Appellate Bench of the Supreme Court with the major aim to "examine and decide the question whether or not any law or provision of law is repugnant to the Injunctions of Islam."[14] In contrast to British law it was observed that:

---

10. Zaman, *Ulama in Contemporary Islam*, 88–89.

11. Among some of the Islamizing goals were: measuring and declaring moral restrictions to radio and television programs, films, newspapers. Making prayers and fasting during the Islamic Ramadan compulsory and declaring punishments to those who do not follow moral standards. Rubya Mehdi, *The Islamization of the Law in Pakistan* (Richmond: Curzon, 1994), 206–209; Musk, *Passionate Believing*, 73.

12. Nasr, *Islamic Leviathan*, 140; Khalid Mahmud Arif, *Working with Zia: Pakistan's Power Politics, 1977-1988* (Karachi: Oxford University Press, 1995), 250.

13. Lau, *Role of Islam*, 9.

14. *Federal Shariat Court* 1998: 414; Saeed, "Politics of Exclusion," 315; Charles H. Kennedy, "Repugnancy to Islam: Who Decides? Islam and Legal Reform in Pakistan," *The International and Comparative Law Quarterly* 41, no.4 (October, 1992): 769–787.

> None of the system of Penal Law established in British India has any claim to our attention except what it may derive from its own intrinsic excellence. All those systems are foreign. All were introduced by conquerors differing in race, manners, language and religion from the great mass of people . . . that of [an Islamic] criminal law which is certainly the last system of criminal law which an enlightened and humane Government would be disposed to receive.[15]

Following the new rules of Islamic law, in 1979 the *Hudood Ordinance*[16] was promulgated to replace the British Criminal Code with an Islamic one, after Zia and the Islamic Council of Islamic Ideology reviewed all laws dating back to 1834 to eliminate those repugnant to Islam.[17]

In 1981 Zia promulgated the provisional Constitutional Order to reconcile military rule with the constitution and limit the power of the judiciary.[18] It was claimed that the dual judicial system would provide speedier justice over the cumbersome Anglo-Saxon law.[19] However, one of the main aims of Federal *Shariat* Court was to reject any law repugnant to Islam and advise the government to alter such laws. According to Anita M. Weiss:

> [The FSC] did not restrict the power of either the civil or military courts operating concurrently in Pakistan, except to ensure that the laws were not repugnant to Islam. Nor was there an overhaul of the legal system, placing all law into conformity at once. Instead, only when a law was challenged as repugnant to Islamic injunction did a *shari'a* bench became involved. In addition, the question of legal derivation was not raised; laws

---

15. Nizami, *The Pakistan Penal Code with Commentary*, quoted in Siddique and Hayat, "Unholy Speech and Holy Laws," 336.

16. In Islam the *hadd* punishments are labelled as rights and claims of God (*huquq Allah*) and not claims of men which includes crimes such as theft (*sarika*); unlawful intercourse (*zina*); its counterpart, false accusation of unlawful intercourse (*kadhf*); drinking wine (*shrub khamr*); highway robbery (*kat al-tariq*) and apostasy (*ridda*). Peters, *Crime and Punishment*, 54; W. M. Watt, *Islamic Political Thought* (Edinburgh: Edinburgh University Press, 1998), 32–33; Mehdi, *Islamization of the Law*, 109–110.

17. Nasr, *Islamic Leviathan*, 139–141.

18. Paula R. Newberg, *Judging the State: Courts and Constitutional Politics in Pakistan* (New York: Cambridge University Press, 1995), 180–181.

19. Nasr, *Islamic Leviathan*, 139–140.

were decreed as conforming to Islamic *shari'a*, but no attempt was made to derive the legal system directly from the *shari'a*.[20]

To Islamize the judiciary, Zia wished to "decolonize" and "Islamize" the judicial system thus, it has been said, "diverting attention from the executive's encroachment on the powers of the judiciary."[21] The new way minimized the High Court's power, especially when it found error in any statute or sentence or intention. For example, the question of abolishing the death sentence for defiling the name of the Prophet and substituting life imprisonment was debated but withdrawn, which will be discussed later. Likewise, the Federal *Shariat* Court intervened to annul any laws seen as not Islamic. The entire Pakistan Penal Code of 1860 was reviewed by the Council, appointed by Zia, who played a significant role in revising many codes as well as adding new ones, significantly to Chapter XV: Of Offences Relating to Religion.

5.3 Amendments in Chapter XV of Pakistan Penal Code from 1980 to 1986

Although the Indian Constitution (which the Pakistan Constitution is based on) does guarantee the right of all citizens to "profess, practice and propogate religion" these rights are increasingly under threat in India and Pakistan today. Initial amendments to Chapter XV: Of Offences Relating to Religion of PPC were by and large a result of the continuing protest against Ahmadis. Though Ahmadis were already considered non-Muslims, their religious practices and expressions were still outrageous to Muslims. For example, anti-Ahmadi agitation concernerod the fact that Mirza and Ahmadi successors use Islamic titles for their own prophets including the prophets such as *Amir-ul-Momineen* (the successors of the Prophet), *Ummul Momineen* (sacred name of Prophet's Wives) or *Sahab-e-Karam* (companions of the Prophet) which became outrageous to Muslims,[22] who insisted only they could use such words, excluding Ahmadis. In 1980, this controversy was controlled through creating section 298-A and inserting the following into Chapter XV of Pakistan Penal Code (added by Ordinance XLV of

---

20. Anita M. Weiss in Saeed, "Politics of Exclusion," 305–306.
21. Nasr, *Islamic Leviathan*, 141.
22. Saeed, "Politics of Exclusion," 197.

1980) which prohibits Ahmadis from linking themselves to the family of the Prophet and the Islamic caliphate:

> Whoever by words, either spoken or written, or by visible representation, or by any imputation, innuendo or insinuation, directly or indirectly, defiles the sacred name of any wife (*Ummel Muminn*), or members of the family (*Ahle-bait*), of the Holy Prophet (peace be upon him), or any of the righteous Caliphs (*Khulfa-e-Rashideen*) or companions (*Sahaba*) of the Holy Prophet (peace be upon him), shall be punished with imprisonment of either description for a term which may extend to three years, or with fine, or with both.[23]

The process of Islamizing the legislation on religious offences and the new additions, in some respect significantly segregated the Ahmadis from the family of the Prophet. Ahmadis as previously self-defined Muslims had various common religious objects and practices such as reading and teachings of the Qur'an which was outrageous to many Muslims of Punjab. In 1982, section 295-B was added to Chapter XV on religious offences, mainly to preserve the Qur'an as a final revealed word of God, as discussed later in the chapter. According to section 295-B, not only Ahmadis but also "anyone" who defiles and damages the Qur'an is liable to be sentenced to life imprisonment.

> Whoever wilfully defiles, damages or desecrates a copy of the Holy Qur'an or of an extract therefrom or uses it in any derogatory manner or for any unlawful purpose shall be punishable with imprisonment for life.[24]

Ordinance XX applied in 1984 cut Ahmadis off from their accustomed social and religious life and practices as, similar to the 1950s and 1970s, anti-Ahmadi demands were again made to the state. Islamic parties, particularly Jamaat-e-Islami, Jamaat-e-Ulama-e-Islam (Society of Ulama of Islam) and

---

23. Taimur Khan, *The Pakistan Penal Code (XLV of 1860)* (Lahore: Al-Noor Law House, 2002), 244.

24. Section 295-B was added in the chapter of religious offence of Pakistan Penal Code (PPC) by Amendment Ordinance 1 on 18 March 1982. The accusation under section 295B is non bailable and non compoundable. Khan and Khan, *Pakistan Penal Code*, 238.

Jamaat-e-Ulama-e-Pakistan (Society of Ulama of Pakistan), re-launched the *Tehrrik-e-Khatam-e-Nubuwwat* (movement to protect the finality of prophethood). *Tehrrik-e-Khatam-e-Nubuwwat* was the leading movement which was used to declare Ahmadis non-Muslims and changed the constitution of 1974 as already discussed. In the 1980s it was re-launched and used by Zia to declare punishment for those who defile Islamic beliefs. Following the previous agitation, they campaigned for the complete removal of Ahmadis from all levels of the bureaucracy and the military on the ground that they were traitors to Pakistan. The demands of religious parties were declared in the meeting held in Rawalpindi on 1–2 January 1984:

> (a) Introduction of death sentence for apostasy; (b) complete ban on publication and distribution of Ahmadi literature; and (c) state take steps to curb the anti-Islamic and anti-national activities of Ahmadis. (d) Ahmadis should be prohibited from naming their places of worship as mosques and their call for prayer as Azaan; and (e) implementation of death sentence for those who use derogatory language about Prophet Mohammad.[25]

This protest was by and large similar to those occurring between 1950 and 1974, but went further, demanding separate legislation to punish these "non-Muslims" as blasphemers. The Islamic parties not only demanded such legislation but also threatened the government that they would take action, even breaking the law, to achieve their aim. For example, in February 1984, the *ulama* threatened to launch a nationwide, anti-Ahmadi campaign and pushed the government to demolish all Ahmadi mosques by 30 April 1984, insisting that if it this was not done by the government the *ulama* would be compelled to do so themselves.[26] Like the previous agitation discussed above, in the 1980s publications also played a role in inciting people. For example, one of Pakistan's official newspapers (*Nawa-e-Waqt*) wrote that Ahmadis should not be allowed to preach against Islam (Lahore, 4 April

---

25. Kaushik, *Ahmadiya Community in Pakistan* quoted by Sadia in, "Politics of Exclusion," 260.

26. Saeed, "Politics of Exclusion," 260.

1984), they should not be allowed to distribute their pamphlets (Lahore, 14 April 1984) and they should stop proselytizing (Lahore, 15 April 1984).[27]

Clearly, religious tension, public agitation, threats and violence came together in Punjab province to affect and even alter long-standing legislation clearly intended to deal with religious offences and conflict. While the label of mob-rule would be inaccurate, as the government itself was part of the agitation, pressure from below, from religious authorities and from pragmatic politicians, did encourage the government to accept their demands even though the government itself thereby broke current laws. For example, at the point when attacks on Ahmadi buildings began, damaging and breaking any places of worship was still punishable under section 295 of Chapter XV of PPC and prohibiting them from preaching and practising their faith violated section 298 of Chapter XV as well as Article 18, 19 and 20 of the UDHR, which Pakistan supported in 1948. The religious demands for more laws to punish Ahmadi demands were a threat to religious freedom.

However, Zia, by following the Islamic parties' demands and in line with the policy to Islamize Pakistan, created a space to discuss "the relationship between Islam and state and the basis of Pakistan's national identity."[28] Ordinance XX of 1984 was promulgated on 26 April, prepared by Raja Zaffarul Haq,[29] with the intention of prohibiting and punishing non-Muslims, entitled "Anti-Islamic Activities of Qadiani group, Lahori Group and Ahmadies."[30] The new ordinance, Section 298-B of Chapter XV: Of Offences Relating to Religion, provides for punishment for the use of derogatory remarks and writing with respect of holy personages. According to section 298-B:

---

27. *Nawa-e-Waqt*, translated and quoted by Saeed, "Politics of Exclusion," 260–261.

28. Saeed, "Politics of Exclusion," 297.

29. Raja Zaffarul Haq, whose anti-Ahmadi prejudice developed in 1970s, later worked in the Federal Cabinet and played an important role in preparing an Ordinance XX of 1984 intending that Islamic countries should collectively strive to eradicate the Ahmadi community. (*Pakistan Times*, 12 May 1984, available at http://www.thepersecution.org/archive/pl_xrzh.html).

30. From 1909, after the death of Ghulam Ahmad, the Ahmadi movement was run by its successors later splitting in two groups called Qadiani and Lahori. The main disagreement between two groups is based on the claims of Ahmad as Prophet. The Qadiani stressed Ghulam Ahmad's claim as Prophet whereas Lahori held that Ahmad never claimed to more than a *mujaddid*, re-appearance of Prophet Muhammad. Friedmann, "Ahmadiyya."

1. Any person of the Qadiani group or the Lahori group (who call themselves Ahmadis or by any other name) who by words, either spoken or written or by visible representation:
   a. refers to or addresses, any person, other than a Caliph or companion of the Holy Prophet Mohammad (PBUH), as "*Ameerul Momineen*", "*Khalifat-ul-Momneen*", "*Khalifat-ul-Muslimeen*", "*Sahaabi*" or "*Razi Allah Anho*";
   b. refers to or addresses, any person, other than a wife of the Holy Prophet Mohammed (PBUH), as *Ummul-Mumineen*;
   c. refers to, or addresses, any person, other than a member of the family (*Ahle-Bait*) of the Holy Prophet Mohammed (PBUH), as Ahle-Bait; or
   d. refers to, or names, or calls, his place of worship as Masjid; shall be punished with imprisonment or either description for a term which may extend to three years, and shall also be liable to fine.
2. Any person of the Qadiani group or Lahore group, (who call themselves Ahmadis or by any other names), who by words, either spoken or written, or by visible representations, refers to the mode or from of call to prayers followed by his faith as "*Azan*" or recites Azan as used by the Muslims, shall be punished with imprisonment of either description for a term which may extend to three years and shall also be liable to fine.[31]

Section 298-B is based on the misuse of epithets, descriptions and titles reserved for a certain holy personage of the Islamic faith. But in the following addition, section 298-C, Ahmadis were prohibited from calling themselves Muslim or preaching and propagating their faith:

> Any person of the Qadiani group or the Lahori group (who call themselves Ahmadis or any other name), who directly or indirectly, posses himself as a Muslim, or calls, or refers to, his faith as Islam, or preaches or propagates his faith, or invites others to accept his faith, by words, either spoken or written, or

---

31. Abdullah Saeed and Hassan Saeed, *Freedom of Religion, Apostasy and Islam* (Aldershot: Ashgate, 2004), 184–185.

by visible representation or in any manner whatsoever outrages the religious feelings of Muslims, shall be punished with imprisonment of either description for a term which may extend to three years and shall also be liable to fine.[32]

It was explained in the previous chapter how groups and agitators were not properly prosecuted for delivering offensive speech and publishing offensive matter in the 1950s and 1970s. After new additions to the law, the government of Pakistan printed a short pamphlet *Qadianis: Threat to Islamic Solidarity* which asserted that imposing conditions on Ahmadis was due to their anti-Islamic activities and faith being repugnant to Islam, insisting that anyone who denied the absolute finality of the Prophet Muhammad "is not a Muslim for the purpose of the constitution or law."[33]

It is also worth reviewing one case, *Mujibur Rehman v. Federal Government of Pakistan*, tried in the Federal *Shariat* Court in 1985 after the promulgation of Ordinance XX which dealt with the question whether the new law violated the constitutional fundamental rights of Ahmadis to profess as well as propagate their faith.[34] The case resembles *Abdur Rahman Mobashir v. Amir Ali Shah* tried by the Lahore High Court in 1978 which was prosecuted after the declaration of Ahmadis' non-Muslim status in 1974, discussing the similar question of their religious rights to profess their faith as mentioned in the previous chapter. The judgment declared in the latter case, that non-Muslims' rights were fully protected, is significantly different from the judgment declared in the subsequent case in 1985 which revoked Ahmadis' religious rights on the basis of their beliefs especially their violation of the core belief in the finality of the prophethood of Mohammed by Ahmadis calling Ahmad the last prophet.[35] The review of both cases reveals significantly different and controversial judgements. In 1979 the first judgement made it legal for Ahmadis to use mosques, profess faith and call *azan* (prayer), whereas the second judgment forbade them to practice such religious rituals or even prohibited them from calling themselves Muslim

---

32. Saeed and Saeed, *Freedom of Religion*, 184–185.
33. Government of Pakistan, *Qadianis: Threat to Islamic Solidarity* (Islamabad: Pakistan Publications, 1984), 5, 28.
34. Mujibur Rehman v. Federal Government of Pakistan, PLD (1985) FSC 8.
35. *Mujibur Rehman v. Federal Government of Pakistan*.

in 1985.[36] The gradual change in judicial outcomes also shows the tension between the Islamic Courts and High Courts dealing with existing law and its practice, the difference between secular and Islamic law and its previous applications, and the future of religious freedom and protection of minorities of Pakistan which will be discussed later in the chapter.

Though the promulgation of Ordinance XX was alarming for Ahmadis, given that they could be accused of numerous religious offences and practices, the final amendment in the law in 1986 affected not only Ahmadis but also all religious communities including Muslims of Pakistan. The core belief in the prophethood of Islam was finally codified in 1986 as section 295-C, known as "the blasphemy law," which prescribed the punishment of death for those who defile the Prophet Muhammad. Before discussing the procedure for prosecution and exacting of the penalty, it is important to note that the word "blasphemy" was not used in Chapter XV: Of Offences Relating to Religion as applied in British India but has become so known in contemporary Pakistan. The term "blasphemy" was also not used in various historical cases and publications in which Arya Samaj published offensive books against the Prophet Muhammad in 1920s as the courts usually declared that the offence had wounded the feelings of Muslims. Likewise, the term "blasphemy" was not used for anti-Christian pamphlets and books published and banned in British India,[37] nor when Chapter XV on religious offences was adopted in India and Pakistan after 1947.[38] "Blasphemy" was not adopted because Macaulay as a legislator involved in framing the law in India, regarded it as necessary to protect the religious feelings of diverse

---

36. The case has discussed in detail by Saeed, "Politics of Exclusion," 328–341.

37. For example, an anti-Christian tract was written by Ganga Prasad Upadhyaya, ed. *Padri Se Bacho* (avoid the missionary) (Allahabad: Arya Samaj Sarju Press, 1941); another anti-Christian tract by Muslim publisher, Muhammad Abdul Razak Hashmi, *Bhonchal Bir Lashkar* (Rawalpindi: Lakshmi Art Steam Press, 1934); another banned tract was regarded as anti-Muslim and anti-Christian in terms of Hindu lower castes' conversion: Dayal Jhalu, *Shuddi se nak mien dam* (Urdu) (Lukhnow: Talkudar Press, 1930). See Barrier, *Banned*, 181.

38. The word blasphemy was not used by Lahore High Court in *Muhammad Khalil v. The State*, against *Development of Muslim Theology* or in *Punjab Religious Book Society v. The State* against *Mizan ul-Haqq*. Both books were alleged to defile the Prophet as discussed in detail in chapter 4.

religious communities rather than following the same "blasphemy act" which had protected only Christianity in the history of the United Kingdom.[39]

Giving full details of the meaning of blasphemy in the Islamic context is beyond the scope of this research. Yet the death sentence for defiling the Prophet Muhammad has been discussed in various sources but with different arguments. For example, Mohammad Hashim Kamali notes that the record of the Prophet's early life does not show blasphemy punishments and also the Qur'an does not prescribe punishments of blasphemy against the Prophet (*sabb al-nabi*) and his companions (*sabb al-sahabah*).[40] Wiederhold comments that according to the collected canonical *Hadiths*, the vilification of the Prophet and his companions was "considered intolerable and therefore forbidden by some of the religious leaders at the time."[41] Abdullah Saeed and Hasan Saeed note that blasphemy has been established as derived from the idea of apostasy (*riddah*) which results in the death penalty under *sharia* law.[42] Before the enforcement of the law of blasphemy in Pakistan, various Pakistani scholars and law enforcers were also concerned with whether the death sentence is according to Islam and can be legalised or not which, as we shall see, has become a crucial question in contemporary Pakistan. However, the death sentence was significantly supported by various Islamic scholars and Ismail Qureshi who played an important role in promulgating this law by arguing that blasphemy in Islam is punishable with death and "the blasphemy law" should be accepted and respected internationally as now it punishes all "words written or spoken" against the Prophet Muhammad as it was used for Jesus Christ.[43]

Though the blasphemy law remained on the statute books in Britain, it was later regarded as "ancient, discriminatory, unnecessary [and]

---

39. Kevin Smullin Brown, "Reforming England's Blasphemy Law to Protect the Individual," *Islam and Christian-Muslim Relations* 14, no. 2 (2003): 188–203.

40. Mohammad Hashim Kamali, *Freedom of Expression in Islam* (Cambridge: Islamic Texts Society, 1997).

41. L. Wiederhold, "Blasphemy against the Prophet Muhammad and his Companions (*sabb al-rasul, sabb al-sahabah*): The Introduction of the Topic into Shaf'i Legal Literature and Its Relevance for Legal Practice under Mamluk Rule," *Semitic Studies* 42, no. 1 (March 1997): 40–41.

42. Saeed and Saeed, *Freedom of Religion*, 36.

43. Qureshi, *Muhammad: The Messenger*, 69.

illiberal"[44] and finally abolished on 8 May 2008 by the Criminal Justice and Immigration Act 2008 on the basis of the religious diversity, immigration policy and cultural pluralism of the United Kingdom which had increased after the 1950s.[45] The abolition of the British blasphemy law was in part a result of discussion about the question whether the law could be extended to protect other religions in the United Kingdom. In 1991, in the case of Salman Rushdie, it was argued by some British Muslims that the law of blasphemy should be amended to apply to books such as *The Satanic Verses* in United Kingdom which was originally written in 1988 in India and was later regarded as offensive to Muslims of India and South Asia and regarded as a serious blasphemy offence in the Islamic world.[46] After viewing the case, the law commissioner noted "the duty of all citizens in our society of different races and people of different faiths and of no faith, not purposely to insult or outrage the religious feelings of others."[47] The case was regarded as inadmissible on the uncertain argument of whether "the law should be reformed or repealed" because of the new make-up of the United Kingdom and the fact that blasphemy only referred to Christianity in general and the Church of England in particular.[48] It is beyond the concerns of this thesis to comment on whether the subsequent British law known as Incitement to Religious Hatred differentiates various ethnic, religious or cultural groups[49] or treats

---

44. Norman Doe and Russell Sandberg, eds., *Law and Religion: New Horizons* (Leuven: Peeters, 2009), 89.

45. Doe and Sandberg, *Law and Religion*; Ivan Hare, "Blasphemy and Incitement to Religious Hatred: Free Speech Dogma and Doctrine," in *Extreme Speech and Democracy*, eds. James Weinstein and Ivan Hare (Oxford: Oxford University Press, 2010), 289–310.

46. Though the debate took place in Rushdie's case but it drew serious attention after the September 11 attacks in New York and later in 2008 the blasphemy was finally abolished and now it is known as the law of "Incitement to Religious Hatred."

47. Law Commission 19, 85. 4. 3. 1; Salman Rushdie cases in Choudry v. United Kingdom, 1991 (Whitehouse v. Lemon. 1 QB 10, AC 617, 1979).

48. Later, the Muslim community of England filed a petition in the European Court of Human Rights to challenge the rejection of their blasphemy case, on the grounds that the then British Blasphemy Law was discriminatory because it did not treat different religions in the United Kingdom equally: the challenge failed. Qureshi, *Muhammad: The Messenger*, 178; Rick Simpson, *Blasphemy and the Law in a Plural Society*, Grove Ethical Studies, no. 90 (Cambridge: Grove Boooks, 1993), 3–25.

49. Kay Goodall, "Incitement to Religious Hatred, All Talk and No Substance?" *Modern Law Review* 70, no. 1 (2007): 89–113.

Christianity like other religions[50] or may be described as a secular approach to protect religious pluralism.[51] However, it is indeed important to note that the British blasphemy law is no longer alive but the British Indian law of 1860 known as Offences Relating to Religion though still existing with the same title, after amendments, especially including the death sentence for defiling the name of the Prophet Muhammad, has generally come to be known in Pakistan after 1986 as the "blasphemy law."

The promulgation of section 295-C marks the first time in Pakistan that the death penalty was added to Chapter XV: Of Offences Relating to Religion, to punish an accused for defiling the name of the Prophet. The question arises of why Pakistan needed another law when section 295-A was already available in practice to protect the religious feelings of Muslims. According to some sources the question of the punishment awarded to an accused for allegedly defiling the Prophet under section 295-A was regarded not as accordance with Islam. Ismail Qureshi notes that the need to apply the blasphemy law with full severity was made clear when a book entitled *Heavenly Communalism* written by a lawyer, Mushtaq Raj, was published in Lahore, Punjab in 1983, containing offensive matter against Islam and its beliefs. Though the author was prosecuted and the book banned under section 295-A for outraging the feelings of Muslims, the main concern was that the "blasphemy law" should be enacted to protect the Prophet Muhammad with severe punishment regarding the intensity of religious insult. Therefore, section 295-A was challenged in the first petition, moved by Ismail Qureshi, held for hearing at the Federal *Shariat* Court (FSC) in 1984 when it was stated that a punishment of two years and a fine or both was not adequate and is repugnant to Islam, and that only the death penalty was adequate punishment for defiling the name of the Prophet Muhammad.[52]

Later, with political and official approval, the bill was moved by Jamaat-e-Islami's Apa Nisar Fatima, MNA (Member of National Assembly) seeking the addition of Section 295-C in Chapter XV: Of Offences Relating to Religion and provided for the death sentence alone for acts constituting

---

50. Brown, "Reforming England's Blasphemy Law," 195.

51. Anthony Jeremy, "Practical Implications of the Racial and Religious Hatred Act 2006," *The Ecclesiastical Law Society* 9, no. 2 (2007): 187–201.

52. Qureshi, *Namoos-e-Rasalat*, 361.

insult to the prophet Muhammad.[53] Although this did not go unchallenged, as some National Assembly members including the law minister, Khan Iqbal A. Khan, were not in favour of it, especially the vexed issue of whether it was in accordance with the Qur'an or Sunna as already noted.[54] After much discussion the bill was passed by the Criminal Law (Amendment) Act 111 of 1986, adding Section 295-C in Chapter XV of PPC that prescribes the mandatory death penalty, with life imprisonment as an alternative punishment, for defiling the name of the Prophet Muhammad.[55]

> Whoever by word, either spoken or written, or by visible representation, or by any imputation, innuendo, or insinuation, directly or indirectly, defiles the sacred name of Holy Prophet Muhammad (peace be upon him) shall be punished with death, or imprisonment for life, and shall also be liable to fine.[56]

It cannot be denied that new additions in Chapter XV were initially added to punish Ahmadis and protect the Islamic faith from them or to protect Islamic faith from future written or spoken blasphemies. Since the law has been amended, it has become a challenge for other religious communities, the judiciary as well as for the government to deal with blasphemy accusations. It affected all religious communities and the many additions contravened, and thus annulled, sections of Chapter XV: Of Offences Relating to Religion of 1860 applied by the British. Before reviewing the relevant original 1860 sections, we should first focus more thoroughly on additions 295-B with the mandatory punishment of life imprisonment for defiling the Qur'an and 295-C with the death sentence for defiling the Prophet Muhammad. These were what gave rise to the accusations known as "blasphemy," which have significantly increased since 1984 in Pakistan legal history and have seriously affected all religious communities. Though all religious communities, including Muslims, are also vulnerable to accusations of blasphemy for defiling the copy of Qur'an and the name of the Prophet, it has been observed how the accusations against minorities such as

---

53. Qureshi, *Muhammad: The Messenger*, 65–67.
54. Qureshi, *Namoos-e-Rasalat*, 48–49, 358, 361.
55. Khan, *Pakistan Penal Code*, 239.
56. The offence under section 295-C is cognisable and non-bailable. Khan and Khan, *Pakistan Penal Code*, 239.

Christians, Ahmadis and Hindus, largely in Punjab province, have brought a level of chaos which breaches the peace of the society.

To understand exactly how this 1984 addition to Chapter XV changed the aim and therefore the practice of the religious conflict law embedded in the 1860 Act, we need to look carefully at the legal meaning of and procedures for Section 295-B and Section 295-C, describing how an accusation for blasphemy can be made, and what areas of dispute have arisen since 1984 in the application of the law. The use of the law as a tool by individuals is one problem. The earlier judges of the Chapter, especially Section 295-A had insisted on examining the context of an accusation to ensure personal vendettas were not unwittingly advanced by the court. Chapter 4 has already pointed out that attention to this issue saw a plaintiff's accusation of religious bias rejected by the court. Clearly from the 1920s if not before, the courts were aware of the controversial nature of these laws and the fact that their application could result in extreme violence; the intention of both Chapter XV and the judiciary had been to maintain community cohesion or at least avoid violence. Arising from this point, not only have the objectives of Chapter XV been changed but also these changes have affected the judgements, the judicial system and the religious communities of Pakistan. Most importantly, the crucial issue of "intention" in the original law of religious offence linked to what became called blasphemy in 1984 has been radically changed. Results of this change include not only the effect on the person accused of blasphemy but also the political leaders, police and most of the lower courts and lawyers, all of whom are at risk if they act in any way judged by the accusers to be less than harsh to the accused. These three areas are the key to understanding the problems which were not thrashed out in the initial 1984 decision, and which over the years have increasingly come to haunt the judicial system of Pakistan and the lives of minorities as well as more critical, reflective or vulnerable members of the majority. Before setting out and analyzing these various issues, it will be helpful to discuss the contents and objectives of the new blasphemy section 295-B.

5.4 Section 295-B

The main objective of section 295-B is to protect the sanctity of the Qur'an from any usage in a derogatory manner with the punishment of life imprisonment. According to Sections 295-B:

> Whoever wilfully defiles, damages or desecrates a copy of the Holy Qur'an or of an extract therefrom or uses it in any derogatory manner or for any unlawful purpose shall be punishable with imprisonment for life.

Section 295-B of PPC can be applied where the Qur'an has been defiled, damaged or desecrated in any derogatory manner or for any unlawful purpose. Second, the prosecution can be brought where such acts have been done "wilfully" to defile or damage the Qur'an.

5.4.1 The Meaning of Defile and Damage in Section 295-B

The words "defile" and "damage" in section 295-B were previously mentioned in section 295 applied by the British in 1860 in the Indian Penal Code, used for the physical protection of sacred places such as mosques, churches and temples and also for any necessary ceremonial or ritual protection to keep the sanctity of any objects held in such sacred places. It is also important to note that words "defile and damage" in section 295-B includes both physical as well as spiritual dimensions.

Before viewing the legal procedure it will be helpful to recollect that Muslims esteem the Qur'an, the Book (*al-Kitab*) as Allah's revelation for moral and spiritual guidance, and as highly respected both spiritually and physically.[57] There are some physical rules that Muslims follow when holding, handling, touching, or reading from the *mus-haf* (the pages) of the Qur'an. Being in a state of ritual purity is mentioned in sura 56:79, "none shall touch it [the Qur'an] save for those who are ritually pure." Some rules have been interpreted and reiterated from early Islamic scholars: *Wudu*, (washing) is necessary before prayer as well as before touching the text of the Qur'an. Al-Hilli deems it reprehensible for a ritually impure person to

---

57. For more about the revelations and theology of the word of God see, Morris S. Seale, *Muslim Theology: A Study of Origins with Reference to the Church Fathers* (London: Luzac, 1964), 69; John L. Esposito, *Islam: The Strait Path*, 3rd ed. (Oxford: Oxford University Press, 1998), 11.

touch the Qur'an and Abu-l-Qasim al-Khudu'i mentions that one who is in a state of ritual impurity is not permitted to touch the writing of the codex or the vocalization signs.[58] There are different explanations as some argue that purity or cleanliness of the heart is necessary.

As a result of this general understanding, the following rules are usually followed in respect of reading and touching the Qur'an. Physical respect is maintained by keeping the Qur'an properly wrapped on a high place either a high shelf or on top of a bookshelf but never on the floor or an unclean place. The Qur'an should be handled with respect and should not be thrown or torn, and anyone touching or reading it must be ritually clean, if necessary performing *wudu* or washing. Ignoring such rules comes close to the word "defile" used in section 295-B of PPC, meaning treating something holy with a lack of respect or making something foul or impure, filthy and polluted.[59] According to Saeed, the Arabic word *sabb* similarly implies that "deliberately throwing a copy of the Qur'an into a dirty place such as a rubbish place" is offensive.[60] In short, physical respect includes certain rules for placing the Qur'an and physical purity for touching or reading it.

Section 295-B sets out both physical respect for the Qur'an, and for its spiritual meaning which is inseparable from the former.[61] To describe the spiritual meaning for example, in Islam, the Qur'an, meaning to read or to recite, is the culmination or final revelation, *wahy*, of Allah that has been revealed to the Prophet Muhammad.[62] Muslims believe that the Qur'an is the only accurately preserved word of God as well as the ultimate moral and spiritual guide in its nature and scope. Disregarding or denying such realties can be considered offensive. These physical and spiritual meanings were described by the Lahore High Court in one case, *Syed Ijaz Husain alias Tahir Pir v. The State* brought under section 295-B in 1992. A Muslim

---

58. Al-Hilli l-Allama, Hasan b. Yusuf b. Ali b. al-Mutahhar, "Tadhkirat al-fuqaha fi talkhis fatawail-ulama," in Joseph W. Meri, "Ritual and the Quran," in *Encyclopaedia of the Quran*, ed. Jane Dammen McAuliffe, Brill Online, accessed 28 November 2012, http://dx.doi.org/10.1163/1875-3922_q3_EQCOM_00177.

59. Catherine Soanes and Sarah Hawker, eds., *Oxford English Dictionary* (Oxford: Oxford Press, 2006), 259; "Defile," *Merriam-Webster*, accessed 7 May 2011, https://www.merriam-webster.com/dictionary/defile.

60. Saeed and Saeed, *Freedom of Religion*, 36.

61. Syed Ijaz Husain Alias Tahir Pir v. The State, (1994) MLD, 15 Lahore.

62. Esposito, *Islam: The Strait Path*, 11.

putting the Qur'an in a bag with a pair of embroidered shoes lying near the accuser's feet, on the bus, was guilty of committing blasphemy by physically disrespecting the Qur'an. Apart from the physical disrespect, he was also guilty of defiling the spiritual meaning of Qur'an by introducing himself as a *Mureed*, follower of a Pir or old person known as a master or Saint who guides and instructs followers in a *sufi* path: the perpetrator apparently claimed a book containing film songs was more sacred than the Holy Qur'an.[63] Though, in this case, physical and spiritual aspects were given as the basis for prosecution under section 295-B, most cases discussed below concern only physical respect for the Qur'an in Pakistan.

Apart from discussing the meaning of "defiling the Qur'an" it is also necessary to review the word "damage," used in section 295-B in making an accusation. The word "damage" according to the Law Dictionary means loss or harm to person, property as well as reputation but in the legal sense not all forms of damage give rise to a right of action. For example, the law generally gives no compensation to the loss of particular material things or people that occurred accidentally, but it is actionable where "damage" has been caused.[64] Section 295-B does not indicate exactly what "acts of damage" are liable to prosecution, perhaps to catch any and every act due to possible shortcomings in the drafting of the law. However, according to some blasphemy cases discussed in the following points, section 295-B was used where the whole or any page of the Qur'an was found torn, burnt or thrown. In many cases, such physical damage to the Qur'an or parts or pages of the Qur'an have been regarded as blasphemy under section 295-B.

Even though it is clear that 295-B of the Pakistan Penal Code for defiling the Qur'an, as discussed above, is applicable either for physical or spiritual damage, such allegations should not be declared as blasphemy unless done "wilfully" to defile or damage the Qur'an, thus maintaining the 1860 basis for guilt.

---

63. *Syed Ijaz Husain Alias Tahir Pir v. The State*.

64. "Damage," *A Dictionary of Law* by Jonathan Law and Elizabeth A. Martin (Oxford University Press 2009), *Oxford Reference Online*, 3 September 2011 http://www.oxfordreference.com/views

5.4.2 The Meaning of "Wilful" Action in Section 295-B

"Wilful" action to defile the Qur'an is the core clause necessary for conviction on the grounds of the defilement or damage of the Qur'an under section 295-B. According to the Law Dictionary, the word "wilfully" means a deliberately intended act which is "usually used of wrongful actions in which the conduct is intended and executed by a free agent."[65] According to the Peshawar Court:

> Wilfully means the act of defiling, damaging and desecrating or distorting the original texts of the Holy Quran or part of it must be with intention to achieve a nefarious objective contemptuously and showing disrespect to Holy Quran which he has forbidding by law to do. Act to wilfully defiling, damaging and desecrating of the Holy Quran or part of it, would constitute the offence committed intentionally, knowingly, purposely for achieving the detestable objectives while in the absence of such intention, necessary *"mens rea"* would be absolutely lacking and in that eventually the person accused for such an offence cannot be held guilty except in a very rare and exceptional circumstances.[66]

This means that if "wilfully" is accepted as essential for successful prosecution, not every incorrect physical or spiritual action or act can be regarded as blasphemy. For example, a Muslim who reads the Qur'an badly, or drops the copy of Qur'an by accident without any malicious intention of defiling the text, should not be held guilty of blasphemy. In one case before the new law came in, Ubaid Ullah, a Muslim was found throwing a booklet entitled *Nizam Mutarajjam* on the ground and trampling it, on 6 April 1982. He was accused under section 295-B in Bahawalpur, Punjab of defiling a copy of the Qur'an. Ubaid denied the allegations and said in his defence that on the day of the incident some unknown persons had given him cigarette filled with *charas*, a drug which made him senseless, and they put the booklet in

---

65. "Wilful" *A Dictionary of Law* by Jonathan Law and Elizabeth A. Martin (Oxford University Press 2009), *Oxford Reference Online*; John Bouvier, *A Law Dictionary* (Adapted to the Constitution and Laws of the United States), 1856.

66. PLD, 2007 Peshawar 83 in Fazal Zada Khan and Touseef Zada Khan, *Pakistan Penal Code: XLV of 1860* (Lahore: Touseef Zada Khan Publication, 2011), 447.

his pocket. After thorough examination in court, it was declared that the statement of the accused seemed both reasonable and plausible and the record of the accused revealed that he was absolutely illiterate and had no reason to carry the booklet. On these grounds it was held that the accused had not committed blasphemy under section 295-B as no defilement or damage of the Qur'an was found in the case.[67]

Likewise, in another case a Qadiani, Muzaffer Iqbal, was accused when it was reported that a copy of the Qur'an was desecrated in the Mosque in Sanghar and Muzaffer was standing near the Mosque. In 1993, the judge set the case aside by declaring that Section 295-B applied to the circumstances and he thus had no jurisdiction in the matter as the initial report was filed under section 295 for defiling a sacred place of worship rather than under section 295-B for defiling the Qur'an. The case was dismissed.[68]

The above cases clearly reveal that without wilful intention of defiling the Qur'an an accusation cannot be maintained under section 295-B but cases have been successfully tried where such intention is present. For example, Muhammad Asghar and Zafar Mehmood, two Muslim accused, were prosecuted under section 295-B when they burnt the Holy Qur'an along with other Islamic books in Lahore on 20 October 1999. It was declared that they were aware of the sanctity of the Qur'an and yet intentionally committed the act which is liable to be accused section 295-B.[69]

There are some notable points in the above cases such as how the judiciary deals with cases and how people bring accusations. The first two cases clearly show that people can easily misunderstand what is sacred or not and in what condition anyone can be said to defile a copy or sacred pages of the Qur'an. It also reveals that merely being in the vicinity can lead to prosecution, such as the Qadiani (an Ahmadi) standing nearby the mosque. There are two areas of concern here. First, while the latter case was thrown out, that depends on the attitude and might one say the integrity of the judge, not on the actual law, and thus not all accused people may be treated fairly. Second, and just as important, in many cases people do not wait for the judicial verdict as to whether a certain act has been done or not, or even if

---

67. Ubaid Ulla v. The State, (1991) SCMR 1734.
68. Muzaffar Iqbal v. The State, (1993) P. Cr. LJ 1993.
69. Muhammad Asghar v. The State in Janahgir, *From Protection to Exploitation*, 57.

there is merely suspicion: they, the mob take the law into their own hands, judge and then act as discussed later in the chapter.

5.4.3 The Prosecution on Suspicion under Section 295-B and Mob Violence

Historically social protest and mob violence over religious issues have occurred in the Punjab province as discussed earlier. Such patterns of mob protest have been revived by blasphemy accusations which resulted in riots, protest and violence. Though all religious communities are equally vulnerable to accusation, given the unclear meaning of section 295-B, minorities such as Christians, Hindus and Ahmadis have been punished by the mob, their places of worship, religious books and other property belonging to them damaged. The most critical examples can be seen where section 298-B and the execution of the law falls into the hands of local communities.

Whether unintentional or wilful, it is useful to see how easily accusations under 295-B became explosive and where the merest suspicion of defiling the Qur'an is enough to punish the supposed miscreant. For example, on 11 November 1995, Yousaf Masih, a Christian resident of Sangla Hill, was accused of burning a few pages of the Qur'an, charged and arrested by local police. Even though he had been arrested and the case was under inquiry, the Christian community of Sangla Hill in the Nankana District in Punjab Pakistan experienced the effects of this "blasphemy" defilement accusation on the following day, when a mob burnt down three churches, a missionary run school, two hostels, and several houses belonging to the Christian community.[70] According to the National Commission of Peace and Justice (NCP), which provided legal aid to the accused, eighty-eight Muslims were arrested on charges of taking the law into their own hands and damaging the Christian community.[71] According to the commission, the matter was first brought up to the Sessions Court, referred to as an Anti Terror Court. The complainant testified in the court that he had accused Yousaf on a mere

---

70. Ata ur Rehman, *Souls on Fire: A Collection of Articles and Editorials Published in Newspapers and Magazines on Gujra Incident* (Lahore: National Commission for Justice and Peace, 2009), 8.

71. Bishop John Joseph established the National Commission of Peace and Justice in 1991 and its main offices were open in Lahore and Faisalabad. It is also called Human Rights Commission that supports and provides legal aid to the people victimized by blasphemy law. Rashid, *A Peaceful Struggle*, 31–33.

suspicion.[72] This kind of incident illustrates the problematic application of the law where punishment for defiling the Qur'an has been inflicted on the Christian community that had nothing to do with it, without a trial, much less a conviction.

One of the most critical and sensitive examples can be seen where any page on the ground with Arabic text is assumed to be Qur'anic, resulting in an accusation of defilement easily made against any local, usually a non-Muslim. It is important to make clear that before asking whether an act represents the religious offence of defiling the Qur'an, there has been a clear tendency for local Muslims to make announcements from mosques to incite followers to judge the accused, usually from a minority, with dramatic and often violent consequences. The following is a typical example of the process.

Near and in Gojra, Punjab in August 2009, an incident targeted the Christian community. According to the case, Imran Aslam, a local Muslim cleric, and his two followers first alleged that three Christians, Mukhtar Masih, Talib Masih and his son, Imran Masih, had defiled sheets of paper inscribed with Arabic verses of the Qur'an by throwing them up in the air during a wedding. However, other accounts of the situation state that children were celebrating by throwing papers in the air that, again according to the accuser's claim, were bits and pieces of pages of the Qur'an. According to Inkisar Khan, District Police Officer, this blasphemy case was registered under section 295-B for defiling the Qur'an. The allegations were not investigated by the police and no evidence was ever found as to whether pages of the Qur'an were actually thrown or not.[73] After the accusation, the local cleric spoke through loudspeakers and asked Muslims to attack Christians instead of waiting for the proper trial. Mostly Christian residents therefore fled to safety. Later, a group of masked men, armed with firearms and

---

72. Emmanuel Yousaf Mani, *Human Rights Monitor 2006: A Report on the Religious Minorities in Pakistan* (Lahore: National Commision of Justice and Peace, 2006), 27–28. A similar application can be seen in Shantinagar case in 1997 when burnt and torn pages of the Qur'an with blasphemous statements were found near a bridge, and both Christians and Muslims denied the truth of the allegation but later a riot attacked Shanitnagarr and set the village, churches, school and shops on fire after an incident of alleged desecration of the Qur'an. Ramnit Lall Rahi, *The Invisibles: The Plight of Christians in Pakistan* (Essex: SPS Communication, 2000), 81; Sookhdeo, *People Betrayed*, 268–274; Rehman, *Souls on Fire*, 8.

73. "Christians' Homes Burnt Over Desecration," *Dawn*, 1 August 2009, available at https://www.dawn.com/news/964049.

explosives, came from Jhang to lead the violence against Christians on the pretext of their having defiled the Holy Qur'an.[74] According to Rafiq Masih, a local resident, "they were shouting anti-Christian slogans and attacking our houses" while the uncontrollable mob went on a violent rampage.[75] Approximately forty houses and a church were set on fire by a mob. The most shocking outcome of this incident was that eight innocent Christians, including two children and an elderly man, were burnt to death.[76]

In this blasphemy case it was not clear whether the papers were really inscribed with verses of the Qur'an and thrown up in the air during a wedding or whether children were celebrating simply by throwing papers in the air which were assumed to be scraps or pages of the Qur'an. However, it is clear that the blasphemy accusation under section 295-B radically disadvantaged the Christian minority which is vulnerable to lynch-justice in the absence of effective rights and protection. Whether or not the case is dealt with in the courts, the existence of 295-B seems to incite those opposed to minorities to take direct action.

There is no doubt that section 295-B has been misused by accusers, by mobs, and even by the judiciary (who usually strive to stay above the fray) and has changed the application of religious offences and the legal history of Pakistan. The actual meaning of defiling and damaging the Qur'an with "wilful" intention is totally ignored and rarely used beyond making an accusation – if the process reaches that level of formality. Before analyzing the implications of this statement, it is important to see the effect on religious freedom of expression and practice, a serious issue under section 295-C of Chapter XV which prescribes the death sentence for those who defile the name of Prophet Muhammad.

---

74. "Outlawed Terrorists in Gojra," editorial in, *Daily Times*, 4 August 2009; Rehman, *Souls on Fire*, 30; Syed Mohammad Ali, Repeal Discriminatory Legislation, published in *Daily Times*, 11 August 2009.

75. Rafiq Masih in Zahid Hussain, "Eight Christians Mercilessly Burn to Death in Pakistan," *The Times*, 3 August 2009.

76. Those who were burnt during the riot were: Hameed Masih, 50, Asia Mohsin, 20, Asifa Almas, 19, Ummia Almas, 9, Musa Almas, 7, Akhlas Hameed, 40, Parveen Victor, 50 and master Riaz. Rehman, *Souls on Fire*.

5.5 Section 295-C

> Whoever by word, either spoken or written, or by visible representation, or by any imputation, innuendo, or insinuation, directly or indirectly, defiles the sacred name of Holy Prophet Muhammad (peace be upon him) shall be punished with death, or imprisonment for life, and shall also be liable to fine.[77]

Generally, defiling the name of the Prophet is offensive for Muslims to whom the Prophet Muhammad is the last prophet as well as the bearer of the final revelation of Allah. Anyone is liable to be punished with death who "defiles" the name of the Prophet Muhammad in various conditions such as "by word, either spoken or written, or by visible representation, or by any imputation, innuendo, or insinuation, directly or indirectly" as described in section 295-C.

For example, "innuendo" means an oblique allusion, hint or insinuation, particularly a veiled or equivocal reflection on character or reputation by using such allusions. In law, it means "an indirect hint or remark" used in lawsuits for defamation (libel or slander), usually to show that the party suing was the person about whom the insulting statements were made or to make clear why the comments were defamatory.[78] Another word in section 295-C, "insinuation," generally gives a similar meaning such as an indirect sly expression, subtle, and usually derogatory utterance or suggestion.[79] Regarding the meaning of terms used in section 295-C, it can be said that any hint, doubt, imagination, or statement of a single witness who has seen an incident either directly or indirectly can bring punishments on those who are thereby assumed to have made an utterance in contempt of the Holy Prophet. The Federal *Shariat* Court gives a definition of blasphemy law:

> Reviling or insulting the Prophet (peace be upon him) in writing or speech; speaking profanity or contemptuously about him

---

77. Sookhdeo, *People Betrayed*, 250–251.

78. "Innuendo," *Burton's Legal Thesaurus, 4E* (2007), accessed 26 March 2013, from http://legal-dictionary.thefreedictionary.com/Innuendo.

79. "Insinuation," *A Law Dictionary, Adapted to the Constitution and Laws of the United States*, John Bouvier (1856), accessed 26 March 2013, from http://legal-dictionary.thefreedictionary.com/Insinuation.

or his family; attacking the prophet's dignity and honour in an abusive manner; vilifying him or making an ugly face when his name is mentioned' showing enmity or hatred towards him, his family, his companions and the Muslims; accusing or slandering the prophet and his family, defaming the prophet, refusing the prophet's jurisprudence or judgment in any matter; rejecting the *Sunnah al-Nabawiyya*; showing disrespect, contempt for or rejection of the rights of Allah and His prophet or rebelling against Allah and His prophet.[80]

Though such conditions can bring various accusations other than that of blasphemy, the crucial issue regards the death sentence for any gesture even if it is done unintentionally. Prescribing the death sentence under section 295-C was initially debated and discussed in the National Assembly but was not a foregone conclusion and only passed into law in 1986. The death penalty has later generated a lot of discussion in Pakistani media, mainly revolving around whether the punishment of death is justified in light of Islamic injunctions.[81] Let us consider the background to the debate over the death sentence given under section 295-C.

5.5.1 The Discussion over the Death Sentence and Life Imprisonment and the Issue of "Intention" in Section 295-C

In 1983–1984, Ismail Qureshi campaigned to enact section 295-C which was later applied in 1986 with the death sentence for defiling the name of the Prophet. Later he attempted to move the Federal *Shariat* Court (FSC) to make further changes to section 295-C such as reviewing the death sentence and clarifying the proof of an intention for accusation of blasphemy in 1991. He clearly mentioned his assumption of the misuse of the law in future when he said:

> In my opinion, it is absolutely necessary to further amend section 295-C so as to bring it in harmony with the Quran and

---

80. This statement was followed by Madni, a Muslim Pakistani scholar. Muhammad Asrar Madani, *Verdict of Islamic Law on Blasphemy and Apostasy* (Lahore: Idara-e-Islamiat, 1994), 19–20.

81. Mehdi, *Islamization of the Law*, 150.

Sunna. Otherwise if this section stands in its present form, there is a danger of it giving birth to ambiguity and legal complications. Quran and Sunna have laid down certain conditions for *hadd* and *tazir* punishments. Islam took the lead in the world to make intention and objective as basic components of an offence[82]

Qureshi also insisted that evidence of *tazkiat ush-shahood* (purity of the witnesses) should have been held essential for the legal prosecution. Some *ulema* appointed to discuss the death sentence, argued that blasphemy was a forgivable offence and some even said that the ruler could award a lesser punishment than death.[83] Various references were discussed, where it was stated that the Prophet himself had condoned the killing of those who offended him. Some references were also given where the companions of the Prophet, *Khulfa-e-Rashdeen* killed such people who had defiled the name of the Prophet.[84]

The council relied on the Qur'an *Surah Anfal* verse 13, "That is because they opposed Allah and His Messenger and whoever opposes Allah and His Messenger – indeed, Allah is severe in Penalty,"[85] and *Surah al-Nisa* verse 65, "But no, by your Lord, they will not [truly] believe until they make you, [O Muhammad], judge concerning that over which they dispute among themselves and then find within themselves no discomfort from what you have judged and submit in [full, willing] submission."[86] The council also relied on some traditions of the Prophet called *Hadith* in support of his pleas that only a sentence of death is the appropriate punishment and no court should be given the authority to pronounce the lesser sentence of life imprisonment. Efforts were made to discuss and even change the sentence but those forwarding the debate withdrew their opposition.[87]

---

82. Qureshi, *Namoos-e-Rasalat*, 328–230; I. R. Rehman, "Jumping the Gun: Award of Death Penalty Without Establishing Intent Contradicts the Federal Shariat Court Ruling" and "The Flaw of the Law of Blasphemy," *Newsline*, June 1998.
83. *Muhammad Ismail Qureshi v. Pakistan*.
84. *Muhammad Ismail Qureshi v. Pakistan*.
85. Qur'anic quote taken from *Muhammad Ismail Qureshi v. Pakistan*.
86. Qur'anic quote taken from *Muhammad Ismail Qureshi v. Pakistan*.
87. *Muhammad Ismail Qureshi v. Pakistan*; Jahangir, *From Protection to Exploitation*, 24.

Amid the argument over the death sentence, the omission of the crucial legal ingredient of "intention" from the code has been debated. While in the various references given by all the judges and lawyers, the central question is whether blasphemy under section 295-C could be committed intentionally or unintentionally. Qureshi notes that in the discussion on intentional prosecution, Muhammad Tahir-ul-Qadir, one of the best-known politicians and religious scholars in the Federal *Shariat* Court, not only supported the death sentence in section 295-C but also argued that "the intention and the motive of the offender are irrelevant and cannot be taken into consideration while deciding the case [and] a blasphemer must not be given an opportunity of a hearing to prove his intention and motive in his defence."[88] Ismail Qureshi argued, following the *Hadith* of the Prophet advising Hazarat Ali when appointing a Judge of Yaman to "decide the cases after hearing both parties" as "according to Islamic injunctions an accused person has the right to defend himself and no one could be condemned unheard."[89] Qureshi noted some of the traditions of the Prophet that "certainly all actions are to be judged by intention."[90] Even "*Hudood* punishments should be avoided where there is doubt."[91]

The FSC discussed the importance of "intention" and, as discussed in the case of *Qureshi v. The State*, how it plays a role in convicting the blasphemer. It was declared that "the mere fact that words uttered sounded contemptuous of the Prophet is not an offence until it is based on malicious action."[92] In some of the jurists' opinion, if contempt for the Prophet has been expressed in "words either spoken or written" the contemnor will not be asked what was his intention but if the words are such which bear or have the capacity of bearing different meanings and senses out of which only one amounts to contempt, he will be asked as to what was his "intention."[93] Some even discussed that the meaning and import of words in different regions and contexts may also suggest different meaning, so that an accused must be

---

88. Qureshi, *Muhammad: The Messenger*, 178.
89. Qureshi, 178.
90. Al Bukhari Kitabul Hadith in Qureshi, *Muhammad: The Messenger*, 67.
91. Kanzul-Ummal-Hadith in Qureshi, 67.
92. *Muhammad Ismail Qureshi v. Pakistan*.
93. Al-Shifa, *Qazi Ayaz*, vol. 11 in *Muhammad Ismail Qureshi v. Pakistan*.

allowed an opportunity to explain lest an innocent person is punished. It is related to the tradition of the Prophet saying that: "The mistake of *qazi* (judge) in releasing a criminal is better than his mistake in punishing an innocent."[94]

Some Qur'anic references were also mentioned to support the argument to provide evidence in blasphemy accusation, such as "there is no sin for you in the mistakes that ye make unintentionally, but what your hearts purpose (that will be a sin for you), Allah is forgiving, merciful" (Q. 33.5). Likewise, "anyone who, after accepting faith in Allah, utters unbelief, except under compulsion, His heart remaining firm in faith but such as open their breast to unbelief, on them is Wrath from Allah, and theirs will be a dreadful penalty" (Q. 16:106).[95]

It is also significant to note the legislature's discussions regarding the tradition of the Prophet in relation to dealing with non-Muslims and their subjects in Islamic territory. For example, Islamic principles of justice were expressed such as Islam does not advocate aggression, extremism and injustice to others or killing innocent people. It is a religion of peace (*Salamah*) and moderation in every aspect of life as described in the Qur'an (2:143): "Thus we have appointed Muslims a midmost nation that you might be witness to mankind."[96] Likewise, one of the references was mentioned: "We believe in Allah and the revelation given to us, and to Abraham, Ismail, Isaac, Jacob, and the Tribes, and that given to Moses and Jesus and that given to the Prophet from their Lord. We make no difference between one another of them; and we bow to Allah" (Q. 2:136).[97] Significantly, various scholars were agreed that minorities should be given equal status and should be protected where necessary. In view of the above discussion, it can be clearly seen that many scholars and lawyers as well as many members of the government assembly were not fully in favour of the death sentence, many supporting and declaring "intention" as an important judicial element for blasphemy prosecution.

---

94. *Sunan Al-Bayhaqi*, vol. 8, 184, quoted in *Muhammad Ismail Qureshi v. Pakistan*.
95. *Muhammad Ismail Qureshi v. Pakistan*.
96. Qureshi, *Muhammad: The Messenger*, 194.
97. Qureshi, 194.

Despite these various arguments, it was declared that the alternate punishment of life imprisonment as provided in section 295-C was "repugnant to the Injunctions of Islam as given in Holy Qur'an and Sunnah."[98] It was suggested that a section may further be added "to make the same acts or things when said about other Prophets."[99] A copy was sent to the President of Pakistan under Article 203-D to take steps to amend the law so as "to bring the same conformity with the injunctions of Islam."[100] The government could have filed an appeal to challenge the decision but it did not and, according to the upheld judgment, "the penalty for contempt of the Holy Prophet . . . is death and nothing else . . . no one after the Holy Prophet . . . exercised or was authorised the right of reprieve or pardon."[101] An offence committed under section 295-C has been regarded as *hadd* which means no one can change or amend it as it is a commandment of Allah. This means that neither the courts nor the government have an obligation or capacity to reduce or do away with the penalty imposed by law of *Hudood*.[102]

Not only the death sentence and failure to consider intention in section 295-C was upheld but also section 295-A, a clause added by the British in 1927 that originally prescribed punishment of two years and fine for outraging the feelings of any class, was also edited. Its punishment was amended from two years to ten years by the Criminal Law (Second Amendment) Act, XVI of 1991.[103] As discussed earlier in the chapter, Qureshi challenged the two years of sentence under section 295-A as not enough for those who defile the name of the Prophet or subsequently other Prophets such as Jesus Christ. Though it can be claimed that Pakistan protects other religions under section 295-A, in practice it has been rarely used in Pakistan to protect minorities especially Ahmadis as discussed in the fourth chapter. After the 1990s, this section was rarely used to protect Christian and Hindu communities, as we shall see below.

---

98. *Muhammad Ismail Qureshi v. Pakistan.*

99. *Muhammad Ismail Qureshi v. Pakistan.*

100. *Muhammad Ismail Qureshi v. Pakistan.*

101. *Muhammad Ismail Qureshi v. Pakistan*; Patrick Sookhdeo, *Freedom to Believe: Challenging Islam's Apostasy Law* (McLean, VA: Isaac, 2009), 65.

102. Qureshi, *Namoos-e-Rasalat*, 104; Qureshi, *Muhammad: The Messenger*, 178.

103. Muhammad Taimur Khan, *Pakistan Penal Code*, 238.

It is clear that the death sentence is the final verdict for defiling the name of the Prophet under section 295-C, which is and will be hard to repeal, even though the fact that under section 295-C, unintentional acts also deserve death for anyone, including Muslims, threatens all religious communities. Subsequently the law has been debated by national and human rights activists and by representatives of the minority religious communities of Pakistan who have regarded it as a threat to religious expression as well as freedom, not to mention an issue of life and death, especially where the context of the law is misunderstood as discussed below. Yet despite intention being omitted from section 295-C, the judiciary, particularly the High Court, has endeavoured to test the evidence and released many who were mistakenly accused. Upon the approval of the death sentence, and given the omission of intention, registrations of blasphemy cases under section 295-C increased, and became another tool to harass and persecute all religious communities and citizens of Pakistan. Let us now examine section 295-C as far as it pertains to the major ingredient, offensive "writing or speech."

5.5.2 The Meaning of Defiling the Prophet in Speech and Writing in Section 295-C

According to section 295-C, anyone can be prosecuted for blasphemy who defiles the Prophet Muhammad by word, either spoken or written, or by visible representation. The words described in section 295-A, applied by the British in 1927, "by words, either spoken or written, or by visible representation" have been adopted and added to section 295-C. The question arises whether section 295-C has the same meaning and therefore application as 295-A. In section 295-A, "words" covers an attempt to write a book or to voice a religious opinion but the offensive speech and writing must have been done with deliberate and malicious intention to outrage the religious feelings of any religious class of citizens.[104] "Outrageous and malicious attention" was added to section 295-A to prosecute written books such as *Rangila Rasool* and *Trip to Hell* that actually offended the Muslim community of Punjab province in British India in the 1920s as discussed in the second chapter. From 1947, in some cases section 295-A was successfully used for any offensive "words, either written or spoken," lest they should

---

104. Phillips, *Comparative Criminal Jurisprudence*, 130.

insult through malicious intention as discussed in the fourth chapter. New sections by and large contain the same description as they were recorded in Chapter XV: Of Offences Relating to Religion of 1860. For example, offensive speech, opinion or publication clearly fall under section 295-C just as under 295-A: publications or speeches which critique the Prophet's life, such as challenging and changing the meaning of the *rasalat*, prophethood and *toheed*, believing in one God, in Islamic belief and similar themes are offensive in both sections. However, the punishment for such blasphemies under section 295-A is not according to Islam.[105]

It is clear that section 295-A is now effectively in abeyance, and the question arises concerning the execution of 295-C, which is the only section in Chapter XV that does not include any reference to "intention" in connection with defiling the name of the Prophet Muhammad. Given this omission, the prosecution of offensive writing and speech under section 295-C after 1986 became highly contested.

First, it is important to view how religious freedom, discussions and speeches were gradually discouraged and later became vulnerable to accusation for blasphemy under section 295-C. Let us examine the first case where a Christian, Daniel Scot, from Punjab, a student at Islamia College Guru Mandir Karachi, had already had difficulties when speaking about his faith in the 1960s. Daniel had entered into debate with Ahmadi students who criticized both him and Jesus, and responded by criticizing the founder of the Ahmadiyya sect. As a result, approximately twenty-five students gathered to harm him, but he was saved when a professor intervened. Daniel was accused in 1969 by Muslim students of being an American spy propagating a Western religion.[106] Before the 1986 amendments, though Christians or other minorities came under pressure for expressing religious matters, religious controversies were still controllable without violence.

However, in later years his speech and words on religion were to be turned into "blasphemy" when he started teaching at Government Degree College Okara, Punjab in 1986. He was asked what he thought about the Qur'an and he answered by giving differences between the Bible and the Qur'an

---

105. Qureshi, *Namoos-e-Rasalat*, 361; Saeed and Saeed, *Freedom of Religion*, 40.
106. Sookhdeo, *People Betrayed*, 258.

concluding that both could not have had the same source. In response he was asked to give up preaching Christianity and convert to Islam which he refused to do. Later, a case was registered under the newly passed section 295-C and later the First Information Report (FIR) was registered on 24/26 September 1986.[107] In response to this, he and his family hid in various places and he eventually fled to Australia. This first case was on the basis of making derogatory remarks against the Prophet Muhammad, which he was said to have done. Thus not only were he and others discouraged from general dialoguing with their Muslim neighbours, but the application of the law prevented him from being open about his faith.[108] It is also important to mention that according to the 1860 previous section 298, utterances made during the course of religious discussion or argument could not be constituted as religious offence unless based on threatening or insulting language. There was no legal clarification of any malicious intention to wound the feelings of Muslims in this early example of the prosecution of religious discussion or personal opinion, which may not intentionally have insulted the Prophet under section 295-C.

Apart from religious expression or speech, it is also important to see how writing was judged offensive under section 295-C. For example, in 1988, in another early case, Emmanuel Luther, sub-editor of the daily *Jhang* newspaper of Lahore, was accused of committing blasphemy under 295-C for using insulting remarks about the Prophet Muhammad, about whom he had earlier written a book in English, *A Lamp Spreading Light* and been given an award for it by Zia-ul-Haq. Some Muslim clerics later claimed that Emmanuel used derogatory remarks about the Prophet and Islam in the Urdu translation of the book.[109] The writing of Emmanuel Luther could have been prosecuted under section 295-A, which is still on the statute book although in abeyance after section 295-C. Luther was threatened and urged to convert to Islam, which he refused. Initially after the allegation, he was forced to leave his job and hid in different places. A Muslim, Maulana Abdul

---

107. Sookhdeo, *People Betrayed*, 258.
108. Sookhdeo, 260.
109. Dildar and Mughal, *Section 295-C Pakistan Penal Code*, 28; National Commission for Peace and Justice, *Human Rights Monitor 2008: A Report on the Religious Minorities in Pakistan* (Lahore: NCJP, 2008), 63.

Rehman Luter, was killed in Gujranwala, in mistake for Emmanuel Luther, who then went into exile and did not return to Pakistan to see his family again.[110] This and other examples illustrate how religious communities and individuals became vulnerable if they discussed Islam even if their writing was not obviously offensive. One of the crucial issues was that accusation of blasphemy created a climate and led people to declare an accused guilty without hearing their case. This and other early examples of the 1986 amendment shows the changed milieu, very different from the period when the accused had a proper trial to review offensive books in Pakistan as discussed in the previous chapter.

Some case studies show that the use of "writing and speech" on any surface, papers or walls could be used as the basis for an accusation. Such prosecuting of "writing and speech" not only changed the mode of prosecution but also the procedure of the trial, the liberty of courts and lawyers as well as bringing extra-judicial judgments from society. One important case which received national and international attention, in which thirteen-year-old Salamat Masih was sentenced to death under section 295-C for writing offensive words on the wall of a mosque in 1995, illustrates the problem.[111]

According to the case, *Salamat Masih v. The State*, three accused, Salamat Masih, aged thirteen, and thirty-seven-year-old Manzoor Masih, both residents of Ratta Thodran, and forty-eight-year-old Rehmat Masih, resident of Phokarpur, District Gujranwala, were seen writing derogatory words with stone on the wall of mosque on 9 May 1993.[112] It was also reported that objectionable words about the Prophet were discovered written in the mosque's toilet and after some time a piece of paper containing "derogatory words about the Holy Prophet" was thrown at the door of the mosque. After some days, offensive words were written in another mosque on a poster displaying a *Kalima Tayyiba*.[113] The complainants: Fazal-e-Haq, an *imam* of the mosque, along with witnesses Haji Muhammad Akram and

---

110. National Commission for Peace and Justice, *Human Rights Monitor 2008*, 63.

111. Salamat was also convicted under section 298-A for insulting the family of the Prophet, however throughout the trial his conviction under section 295-C with death penalty was mostly discussed. Salamat Masih v. The State, (1995) 28 P. Cr. LJ 813 (Lahore).

112. *Salamat Masih v. The State*; Jahangir, *From Protection to Exploitation*, 80–81.

113. Kalima Tayyiba is a Muslim creed meaning "there is no God but Allah and Muhammad is the Prophet of Allah." *Salamat Masih v. The State.*

Muhammad Bakhsh Lamberdar, claimed to have seen all the offensive acts. Though the case was filed at the police station of Kot Ladha in May 1993, the three accused did not plead until 1 January 1994.[114]

Salamat's statement in his defence was recorded in which he denied all allegations imposed on him. He denied writing anything on the wall of the mosque, as he was illiterate, and said the case had been filed because of his quarrel with Mujahid, a nephew of Muhammad Akram, one of the witnesses of the case.[115] Likewise, Rehmat Masih also denied the allegations and gave an explanation of why he was accused of blasphemy: Master Inayat, a teacher and resident of Kot Ladha, had refused to teach Christian children and complained about the loud speaker in the church and its effect on his students. He further stated that he respects all religions and refused to produce any further evidence in his defence.[116]

All statements concerning the blasphemy allegations of the case were discussed in the trial. Before any verdict was passed on the accused, on 5 April 1994 three armed men attacked them after a hearing of the case as they were leaving the district and session court. Manzoor Masih died on the spot, but Salamat and Rehmat were injured. Though Manzoor Masih's case was closed with his sudden death, Salamat and Rehmat's trial continued.

Haji Fazal-e-Haq, a complainant and the first witness in the blasphemy case, stated that his allegation of blasphemy was correct but that he did not wish to pursue the case, fearing for his life, although not directly from the accused.[117] Likewise, the second witness, Muhammad Akram, described the blasphemy incident, saying that he, along with Muhammad Fazal-e-Haq and Muhammad Bakhsh, had seen Salamat Masih writing offensive words on the wall with a stone while the other two were standing nearby. He further stated they read those words written on the wall by the accused but refused to express the words to keep the sanctity of the prophet. Even though he did not say those words, he admitted that the local cleric Fazal-e-Haq had wiped out those sentences, which contain five or six words, with a piece of cloth. He also claimed that "unknown persons used to throw chits in the

---

114. Jahangir, *From Protection to Exploitation*, 80; *Salamat Masih v. The State*.
115. Salamat's statement recorded by Jahangir, *From Protection to Exploitation*, 81.
116. Rehmat's statement in Jahangir, 81–82.
117. Jahangir, *From Protection to Exploitation*, 80.

toilets" but no action was taken as it was not known who was behind these acts. During cross examination, he agreed he first mentioned the chits two days after registering the case.[118]

The third witness, Muhammad Bakhsh, gave the same story under examination of how he, along with Fazal-e-Haq and Muhammad Akram, saw all three accused writing remarks on the wall. He also said that he could not speak those words out of respect for the Prophet Muhammad.[119] He admitted that two chits with offensive words that were found in the Mosque's toilet were produced by Fazal-e-Haq before the police in his presence. In the cross-examination regarding the quarrel of Salamat Masih with Mujahid, he insisted the blasphemy accusation was not linked to religion or to a quarrel as stated by the accused, that Mujahid, his nephew, had no dispute with Salamat, who was not illiterate. He also rejected Rehamat's evidence that Master Inayat had refused to teach Christian children as well as stated that there had been no dispute before the blasphemy accusation between Christian and Muslim communities.[120]

The fourth witness, the police officer Aman Ulla Khan, stated that he investigated the case on the basis of and after the registration of the FIR and kept two chits in his possession. Like the first three witnesses, he also said that written words on the wall were not readable. Notably, the most important question was raised whether anyone can be convicted for blasphemy under section 295-C if the accuser out of reverence for the Prophet, refused to read or say the derogatory remarks said or written by the accused. After reviewing all statements given by the four witnesses and not finding enough evidence, Asma Jahangir, council for the appellants, stated that: The case against the accused was false and frivolous and the court suffered from several flaws. She elaborated that:

---

118. *Salamat Masih v. The State.*

119. Muhammad Bakhsh statement recorded in *Salamat Masih v. The State.* On the hearing of the timing of the prayer, Asma Jahangir argued that each of the witnesses narrated a similar story of the incident but none of them could tell the exact time of the prayers for which they were present at the Mosque at the time of the occurrence of the incident of blasphemy. See Jahangir, *From Protection to Exploitation*, 82.

120. Muhammad Bakhsh statement as a third witness, recorded in Jahangir, *From Protection to Exploitation*, 81.

> The first complainant, Fazal-e-Haq, stated on oath that he did not want to pursue the case and was declared hostile on the ground of intentionally suppressing the truth. In cross-examination . . . he was a hostile witness and his statement lost all its evidentiary value . . . He stated nothing in the court regarding the occurrence concerning writing on the wall or the production of the chits . . . therefore his evidence was of no value . . . There is a serious contradiction between the versions of the P.W.2 and P.W.3 [Witnesses]. P.W.2 stated that Salamat Masih was writing something of the wall with a stone. Rehmat Masih and Manzoor Masih were also standing there. While P.W.3 Muhammad Bakhsh stated that Salamat Masih, Rehmat Masih and Manzoor Masih were writing on the wall with stones in their hands. It is a serious contradiction between the versions of two eye-witnesses which makes their evidence doubtful and unreliable . . . they have said nothing with regard to the offence under section 295-C and 298-A, P.P.C . . . [Objectionable] words were not reproduced and stated in court by witnesses. The impressions and opinions of these witnesses cannot be made the basis for a judicial finding under the law. With regard to chits . . . the prosecution has failed to prove that these were written by the appellants or recovered from them or had any connection whatsoever. This objectionable material was kept . . . for a year and was produced for first time on 11-5-93 at the police station . . . after two days of the occurrence.[121]

It is critical to note that the Judge declared the sentence of death on Salamat and Rehmat with the following words:

> He had no doubt from the overall appraisal of the evidence that in fact the accused had written objectionable material to defile the sacred name of the Holy Prophet (PBUH) on account of minor disputes. He further stated that if the stone with which the words were written on the wall or the cloth—with which the words were wiped off—was not taken into possession, it

---

121. *Salamat Masih v. The State*, 817–818.

did not have any effect on the prosecution. Salamat had specifically stated that he was illiterate but a judicial notice of School Leaving Certificate was produced before the court which showed that he had studied in school up to class 11.[122]

Mujahid Husain Shiekh, the Additional Sessions Judge, declared the death sentence on Salamat (at that time only fourteen years old) and Rehmat, under section 295-C on 9 February 1995. The judgement shook the nation, particularly minorities, and it was realized that anyone even young children can be awarded with death sentence.

On 13 February 1995, the case was filed for appeal at Lahore High Court. Justice Muhammad Ilyas, the chief Justice of Lahore High Court, heard the appeal.[123] The High Court declared all witnesses as "unreliable" and announced a review of the case, after which it declared that there are "serious contradictions which reflect on the veracity of these witnesses and makes their statements doubtful" especially when there is no evidence of exactly what the objectionable words were on the wall about the Prophet Muhammad.[124] It was noted that those words, which according to witnesses were insulting, were rubbed off by the accuser and never described clearly throughout the blasphemy trial.[125] Seven lawyers present before the High Court argued that the case the appellants were convicted of was founded on baseless evidence. They also criticized the negligence of the lower judicial authorities for declaring a blasphemy death punishment on such uncertain evidence.[126] Most importantly, it was discussed whether if a Muslim cannot repeat aloud any blasphemous words about the Prophet when it is required by the court, what kind of evidence would be required in future blasphemy cases? Here it is important to see though although section 295-C does not include intention the courts still struggled to investigate the evidence on the basis of something very close to intention. Advocate Abid Hassan Minto, senior advocate of the bench, referred to the principles of

---

122. Jahangir, *From Protection to Exploitation*, 82–83.
123. Aftab Alexander Mughal, *Death or Exile: The Story of Salamat Masih's Case* (Multan: National Commission of Justice and Peace, 1995), 5, 8.
124. *Salamat Masih v. The State*, 824–825.
125. Jahangir, *From Protection to Exploitation*, 29.
126. *Salamat Masih v. The State*, 818–823.

Criminal Jurisprudence, saying that according to *Qanoon-e-Shahadat*, the law of evidence:

> The court decision must rest upon a legal grounds established by legal testimony. The prosecution must prove its case beyond all reasonable doubts and the benefits of doubt had to go to the accused as in Islamic Law he is presumed to be innocent . . . the evidence should direct and the circumstances corroborating the evidence must be cogent.[127]

Apart from the written words on the wall, the court also observed that the offensive writing, on chits found in the mosque's toilet, was indeed offensive but was apparently planted by some person motivated to bring or to investigate the case. Advocate Sultan Ahmad referred to the investigating agencies such as police and court who failed to take samples of the writing, clearly not written by the accused.[128] On 23 February 1995, the Lahore High Court set aside the death sentence for blasphemy imposed on Salamat Masih and Rehmat Masih as the prosecution had failed to prove the charge. The lower court, while accepting the appeal, declared that "we will be successful in the eye of Allah and his Prophet. We are sure our decision is in accordance with the principles of the prophet's teachings."[129]

Salamat and Rehmat were free at last – yet they continued to receive threats. The religious organization Ahl-e-Sunnat, announced a price of one million rupees while another religious party, Mutthida Ulema of Sarghodha, offered three hundred thousand rupees for killing them.[130] It was clear that Salamat and Rehmat could not live in Pakistan even though they had been freed by the High Court. Their families were forced to leave the village and settle elsewhere. Salamat and Rehmat, fled the country, finding asylum in Germany to this day.

Not only the accused but also their legal advisor, Asma Jahangir, was threatened and Iqbal Bhati, the senior member of the high court, continued to receive threats after acquitting Salamat and Rehmat, and was later

---

127. Abid Hassan Minto recorded in *Salamat Masih v. The State*, 818–819.

128. *Salamat Masih v. The State*, 823; Mughal, *Death or Exile*, 5.

129. Justice Arif Iqbal and Falik Sher's declaration of the judgment in *Salamat Masih v. The State*.

130. Siddique and Hayat, "Unholy Speech," 333.

murdered for his judgement, on 10 October 1997.[131] This murder shows the risk of handling blasphemy cases by session courts and lawyers. The critical events of this case – such as the murder of Judge Bhatti and of the accused, Manzoor (during the trial); the serious threats and injuries to Salamat and Rehmat; and the uncertain justice meted out to and the insecurity of religious communities – led the National Assembly of Pakistan to debate the issue. Supreme Court Justice Dorab Patel (also Chairman of the Human Rights Commission of Pakistan) declared that the blasphemy law should be amended as it contributes to religious fanaticism. Before he could finish his statement, a Sunni Muslim shouted, "Anyone who commits blasphemy will meet the fate of Manzoor Masih."[132] This indicates that any comment such as reforming the law for protecting minorities can fall under the catch-all of "blasphemy": all who oppose it must live with insecurity and anxiety.

Like the case of Salamat Masih, many other cases reveal similar applications of the law where "writing and speech" is not actually proper writing, publication or speech: the mere suspicion that something offensive has been written can endanger anyone's life. For example, an incident in Okara, Punjab shows how the use of "word" in section 295-C can be misunderstood. According to the case, a Muslim and five Christian boys who used medicine to treat the wound of a donkey, which then streamed into different shapes, were accused of writing holy names on the donkey in 2001.[133] Though these boys were later released from the jail, and even the donkey was also detained briefly for examination: this is where blind application of the law can end, where shapes resembling words can put even children's lives at risk.

In several cases, the meaning of "writing and speech" has gone beyond reason or propriety, and may not even be offered as evidence in accusations of blasphemy, the accusation being based on different reasons such as conversion or personal enmity. For example, converts run a high risk of a blasphemy accusation, which is an alternative way of disciplining converts given that Pakistan does not have an apostasy law, meaning it is still generally legal to convert from one religion to another. Converts may be accused

---

131. Siddique and Hayat, 335.
132. Amnesty International, "Pakistan: Use and Abuse," 2.
133. Marshall and Shea, *Silenced*, 87.

of blasphemous speech against the Prophet.[134] For example, in one such case, thirty-three year old Tahir Iqbal, after his conversion to Christianity in December 1990, was accused of blasphemy in Kot Lakhpat, Lahore. After his conversion, his family broke any relationship with him and he began receiving threats.[135] On 7 December 1990 he was arrested by Peerzada Ali Ahmad Sabir, a local cleric, on blasphemy charges under section 295-C in Kot Lakhpat, Lahore. Patrick Sookhdeo records an accusation:

> Iqbal had converted from Islam to Christianity; that while coaching Muslim children free of charge he would criticise Islam; that he claimed that he could prove from the Quran that "illicit intercourse, drinking and sodomy are justified in Islam;" that he had prepared a list of various chapters and verses in the Quran and marked and underlined those passages in the Quran; and finally that he had abused Islam and Muhammad.[136]

The witnesses in Tahir's case were teenage Muslim boys: Izhar ul-Haq, Dil Muhammad and Maqsood Ahmad. Izhar claimed that Tahir's behaviour was un-Islamic therefore he committed blasphemy. In the beginning of the trial, Tahir did not receive legal assistance and no lawyer was ready to defend his case; however, later the Human Rights commission took this case. Asma Jahangir, who helped, was threatened by Sabir, a cleric who warned her that she could face "dire consequences if [she] continued to defend Tahir."[137] Tahir faced his trial in the court of Fakhar Hayat Chaudrey and an additional session judge in Lahore and pleaded not guilty. However, Tahir's application for bail was rejected by the session court and a subsequent appeal for bail was also rejected by Lahore High Court. In April 1992, it was reported that he was in a critical condition in the Kotlakhpat jail, Lahore. On 23 April, an

---

134. Sookhdeo, *People Betrayed*, 264.

135. According to the National Commission of Justice and Peace, Tahir Iqbal was born into a Muslim family in 1959 and later joined the Pakistan Air Force as an aeronautical mechanic. In 1982, he contracted meningitis and his lower part of the body became paralysed. In 1984 after two years of medical treatment, he retired from the Air Force and started searching and working on a comparative study of Islam and Christianity. In this process he converted into Christianity and was baptised by Nazir Lal, a church minister of United Pentecostal Church Lahore. Dildar and Mughal, *Section 295-C Pakistan Penal Code*, 31–32.

136. Sookhdeo, *Freedom to Believe*, 79, 65–66; Sookhdeo, *People Betrayed*, 264–267.

137. Jahangir in Dildar and Mughal, *Section 295-C Pakistan Penal Code*, 33.

application was given to the additional session court of Sabah Mohayiuddin requesting Tahir's death sentence for converting to Christianity. The court rejected the application as there was no law or code against conversion.

On 21 June 1992, Tahir's lawyer was not present to defend him in the court, and on the same day he told his councillors that his life was in danger and that he was receiving threats. On 1 June, he posted letters to the president, chief minister and inspector general, and police stating that he feared he would be murdered in the jail. The day before his next hearing in the court, Tahir died in the jail on 21 July. Neither the court nor his councillors were officially informed about his death, having to read about it in the newspapers. Jail authorities claimed that he died after a protracted illness: Christian leaders and community suspected that he was murdered. Naeem Shakir, a lawyer, noted that he probably was poisoned just before his scheduled appearance in Sessions Court.[138] However, the prison authorities refused to accept this charge of murder. His funeral was done according to Islamic faith and he was buried in Faisalabad in a Muslim graveyard. According to section 297, it is a religious offence to bury a Christian in a Muslim graveyard. However, the Christian community was mostly silent on the claim that the accused was a Christian and that they therefore had the right to bury him according to Christian custom.

In reviewing this case, it can be said the accusation was simply based on the issue of conversion which was turned into blasphemy for punishment. Tahir's neighbour, Muhammad Saleem said that "Tahir was an intelligent and good person. His only offence was his conversion."[139] Naeem Shakir, a Pakistani lawyer, notes that "conversion from Islam to Christianity in itself is an offence."[140] However, the second crime, blasphemy, became a greater charge.[141]

Continuing the discussion to review how offensive "words either written or spoken" can bring prosecution under section 295-C, there are numerous underlying issues which can put any innocent person at risk of a blasphemy accusation. For example, it has been noticed by the judiciary that economic

---

138. Naeem Shakir in Chunakara, *Blasphemy Law*, 18.
139. Muhammad Saleem in Chunakara, *Blasphemy Law*, 32.
140. Naeem Shakir in Chunakara, *Blasphemy Law*, 32.
141. Sookhdeo, *People Betrayed*, 264.

and poverty issues may lead to a person targeted for their job, land or property dispute if accused of blasphemy.[142] Historically, economic prejudice was seen on a political level when Hindus of East Pakistan and Ahmadis in West Pakistan were forbidden to lead governing offices as discussed earlier. Such tension became a religious slogan to remove them from their offices and prevented these minorities from enjoying full social and economic status. Historically, some Christians who worked as farm labourers for Muslim, Sikh and Hindu landlords also migrated to Pakistan with their employers after independence, to whom they remained in some subjection.[143] For many indigenous local village Christians employed as labourers, by landowning Sikhs, partition also brought hardship, as Muslims replaced them as a workforce.[144] In addition, previous caste influence and background disadvantaged many Christians from gaining new employment during resettlement,[145] forcing most to adopt their traditional job of sweeping in the new Pakistani context.[146] It cannot be denied that Christians in rural areas and large cities with the passage of time made progress economically.

Resentment between Christian employees and Muslim employers and people mostly in rural areas has been linked to blasphemy accusations, playing an important role in settling economic disputes or eliminating opponents. Though all communities are equally vulnerable to this threat however, the consequences surrounding an accusation against Christians and Ahmadis can be fatal. For example in one of the cases Ayub Masih (thirty years old) a Christian resident of Chak 353/E.B, Arifwala, Sahiwal district, Punjab province was sentenced to death on 27 April 1998 on charges of blasphemy under section 295-C of PPC by a court in Sahiwal. On 14 October 1996, Ayub Masih had been arrested following allegations made by a Muslim neighbour, Muhammad Akram, for hurting his religious feelings when he exalted Christianity, maligned Islam, uttered certain derogatory words about the Holy Prophet and advised the complainant to read

---

142. Jahangir, *From Protection to Exploitation*, 30; Ayub Masih v. The State PLD (2002) Supreme Court 1048.

143. Walter P. Hares, *Gojra Jungal Vich Mangal: The Story of a Canal Colony in the Land of the Five Rivers* (Mysore: Wesley Press, 1934), 10.

144. Webster, *Dalit Christians*, 167.

145. Streefland, *Sweepers of Slaughterhouse*, 15.

146. Stock, *People Movements in the Punjab*, 181.

the book, *Satanic Verses*, written by Salman Rushdie. He was sentenced to death by the local court of Sahiwal but later after seven years he was found innocent and acquitted by the Supreme Court on the grounds that there was not enough evidence to prove the case. It was revealed that there was a land dispute between the accuser and Ayub which was the main cause of the accusation.[147] It is also important to note that where such an intention is present, even if the accused person is declared innocent and released, a person from a minority released in such circumstances does not come back to his land or job. Such a person has a long journey to retrieve any social or economic stability they may have had.

The judiciary has observed that the law of blasphemy has threatened some students, and even professors are at risk of being accused, whether for reading, discussing or delivering a lecture. For example, in October 2000 a Muslim lecturer, Dr Younas Sheikh, was accused by his students of saying that the Prophet was not born a Muslim and was not a Prophet until the age of forty. The court agreed that the accusation against the professor had been filed without realizing that indeed there was a non-Muslim period in Arabia before the advent of Islam, a view which the student had rejected.[148] He was found guilty and was sentenced to death on 18 August 2001 but was acquitted by Lahore High Court in November 2003. In a letter he wrote from prison, he called the blasphemy law "wide open to abuse, through and by the miscreant mullahs for political, repressive and vindictive purposes . . . The law's abuse is part of a rising wave of ignorance, incivility and intolerance as well as the medieval theocratic darkness."[149] However, in a number of cases filed under section 295-C, similar claims have been accepted to prove blasphemy.

---

147. For full trial detail see *Ayub Masih v. The State*; In some cases people were not given a chance to be declared as innocent as it happened in Niamat Ahmar's case who was alleged of defiling the name of the Prophet. According to the case, on 18 December 1991, copies of hand written pamphlet with offensive remarks were posted on the walls of the school. Later Niamat Ahmar, a Christian school teacher, was accused of writing and posting offensive remarks. He was forced to leave the job and later was killed without any trial and legal aid. See Dildar and Mughal, *Section 295-C Pakistan Peal Code*, 24–26; Jahangir, *From Protection to Exploitation*, 26–27.

148. Marshall and Shea, *Silenced*, 98; Dr Younas Shekh, "Blasphemy: My Journey," http://www.muktomona.com/Articles/Younus_Sheikh/blasphemy.

149. Akbar S. Ahmed, "Pakistan's Blasphemy Law: Words Fail Me," *The Washington Post*, 19 May 2002.

The decade from the 2000s onwards brought more critical implications for section 295-C where the meaning of "speech" even included severe punishments and the accusation of blasphemy for any, including Muslims, who show compassion for the accused, asked to forgive an accused or for repeal of the law. For example, in November 2010 the death sentence of Asia Bibi, a Christian accused, provoked a storm, particularly when it was argued that she should be pardoned or at least receive a lesser punishment than death. One of the contemporary problems is that court and other legal officials are alleged of committing blasphemy, with fatal consequences, when they talk about the misuse of the law, a point in the next chapter.

Today the application for the prosecution of an offence of writing and speaking offensively about the Prophet shows that "words either spoken or written" of section 295-C are not necessarily the basis for or cause of the accusation. It has been argued by accusers in various cases that those accused of blasphemy must be punished. However, the study of a considerable number of cases has revealed that victims were charged on spurious or questionable grounds and without intention being demonstrated. This has made such judgments controversial. Instead of protecting the innocent in particular and religious communities in general, the intention of Chapter XV maintained between 1860 and the late 1980s, the law has made it legal for extremists to persecute and even kill at will. There is thus a very limited capacity to protect religious communities and their members. Yet protests against the misuse of the law remain and efforts have been and are still being made to ameliorate if not alter the most troubling clauses of the current laws. This will be discussed in the following chapter.

5.6 Conclusion

After reviewing the new additions sections 295-B and C in Chapter XV: Of Offences Relating to Religion, it can be said that the law has brought serious changes to and problems for the application of law in the legal history of Pakistan. Religious communities and minorities face consequences as citizens which, as has been demonstrated, they did not face in the early years of Pakistan. It has been stated by the Lahore High Court that the rising number of blasphemy cases from 1986 "shows that the law was being abused . . . to settle . . . scores."[150] According to Pakistan's National Commission of Justice and Peace from 1986 to August 2009, a large number of cases occurred in Pakistan, of whom 679 were Muslims, 240 were Ahmadis, 119 Christians, 14 Hindus and 10 of unknown religions.[151] It has been argued the law is not discriminatory as it affected all communities and the majority of those accused of blasphemy are Muslim. However, it appears to be a difference in outcome. An individual Muslim who is accused – dreadful though that person's fate may be – is not seen as a representative of all Muslims who are then attacked en masse: the accused represents only themself. Where a member of a minority is accused, the consequence of that accusation affects the entire community in that place and beyond, as that person is taken as a representative of that class, against which vengeance may be exacted.

The introduction of new sections in Chapter XV of the Pakistan Penal Code has resulted mostly in near-anarchy in the country when these clauses are used as a tool to harass, intimidate, discriminate against and persecute religious communities of Pakistan. Though the law, particularly sections 295-B and 295-C, exposes all religious communities to allegations of blasphemy, Muslims rarely face death after such allegations unless they have supported the accused from minority groups. For minorities in Pakistan, in addition to the physical death that threatens accused blasphemers, families are also at risk from social isolation as members scatter into hiding for fear of their lives, as is the property of any from that minority.

The application of the law has also raised the question whether non-Muslims should be judged for blasphemy. It has been argued by Muslim scholars that non-Muslims should not be accused of blasphemy or heresy as "they are by definition unbelievers"[152] and unbelief does not legalize the killing of a person.[153] Moreover, most of the people who die are by definition in Islam "people of the book" (*ahl al-kitab*), Christians. Historically, Muslims have claimed to protect non-Muslims in Islamic countries by declaring their

---

150. Muhammad Mahboob v. The State, (2002) 54 PLD (SC) 587, 16 (Pakistan).
151. Pakistan's National Commission of Justice and Peace in Marshall and Shea, *Silenced*, 87.
152. Saeed and Saeed, *Freedom of Religion*, 49.
153. Burhan al-Din al-Marghinani, *The Hedaya, or Guide: A Commentary on the Mussulman Laws*, vol. 1, trans. Charles Hamilton, (London: T. Bensley, 1791), 577.

status as *ahl al-dhimma* (literally, the people of the protection).[154] In addition to *dhimmi*, there is another proposed class of non-Muslims called *Mu'ahid*, someone not conquered by Muslims but who has chosen to live among Muslims.[155] Non-Muslims, particularly Christians, have debated the status of *dhimmis*, claiming that they are much more than a protected community in contemporary Pakistan. They simply claim to be Pakistani citizens. James Channan comments: "we are Pakistanis and would like to be treated as equal citizens . . . We are not *dhimmis*; we are sons and daughters of the soil."[156] The issue is certainly not just what Christians and other minorities should be called: but the outcome of these laws sits ill with the Muslim claim to protect non-Muslims in Islamic countries.

A further effect of the new additions has been on Pakistan's legal system and the erosion of an independent judiciary. There is a serious struggle in the legal system of Pakistan dealing with blasphemy cases, as we have seen in the tussles between lower courts and the High Court. For example, a person can be charged with blasphemy on testimony alone, without any details whatsoever, and be immediately and arbitrarily detained without opportunity for bail. Trials became rare or controversial and many lawyers who are willing to take cases face "dire consequences if [they] continue to defend [the accused]."[157] The death sentence has been declared by lower local courts in a number of cases but the High Court successfully released the accused.[158] Lower courts rely on one witness to declare guilt and assess punishment, and are vulnerable to local pressure, while the High Court does not just accept a statement to prove the offence.

The working of the 1986 laws clearly show that the religious expression and rights of *all* religious communities been violated. Regarding the human rights of Pakistani citizens, I. A. Rahim, a Muslim human right activist,

---

154. Watt, *Islamic Political Thought*, 49.

155. The *Mu'ahid* is not liable to pay *jizyah*, tax for the protection but rather enters into a contract or agreement (*ahd*) with the Muslims. Abul A'la Maududi, *Human Rights in Islam*, 2nd ed. (Leicester: Islamic Foundation, 1980), 7–9.

156. James Channan, "Human Rights and Situations of Christians in Pakistan," in *Islam in Asia: Perspectives for Christian–Muslim Encounter*, eds. Paul Rajashekar and H. S. Wilson (Geneva: Lutheran World Federation, 1992), 105–109.

157. Jahangir in Dildar and Mughal, *Section 295-C Pakistan Penal Code*, 33.

158. *Ayub Masih v. The State*.

stated that: "these laws are retrogressive, because they discriminate against minorities; impinge on their rights to freedom of belief and pose a serious threat to their right to liberty. So these laws are in conflict with their constitutional and fundamental rights."[159] Though both Muslims and non-Muslim raise their voice, most people have been forced to remain silent. Minorities have been left in a position where they have little or no power for self-protection. The law became a continuing threat to the social and religious life of non-orthodox and indeed even non-Sunni religious communities. The outcome is that "a sense of fundamental entitlement of citizenship in the hearts and minds of the embattled Christians and non-Muslim communities is lost;" to which we must add certain Muslim communities as well.[160] It seems clear that the potential for the misuse of the law is considerable. Consideration of how to control the violence to protect the communities will be discussed in the following chapter.

---

159. I. A. Rahim, quoted in Gabriel, *Christian Citizens*, 67.

160. Sherry Rehman a Muslim former member of the parliament of Pakistan on the deaths of seven Christians in Gojra. See Sherry Rehman, "Gojra and Pakistan's Identity," *The News*, 13 August 2009 quoted in Rehman, *Souls on Fire*, 21.

CHAPTER 6

The Blasphemy Law and the Question of the Protection of Religious Communities and Their Religious Rights

Two issues related to religion have challenged Pakistan since its inception: the exclusion of certain religious communities and the opposition to certain religious beliefs and attitudes. From 1947 to 1974 the question of whether and how to declare Ahmadis non-Muslims became increasingly critical with demands to criminalize their religious practices, ending in their expulsion from the family of Islam in the 1980s. This chapter will pick up on opposition to, and use made of, non-Muslims and minority Muslim groups in the socio-political evolution of the country.

The previous chapters have shown how not only religious parties and communities but also political power was involved in making changes in the legal history of Pakistan. According to Malik, although historically in Pakistan religious agitators were never able to establish a government, Pakistan still remains a country whose establishment was achieved by reformists such as the Muslim League which used Islamic symbols creating a "Muslim identity yet disclaiming any ideas of a theocracy."[1] He further notes that since the later 1980s, the press, the judiciary and numerous volunteer organizations have begun challenging the earlier conformist traditions with the aim of establishing basic human rights. However, rather than consolidating political and constitutional norms through dialogue and consensus, "Pakistani politicians frivolously consume their energies on internecine dissensions, occasionally

---

1. Malik, "State and Civil Society," 676.

resorting to popular appeals for street agitation . . . and trespassing all the parliamentary norms."[2] From the 1990s, religious parties, as well as agitators in general, had the capacity to influence governing officials and politicians to enforce their religious demands and slogans. As in the 1950s, 1970s and 1980s, as discussed in the previous chapters, popular agitation and religious demands still remain powerful. However, the unresolved issue of religious violence motivated by blasphemy accusations from the 1990s has become critical in the protection of minority Muslims and non-Muslims.

The misuse of the law of blasphemy has been recognized by the judiciary, government, non-Muslims and even Muslims of Pakistan but nothing significant has been done to reduce the violence. From time to time, religious communities, government and officials have faced critical situations as well as much criticism concerning any efforts they might make regarding the protection of religious communities. Having shown that the roots and growth of this problem lie clearly in the past, this chapter discusses how the protection of citizens of Pakistan, especially from religiously motivated violence, has become the crucial concern and issue of today and how politics and society are split between those who want reform of the law, especially those passed between 1980 and 1986 and those who agitate to keep all post-1980 clauses. To review this, we first need to see how religious communities of Pakistan raised the issue of their protection.

6.1 The Protest of Religious Communities for their Protection

Even though there is a manifest danger in responding towards blasphemy allegations for all Pakistan's religious communities, a number of political leaders, judges and religious communities, both Muslim and non-Muslim, have expressed their thoughts and concerns either in favour of or to reform the law to control its misuse of Pakistan. The implications of the new sections on blasphemy promulgated between 1980 and 1986 have been discussed in the previous chapter, showing that though all religious communities are equally liable to be accused of blasphemy, minorities are much more vulnerable both to an accusation and to critical and even fatal consequences. Such

---

2. Malik, 681.

communities are concerned that even though Pakistan claims to provide religious protection, they do not feel they are counted as equal to majority-religion citizens in terms of protection. One of the reasons for this may be that it appears the majority of Muslims are in favour of anti-blasphemy laws: in a democratic country officials may claim to protect religious freedom of all but follow the demands of the majority. Despite the negative consequences of condemning the practice of these laws, minorities, along with supporters from the majority, have continually responded to the way the law of blasphemy is used.

Historically Ahmadis were always vulnerable, even before the amendments in the law, and were long accused by the local majority community of Punjab for their unacceptable religious beliefs and practices. From the 1990s, Christians have also been struggling for protection from religious violence. Bishop Samuel Azaraiah, noting one verdict, said "the blasphemy sentence has shocked the Christian community," and another bishop, John Malik, said "the sense of insecurity would increase following the convictions."[3] The Christian community (perhaps strengthened by overseas support) have been most vociferous in protesting the continued risks to their life, seriously threatened by both local communities as well as questionably fair legal trial. Anees Jilani said:

> The blasphemy law now has become a tool in the hands of criminal minded persons. They have now started using them to embroil their opponents in highly questionable litigations which get so controversial and dichotomous during the course of trial that it becomes almost unfeasible to decipher the truth.[4]

While there have been many individual protests against the blasphemy law, the death of Manzoor Masih in 1994 sparked agitation across the country as Christians were demanding repeal of the blasphemy law and security for their lives. The initial conviction and death sentence against twelve-year old Salamat Masih, discussed in the fifth chapter, and rising mob violence against Christians, especially that damaging their property and places of worship

---

3. Bishop Azraiah and Malik quoted in Amritsari, *Blasphemy Law*, vol. 1, 31.
4. Anees Jilani, "Blasphemy Law and the Minorities," *The News*, 14 May 1998.

in Shantinagar in 1997,⁵ drew the attention of human rights activists all over world. Many affected people have expressed how the blasphemy issue has affected the social life and relationship of Christians and Muslims. For example, one of the victims said:

> We [Christians] and Muslims have been living here for generations. Both communities were on good terms, but, due to this incident, we have disconnected forever. In the past, we were friends. Now we are enemies. This incident has left long lasting effects. It is not possible for us to forget what Muslims have done to us. A personal dispute was turned in to a communal dispute and as a result, unending enmity and abhorrence has emerged in the heart of both communities.[6]

Perhaps the most desperate act of protest was by Roman Catholic bishop, John Joseph, a chairman of a Christian-Muslim relation commission and the National Commission for Justice and Peace Pakistan. He said:

> Since the Government failed to fulfil its commitments, we have no alternative but to launch a countrywide agitation and to adopt other tactics for the abolition of blasphemy law . . . such "verdicts" are not only detrimental to national unity, they created hatred among the minority community . . . we are united for our rights and are prepared to sacrifice even our lives.[7]

Four years after witnessing the death of Manzoor Masih, Joseph shot and killed himself outside the Sahiwal Court in Punjab province after Ayub Masih was sentenced to death for blasphemy on the 5 of May 1998, though

---

5. According to this case, rioters attacked Shanitnagar, Punjab and set the village on fire after an incident of alleged desecration of the Qur'an. It was observed that 785 of the 905 houses, churches of these places, schools and shops were burnt where the punishment of defiling the Qur'an had been inflicted without confirmation of blasphemy, even without a trial on the Christian community that had nothing to do with it. Sookhdeo, *People Betrayed*, 268–274; Rehman, *Souls on Fire*, 8.

6. Samuel Masih expressed his thoughts in the interview with Jinnah Institute team after the attack in Bahmni Wali, Kasur, Punjab on 23 January 2009. Fauqi, *Question of Faith*, 45.

7. Bishop John Joseph, reaction to death verdict, Christians to start nation-wide protest in Amritsari, *Blasphemy Law*, vol. 1, 25.

later released by the Supreme Court for lack of evidence of blasphemy.[8] To Bishop Joseph, it became clear that "lives destroyed by false allegations meant nothing to the authority."[9] Bishop Joseph, in his letter, faxed to the press just before his death on 5 May 1998 stated:

> Section 295-C is the greatest block in the good and harmonious relations between Muslims and the religious minorities in Pakistan. In order to achieve national harmony, let us give a push to this immense boulder, before it crushes all of us. Once the obstacle is away, each Pakistani will be able to live and work in peace and our beloved motherland, Pakistan will prosper.[10]

Bishop Joseph hoped his suicide would galvanize authorities and communities of Pakistan for the repeal of the blasphemy in order to create peaceful co-existence. On the one hand, the Christian community discussed whether he was a martyr and great leader and protested against the misuse of the blasphemy law.[11] However, on the other hand, religious and political organizations condemned the act of suicide by claiming that the bishop wanted to embarrass Pakistan in the eyes of the world. Some condemned misusing the law and argued that the law of blasphemy has added to the corpus of discriminatory legislations against minorities and led to distortion.[12] Whatever he may become for future generations of Pakistan, today his death is a symbol for a powerless minority which lives through continuing struggle under the threat of blasphemy laws. The death of John Joseph also represents a loss of religious leadership in the Christian community in Pakistan.

---

8. The point is discussed in detail in the following cases: *Salamat Masih v. The State*, (1995) and *Ayub Masih v. The State* PLD (2002) in chapter 5.

9. Bishop John Joseph in Amritsari, *Blasphemy Law*, vol. 1, xv.

10. Bishop John Joseph's letter, "the Final Step against 295-C," in Amritsari, *Blasphemy Law*, vol. 1, xiii; Bishop wrote various letters to the authorities as well as church authorities about discrimination and the misuse of the law throughout 1990s. See Rashid, *A Peaceful Struggle*.

11. Christians critically protested against blasphemy as observed in Karachi (*The Frontier Post*, 11 May 1998) and across Punjab: in Faisalabad (*The Nation*, 12 May 1998, and *Dawn*, Lahore 12 May 1998), in Multan (*Dawn*, 13 May 1998) in Lahore (*Dawn*, Lahore, 16 May 1998), Christian workers of all corporation and cantonment board were observed on strike pushing government for repealing the law on 15 May (*Dawn*, Lahore, 12 May 1998).

12. *Dawn*, 9 May 1998.

Muslim community and political leaders mostly condemned the death of Bishop Joseph, while sympathizing with his family. For example, in 1998, Prime Minister Nawaz Sharif expressed deep sorrow over the suicide of Bishop John and in a condolence message to the bereaved family and the Christian community, insisted that the constitution of Pakistan guaranteed full freedom and fundamental rights to the minorities.[13] Opposition leader Benazir Bhutto also expressed shock and grief over the tragic death of Bishop John. In a message she said, it is a traumatic event which focuses the deep sense of frustration felt by the members of the minority communities at the misuse of the blasphemy law by extremist and bigoted elements. It also highlights the need for making the law foolproof against misuse as an instrument of personal vendetta and creating mischief in the name of religion. There is, she said, clearly a need to punish false accusers and reform the law.[14]

The question of protecting the minorities, and especially the misuse of the law was mostly condemned by governing officials. The Federal Minister of Religious and Minorities Affairs, Raja Zafer ul-Haq, while insisting that the law is not against particular religions, urged the government to re-examine the law.[15] However, most of those sympathetic to Islamic Parties who wanted the law to remain on the statute book feared that the government might take action towards making changes in the law. They started criticizing Christians' protests over the law and argued that section 295-C is not discriminatory as it is the same for anybody found to have committed blasphemy.[16] All communities are indeed equally vulnerable to accusation but who actually suffers is a critical question which remains unanswered. There are clear attempts to silence people. For example, the Minister for Religious Affairs, Ijazul Haqq stated that "the people of Pakistan would come out on the streets if attempts were made to change the blasphemy law."[17] He also stated vehemently that even if 100, 000 Christians lost their lives under the Blasphemy Law it will not be repealed.[18] The refusal to review

---

13. *The Nations*, 9 May 1998 in Amritsari, *Blasphemy Law*, vol. 1, 24.
14. *Dawn*, Lahore, 11 May 1998.
15. *Dawn*, Lahore, 10 May 1998.
16. *The News International*, 9 May 1998.
17. *The Times*, 11 May 1998 in Gabriel, *Christian Citizens*, 64.
18. *BosNews Life*, 27 June 2006 in Gabriel, *Christian Citizens*, 65.

the blasphemy law in terms of protecting minorities and the insistence on keeping the law even if minorities continue to suffer suggests an uncertain future for the status of minorities, as well as others vulnerable to accusations because they support the repeal of the law. A successful outcome of the argument among Muslim and minority groups on the issue of repeal may take a long time or it may not happen. However, assuming the law stays, it will be helpful to examine how blasphemy accusations are dealt with by the apparently independent judicial system.

6.2 Judicial Concern over the Misuse of the Blasphemy Law and the Safety of Religious Communities

In general, the judicial system of Pakistan claims to follow the rules, providing justice to all, a point insisted upon by Jinnah in his informal talk to civil officers at Peshawar in April 1948, when he said: "you should try to create an atmosphere and work in such a spirit that everybody gets a fair deal and justice is done to everybody. And not merely should justice be done but people should feel that justice has been done to them."[19] However, the justice system of Pakistan, especially the lower courts, has become controversial and some have suggested even notorious in terms of dealing with blasphemy accusations. The judicial system for dealing with blasphemy cases has been affected by the pressure and threats of the masses. Justice Munir, who headed an investigation into anti-Ahmadi agitation in 1953 and reviewed how the legislation on Offences Relating to Religion was misused (discussed in the fourth chapter), commented "Pakistan is being taken [over] by the common man—though it is not—as an Islamic state. This belief has been encouraged by the ceaseless clamour of Islam and an Islamic state that is being heard from all quarters since the establishment of Pakistan."[20]

It has been observed that not only those accused of blasphemy but also the judiciary and courts are exposed to mob pressure. The issue of repealing the law and the threats to the lives of minorities has also split the judiciary.

---

19. Jinnah in Pirzada, *Fundamental Rights*, 86.
20. Muhammad Munir, "Christians in Pakistan Bear the Cross of its Blasphemy Laws," *Navhind Times*, May 1998 quoted in Amritsari, *Blasphemy Law*, vol. 1, 186.

Various lawyers and judges support the inevitably arbitrary imposition of the death sentence under blasphemy accusation but others regard it as discriminatory and unacceptable for non-Muslims to face criticism and threats from Muslims. For example, it was noted that the lower courts in cases such as Salamat Masih's in 1994, discussed in the previous chapter, passed the death sentence against the accused despite inadequate evidence. However, Salamat was released later from the High Court but the judge who ordered his release was threatened and later murdered. We should also note that on 4 September 1999, Lahore High Court Justice, Nazir Akhter reportedly said that those accused of blasphemy "must be punished or killed on the spot without any trial and there is no need of the law."[21] Judgments mentioned above clearly show how the judicial system or individuals in it can fall under suspicion of failing to provide justice in some blasphemy cases. According to Asma Jahangir (1952–2018), former Chairperson of the Human Rights Commission of Pakistan and UN Special Rapporteur on Extrajudicial, Summary or Arbitrary Executions,

> The anti-blasphemy law has tended to be abused. Because of the public sentiment the allegation arouses, the law has also been liable to a miscarriage of justice. Clearly, the incidence of blasphemy was no greater than before the law came in than it is after it. There are certainly more allegations of it now. The experience points to the need for serious rethinking of the law.[22]

Though the judicial system as a whole came under suspicion of not providing full justice to those accused of blasphemy, the High Court has generally struggled to provide justice on the basis of requiring firm evidence to prove the case, provided the accused survives to reach the High Court stage.[23]

It has been expressed by the judiciary that it "must seriously consider the ways it [blasphemy accusation] can badly affect the innocent people."[24]

---

21. Barbara Larkin, ed. *Annual Report on International Religious Freedom 2000* (Washington: US Governing Printing Office, 2000), 519.

22. Human Rights Commission of Pakistan, "State of Human Rights in 1998," Lahore, Pakistan, February 1999, 164.

23. *Ayub Masih v. The State*.

24. Faizan Usmani, "Blasphemy Law: To Repeal or not to Repeal?" posted on 2 December 2010, available on www.pkarticleshub.com.

Ismail Qureshi, though regarding the death sentence as the final verdict and seeing section 295-C as an important piece of legislation to prevent defiling the name of the Prophet, nevertheless emphasizes that Muslims should not take the law into their hands "when there is recourse to a court of law against the contemnor."[25] However, the contemporary practice of the law in the hands of local communities presents just this situation, and due process of law has been critically affected by violence motivated by blasphemy accusations. The most critical examples of this disregard for proper practice can be seen when a local community does not care about the judgment of the courts concerning the innocence of an accused, preferring to kill them.

Some judicial suggestions have been made by judges regarding both the law and its possible amendment, discussed in the case *Riaz Ahmad v. State* in June 1994, particularly the question of whether the language used by the accused which is said to be in accord with the teaching of the founder of any religion, in this case Ghulam Ahmad, is derogatory to the Prophet Muhammad and this constitutes an offence under section 295-C.[26] The case was tried on the behalf of Ahmadi and Christian parties. During the trial, the counsel representing Christian parties discussed and argued that section 295-C should be extended in order to prohibit contumacious reproaches against Jesus Christ so that those who indulge in defiling the name of Christ are also punished with death. The trial Judge Mian Nazir Akhtar expressed his hope that "the provision be made more comprehensive to as to make blasphemy qua other prophets including the Holy Christ, punishable with the same sentence."[27] The first problem here is that under such a suggestion Christians could be alleged to commit blasphemy against Muslim beliefs when they declare their belief that Jesus is the Son of God unless such a statement is allowed – as it would have been under the 1860 law allowing mutual and courteous discussion of faith. Second, religious leaders and founders such

---

25. Qureshi, *Muhammad: The Messenger*, 69.

26. According to the case Riaz Ahmad, an Ahmadi was alleged stating that a number of miracles of Prophet Muhammad was three thousand but that of Ghulam Ahmad was one hundred thousand. With the miraculous power Ahmad associated himself with Christ and called himself the promised Messiah. The court did not accept the intention of defiling the name of the Prophet however bail was rejected and the case is still pending in Supreme Court. Riaz Ahmad v. The State, PLD (1994) Lahore 504.

27. *Riaz Ahmad v. The State.*

as the Prophet Muhammad and Jesus Christ are already included in section 295-A, the clause which can defend any religious community from outrage against their religious personages and faith through malicious speech and writing as discussed in the second chapter. However, this clause was rarely in use in Pakistan, and after 295-C was enacted, it was effectively annulled. Therefore suggestions such as those of Akhtar do not seem particularly useful.

Given the continuing protest and violence concerning whether the law should be repealed or not, a few changes in legal procedure were introduced by governing authorities concerning the procedure for accusation. Abdulfateh Amor, the Special Reporter of UN Commission on Human Rights on the Elimination of All Forms of Religious Intolerance, concludes that "the blasphemy law should not be discriminatory and should not give rise to abuse . . . If offences against belief are made punishable . . . then procedural guarantees must be introduced and a balanced attitude must be maintained."[28] Let us see what kind of procedural changes were made by the government to reduce the critical implications on religious communities.

6.3 Political Efforts to Bring Changes in the Legal Procedure of Blasphemy Accusations

In 1988, Zia-ul-Haq died in a plane crash and whoever came to power later was not able, or did not wish, to repeal the law to protect all citizens of Pakistan from religiously motivated violence, discrimination and persecution. Bringing a few changes in the legal procedure of prosecution was tried by few politicians. In 1988 Benazir Bhutto (1953–2007) chairperson of the Pakistan People's Party (PPP), became prime minister and began arguing that the religious offences law should not be misused. During her regime, political authorities delivered various statements regarding the protection of minorities for religious motivated violence under blasphemy law but her political power collapsed in 1991. In 1992 the Federal Minister of Religious Affairs, Mawlana Abadu Sitar Niazi, issued "a *fatwa* against her declaring her to be a *kafir* [unbeliever] liable to the death penalty."[29] A year later, "a

---

28. Recorded in the report to the 52th Session Commission on Human Rights, E/CN.4/1996/95/Add.3.

29. Sookhdeo, *Freedom to Believe*, 66–67.

case was brought against her in the Lahore High Court under section 295-C . . . accusing her of criticising the blasphemy law."[30] Though she was not convicted of blasphemy, this is an early example to show how the law started to be used against the governing officials to weaken their power.

In early 1994, after being re-elected prime minister, Benazir Bhutto again intended to introduce procedural changes to lessen the possibility of abuse of Section 295-C, and upholding a formal authorization by a judicial magistrate being required before a complaint of blasphemy could be registered and arrests made. As a "false allegation of blasphemy would itself be made a criminal offence to be punished with up to seven years' imprisonment."[31] In February 1994, the Chief Justice of Pakistan, the chairman of the Council of Islamic Ideology and chief justices of the four provincial high courts sent an Amendment Bill to the Council of Islamic Ideology for further revision of the misuse of the law. Maulana Kausur Niazi, chairman of the Council of Islamic Ideology commented that "the law needs modification to ensure that it is not abused . . . The procedure for police registration of a case, the judicial level at which it should be considered and the suitable criteria for admission of witnesses have to be looked at thoroughly."[32] There is no doubt that the judiciary has frequently agreed that the law of blasphemy has been misused, particularly where the accused was sentenced on false allegations, as in cases such as Salamat Masih and the mob violence incited by unproven allegations of blasphemy, which occurred in Shantinagar, and other incidents like this as discussed in the fifth chapter. Making knowingly unfounded allegations a punishable crime may have constrained malicious accusations and protected the innocent to a certain extent: but this proposal did not become law. On 28 May 1995, Bhutto, after facing critical widespread strikes and protests across Pakistan against any changes to the blasphemy laws declared that her government had only envisaged procedural changes, and "will not amend the law."[33]

---

30. Sookhedo, 66–67.

31. Amnesty International, "Pakistan: The Death Penalty," September 1996, AI index: ASA 33/10/96, 9.

32. Maulana Kausur Niazi quoted in Amnesty International, "Pakistan: The Death Penalty," 9.

33. Benazir dealing with section 295-C in Amnesty International, "Pakistan: The Death Penalty," 9.

In the 1990s, Nawaz Shareef, elected twice as prime minister, also faced pressure and demands to apply *Sharia* as it was part of his political manifesto:[34] it was his government which removed the optional sentence, life imprisonment for defiling the name of the Prophet, and imposed the mandatory death sentence in section 295-C of PPC in 1992.[35] Although he was also one of those political leaders who condemned the misuse of the law, he remained convinced that the law should not be repealed. Given this apparent impasse, the question of what should be done to stop the misuse of the law to protect the citizens of Pakistan became increasingly important.

In October 1999, Pakistan's political and constitutional evolution was interrupted by praetorian rule through martial law when General Pervez Musharraf, a military chief army officer, came to power as president of Pakistan, holding his position till 2008. During his presidency, he said publicly on several occasions that there needed to be procedural changes in the existing law to check its frequent misuse.[36] In 1999, shortly after seizing power, Musharraf's political and social agenda appeared to maintain a moderate Pakistan in which "minorities enjoy full rights and protection as equal citizens and in the letter and spirit of true Islam."[37] In 2000 he promised to amend the blasphemy law to allow only senior district officials to register blasphemy cases, but soon withdrew the proposed change under pressure from the religious lobby. In 2004, under critical pressure, he too was forced to back down and stopped reforming the law,[38] although in 2005, parliament passed a law requiring that a senior police official investigate a blasphemy accusation before a complaint was filed in the courts.[39] Later, in May 2007 a bill by a ruling party parliamentarian calling for changes that would make the blasphemy law less discriminatory was rejected. The parliamentary affairs

---

34. Malik, "State and Civil Society," 19.

35. Faruqi, *Question of Faith*, 39.

36. Mani, *Human Rights Monitor 2008*, 44.

37. Musharaf in Amnesty International, "Pakistan: Insufficient Protection," 34; Shaun Gregory, "Under the Shadow of Islam: The Plight of the Christian Minority in Pakistan," *Contemporary South Asia* 20, no. 2 (2012): 203.

38. Gregory, "Under the Shadow of Islam," 203.

39. Amnesty International reported forty-four registered blasphemy cases in 2006. See Amnesty International, "Country Report: Pakistan," *Amnesty International*, 2007, available at http://www.refworld.org/docid/46558edb25.html.

minister was quoted as saying: "Islam is our religion and such bills hurt our feelings. This is not a secular state but [the] Islamic Republic of Pakistan."[40] Musharraf resigned and went into exile in 2008.

Thus from 1988 to 2007, the political and governing power represented by Benazir Bhutto, Nawaz Sharif and Pervez Musharraf all tried making some changes either to uphold the death sentence or making some procedural changes in blasphemy accusation. For example, Bhutto and Musharraf felt that changing the initial procedure of arresting anyone accused of blasphemy, especially giving authority only to the magistrate or the senior police inspector for investigating the reported incident before arrest, would reduce the threat and misuse of the law.[41] The main aim of this change was that the case should be properly investigated before people were arrested on mere suspicion, as clearly occurred in some cases discussed in the fifth chapter. However, it must be noted that this procedural change had little significant effect because it has rarely been implemented, and any blasphemy charge received by police and registered by FIR (First Information Report) immediately leads to the arrest of the accused.[42] There are some reasons for this, the main one being that immediate mob action towards anyone, especially non-Muslim, accused of blasphemy is almost normal, as people do not wait for any police action or arrest. In such circumstances not only the accused person but also the whole community is liable to experience loss of life and property, and even places of worship, all of which of course contravene the earlier religious conflict laws. For example, it is still a general principle inherited from previous versions of Chapter XV that damaging or defiling the place of worship or object (under section 295), disturbing religious assemblies and worship (under section 296), disrespecting funeral rights and burial grounds (under section 297) and wounding religious feelings of any religious class and deliberate offensive action of religious discussion (under section 298) are religious crimes which are still on the statute book. However, on many occasions, especially where non-Muslims are accused

---

40. Sohail Khan, "Government Rejects Bill to Amend Blasphemy Law," *The News*, 9 May 2007; Amnesty International, "Pakistan: Blasphemy Acquittal Welcome but Law Must be Amended," AI index: ASA 33/026/2002.

41. *Riaz Ahmad v. The State*, 485.

42. Mani, *Human Rights Monitor 2008*, 44; Gregory, "Under the Shadow of Islam," 203.

of blasphemy, even mere suspicion brings critical damage to lives and all religious objects of communities. For example, it has been observed in many cases that before any prosecution and legal trial, churches and bibles, Hindu temples and religious deities, Christian schools and hostels, residences or neighbourhoods of an accused or their community are damaged or burnt with consequent loss of property or life of innocent people, as occurred in Gojra, Korian, Shantinagar, Sanglahill, Sialkot and Lahore in Punjab.

Even the dead are attacked, in violation of section 297, such as when in July 2010 the Liaqatabad police station was approached with the demand to remove the Islamic inscriptions such as *kalmia tayaba*, (there is no god but God and Muhammad is His Prophet) from the tombstones of Ahmadis' graves. Later in October, the police was ordered to do this in accordance with section 298-B of Chapter XV which prohibits Ahmadis from using such inscriptions: the words and phrases were painted over or removed from stones.[43] Punishing the dead went further when about fifteen to twenty unknown persons deliberately entered the Ahmadi graveyard in Model Town, Lahore and desecrated and damaged one hundred and twenty Ahmadi graves in December 2012. The police registered the case under section 297 but no one has been charged. Notably, both cases reveal the conflict where on one hand removing the text from tombstones is apparently not a crime, and on other hand that the incident done by the group of people is a religious crime under section 297. As mentioned in the first chapter, section 297 was applied not only for the specific religious community or religious feelings but to respect the dead. However, today it has been expressed that in Pakistan ". . . violence is inflicted on the living as a matter of course, [but] the visceral hatred . . . on Ahmadi graveyard [dead people] . . . is chilling"[44] and such accusations do not allow them "to rest in peace even after [they] are dead."[45]

For the Pakistani government and judiciary, dealing with such conflict in law is not an easy task and it is a challenge whether such conflict and incidents can be controlled by changing the procedure of accusation and

---

43. Shamsul Islam, "Police Removed Quranic Verses from Ahmadi Graves to 'Avert Clashes,'" *The Tribune Express*, 18 August 2012.

44. "Chilling Act," *Dawn*, 5 December 2012, https://www.dawn.com/news/768976.

45. Gulmina Bilal Ahmad, "A New Order?" *Daily Times*, Pakistan, 7 December 2012, https://dailytimes.com.pk/104916/a-new-order/.

arresting accused of blasphemy today in Pakistan. Providing security may be the initial responsibility of the police as proposed by Bhutto and Musharraf, mentioned above. However, it has been observed that the arrest of an accused, their imprisonment and court procedure became controversial and suspicious, particularly where during investigation some accused were killed either by the police authorities or in police custody. For example, according to one of the blasphemy cases, Robert Fanish (nineteen years old), a Christian from Jatheki, Sialkot Punjab, known to be having an affair with a Muslim woman, was accused under section 295-B for throwing down a copy of the Qur'an in September 2009.[46] Before his arrest, the local church, including all religious books and bibles, were set on fire. Fanish was later arrested and before any trial and inquiry was found dead inside his jail cell. All those who spoke at the news conference said that the death of Fanish raised suspicion of the involvement of jail officials in his murder.[47] Suspected of murdering Fanish, assistant Superintendent Sibtain Raza, Head Warden Mohammad Yusuf, and Warden Javed Iqbal Awan were suspended and Salim Shahid Beg of Lahore said that the suspended officials would face an inquiry under the Punjab Employees Efficiency, Discipline and Accountability Act.[48] However, police have not yet arrested anyone in this case. This situation clearly shows that an initial blasphemy accusation can further frustrate and alienate minorities from the legal system, courts and jail custody. Therefore considering these forces and incidents, merely giving authority to investigate the case properly is not enough to rescue the accused and cannot guaranteed the safety of their life. This change has not led to a significant reduction in blasphemy charges.[49]

---

46. Emmanuel Zafar, "The Minorities View," *Hamsookhan* 7, no. 9 (September 2009): 19.

47. On the death of Fanish, Asma Jahangir, a lawyer and chairperson of Human Rights Commission, Secretary-General I. A. Rehman, Muhammad Tehseen, Nadeem Anthony, Shahtaj Qazilbash, Joseph Francis and Farooq Tariq concluded that minorities should be protected either in their homes or in jails. Newsletter of National Commission for Justice and Peace, *The Mirror*, vol. 13, issue 1 (January-March 2010): 4–6.

48. Newsletter of National Commission for Justice and Peace, *Mirror*.

49. Amnesty International reported forty-four registered blasphemy cases in 2006; see "Country Report: Pakistan," *Amnesty International*, 2007, available at http://www.refworld.org/docid/46558edb25.html.

It can be said that governments of recent times have been unsuccessful in following through any agenda they might have had to protect religious communities from violence. Government officials have insisted that the law should not be misused yet they are not able either to demonstrate this or deal with the issue of blasphemy properly to protect all communities. Amnesty International notes that continuing complex religious issues are a result of long negligence of successive governments, demonstrating an overruling concern for power and rule rather than principle.[50] Amnesty International reiterates its call to the government of Pakistan to ensure that:

> While the law remains on the statute book, everyone charged under the blasphemy law receives a fair trial and is not subjected to any form of ill-treatment; to declare a moratorium on carrying out the death penalty under this law and to take steps to abolish the death penalty for this offence; to take adequate steps to ensure the safety of members of the religious minorities in general and anyone at present charged with blasphemy in particular; and to implement international standards for the protection of the rights of religious minorities.[51]

It can be concluded that from 1988 to 2007 religious communities continually faced threats from blasphemy accusations but no proper rules or regulations were applied to protect them. After the assassination of Benazir Bhutto in 2007, once again the government of Pakistan People Party came to power and faced critical problems with the imposition of the blasphemy law, the position of its political leaders, and the question of protecting religious communities and restricting the blasphemy law. One of the most important steps was the tabling of the Amendment of Blasphemy Bill, which is the basis of the following discussion.

---

50. Amnesty International, "Pakistan: Use and Abuse."

51. It was declared during the rule of Musharaf. Amnesty International, "Pakistan: Use and Abuse," 2.

6.4 Critical Implications of Blasphemy and Proposal for the Amendment Bill of Blasphemy from 2007–2012

In February 2008, Asif Ali Zardari, the widower of the assassinated former PM Benazir Bhutto, became president of Pakistan.[52] The period of this government was not free from religious agitation, as killings after accusations of blasphemy continued as did protests against blasphemy and disturbances of the public peace throughout this government's rule. The problem is well illustrated by the threats to the government and the religious communities resulting from the blasphemy accusation of Asia Bibi, a Christian accused, who was sentenced to death for insulting the Prophet Muhammad in 2010. Subsequently, the government was shocked, or frightened, into silence when two prominent members of the Parliament, Sulman Taseer, the Punjab Governor and Shahbaz Bhatti, a Christian leader, human activist and the first Pakistan's Federal Minister of Minorities appointed by Pakistan People Party in 2009, were killed in early 2011 for raising their voice to reform the law of blasphemy and protect the minorities of Pakistan.

According to the case, Asia was accused of committing blasphemy when she was fetching water while working with other women in the field. It was argued that Christian non-Muslims should not drink from the same cup and it was said by other women working in the field that the water was impure, *haraam*, and therefore undrinkable. Amid the subsequent argument, Asia was asked why she would not give up her faith and convert to Islam, to which she replied with another question: why should she want to convert to Islam?[53] Before discussing how this case revived the issue and its impact on the community it is important to recall from the first and second parts of this thesis that there were similar cases during British rule where particularly Christians were targeted for their lower and former caste status of untouchabilty, even after their conversion. Holding fast to this memory, many Muslims in Pakistan, especially in rural areas, regard Christians as a lower caste than Muslims with whom one should not eat and drink – despite the

---

52. Gregory, "Under the Shadow of Islam," 204.
53. For the whole story see the foreword in, Asia Bibi, *Blasphemy: The True Heartbreaking Story of the Woman Sentenced to Death Over a Cup of Water* (London: Virago, 2012).

official absence of caste in Islam.[54] On the issue of drinking water from the same cup, Asia was later accused by the local cleric who was not even present when the supposed incident occurred. She was arrested in June 2009 and received the death sentence in the district court in Nankana Sahib, Punjab on 8 November 2010, based on the allegation that she passed derogatory remarks about the Prophet Muhammad.

Asia's accusation and death sentence was condemned internationally. Amnesty International (a human rights organization) demanded her death sentence be commuted and argued for the law of blasphemy to be reformed.[55] Likewise, Pope Benedict XVI appealed for Asia's release and commented that Pakistani Christians "are often victims of violence and discrimination" and urged that their "dignity and fundamental rights be fully respected."[56] Asia Bibi's case also provoked a storm nationally, when it was argued that she should be pardoned or at least receive a lesser punishment than death. Mariam Faruqi notes that the conviction and death sentence horrified key government leaders and President Zardari ordered a ministerial review, which concluded that "the verdict was legally unsound and sought a presidential pardon for her [Asia]."[57] She further notes, however, that on 26 November, Pakistan's law minister ruled out making any changes in the blasphemy law.

The government gave in to a long-standing demand of its coalition partner; the Jamiat Ulema-e-Islam led by Maulana Fazl-ur-Rehman, and appointed a hard-line cleric from the party to head the Council of Islamic Ideology to decide whether the country's laws are in conformity with Islam. On 29 November 2010, in a clear case of judicial overreach, the Lahore High

---

54. The issue can also be seen where on 12 May 2000 two Christians, Saleem Masih and Rasheed Masih, were each sentenced to thirty-five-years imprisonment and fined on blasphemy charges. According to the case they were arrested following a dispute over ice cream service. Maqsood Ahmed, an ice-cream vendor in the village Sabomahal in Pasroor, district Sialkot refused to serve the Christians in the same bowls used by Muslims and sent them away to get their own utensils. A dispute began and the two parties struck each other in the face. After seeking opinion and advice from the local cleric, the vendor filed a complaint about being assaulted and beaten by the two Christians. Amnesty International, "Pakistan: Insufficient Protection," 10.

55. Amnesty International, "Pakistani Woman Sentenced to Death," 18 November 2010, AI Index: ASA 33/011/2010.

56. "Pope Pleads for Life of Condemned Pakistani Woman," *BBC News*, 17 November 2010, https://www.bbc.co.uk/news/world-south-asia-11777482.

57. Faruqi, *Question of Faith*, 4.

Court barred the president from issuing a pardon despite this privilege being granted to him by the constitution.[58] On 30 November Sherry Rehman, Member of National Assembly (MNA) of Pakistan People's Party, submitted a bill to the National Assembly Secretariat seeking an end to the death penalty under the existing blasphemy laws in order to reduce misuse of the law, discussed below.[59] Faruqi further notes that the Islamic groups and religious political parties intended to use the issue to rally popular support in preparation for the next elections, as a number of public meetings were organized on the issue of amending the law. Finally, on 30 December, faced with a threat to its majority, the government publicly reneged on a commitment to review the blasphemy laws, announcing that it had "no intention" to repeal or amend the law. Sensing the government's lack of resolve and supported by sections of the media, extremists offered head money to anyone who killed Asia Bibi and issued death threats to opponents and critics of the blasphemy law.[60]

Asia's case received serious attention when the Punjabi Governor, Salman Taseer, a Muslim, visited her in jail to help her to get justice.[61] In December

---

58. Faruqi, 4.

59. Sherry Rehman President of the Jinnah Institute, held a conference to engage academics, lawyers and other members of civil society in an open discussion on the amendments to the Blasphemy Laws. The conference highlighted the recent case of Asia Bibi and the blatant abuse of the legislation in bringing false claims against members of minority communities. The discussants included Asma Jahangir (President Supreme Court Bar Association), Hina Jilani (General Secretary, HRCP), Anis Haroon (Chair NCSW), Shahbaz Bhatti (Minister for Minorities Affairs), Ali Dayan Hasan (Human Rights Activist and Board of Advisors, Jinnah Institute), Dr. Khalid Masood (Former Chairman, Council of Islamic Ideology), Prof Ghamdi (religious scholar) and Ashiq Masih (husband of Asia Bibi). See Amir Waseem, "Sherry Submits Bill For Amending Blasphemy Law,'" *Dawn*, 30 November 2010; Rehman, "Amendments to the Blasphemy Laws."

60. In December 2010, a leading Urdu daily published an editorial in support of a Peshawar cleric's call for head money on Asia Bibi. Maulana Yusuf Qureshi, a cleric of the Mohabat Khan mosque in Peshawar, announced a reward of Rs 500,000 for anyone who would kill Asia Bibi. The contentious editorial praised the cleric's move, stating, "What the government couldn't do after a court decision, the nation will." The government did not take any action against the cleric and his incitement to murder, nor against the irresponsible and inflammatory language in local media. At the time of writing Asia Bibi was still in the jail in Shekhupura, Punjab, and had lodged an appeal at the High Court. Faruqi, *Question of Faith*, 4, 43.

61. United States Department of State, Bureau of Democracy, Human Rights and Labor, *International Religious Freedom Report for 2011*, available at http://www.state.gov/documents/organization/193145.pdf; M. A. Niazi, "Blasphemy Case Shakes the Nation," published on 3 December 2010, https://nation.com.pk/03-Dec-2010/blasphemy-case-shakes-

2010, Taseer took a huge step at a political level by asking for Asia's forgiveness. In reviewing religious intolerance and human rights in Pakistan, he concluded that "the sentence against Assia is inhumane . . . I have handed over the appeal (for Assia Bibi) for a presidential pardon, which I will take to the president and soon Assia will be pardoned and will be released from imprisonment."[62] Helping Asia to get justice was offensive enough, but Taseer's criticism of the blasphemy laws and their misuse was itself regarded as blasphemy. He did not live to see any pardon or release of Asia Bibi as he was assassinated by his bodyguard, Malik Mumtaz Hussein Qadri on 4 January 2011, in Islamabad.

The reaction to the murder of Taseer was widespread in social life and the media, much of which supported the murderer. The Jamaat Ahl-e-Sunnat, Pakistan warned that those who expressed grief over the assassination could suffer like Taseer, insisting "no Muslim should attend the funeral or even try to pray for Salman Taseer or even express any kind of regret or sympathy over the incident."[63] Moreover, Qadri's appearance at the court attracted large crowds including lawyers who showered rose petals to welcome him and support him for killing Taseer. Qadri admitted killing the governor and argued in the court that "I did not kill anyone unlawfully. I have taught a lesson to apostate Salman Taseer in the light of the teachings of the Qur'an and the Tradition of the Prophet."[64] This was another in the line of cases showing how one who murders the blasphemer becomes a hero, as did Qadri, following the legacy and example of Illam Din, still known as "the martyr," who killed Rajpal for publishing the offensive pamphlet insulting the Prophet Muhammad in 1927 in Lahore, in British Pakistan.[65] The killing of Taseer and the response to it shocked the government and weakened its

---

the-nation; Zahid Husain and Tom Wright, "Pakistan Killer Had Revealed Plans," *The Wall Street Journal*, 5 January 2011, available at https://www.wsj.com/articles/SB10001424052748703675904576063581434623072.

62. Salman Taseer in "Violence Brings Pakistan's Women Advocates to Aid Religious minorities," *Women News Network*, 19 August 2011, https://womennewsnetwork.net/2011/08/19/violence-pakistans-women-religious-minorities/.

63. "Salman Taseer: Thousands Mourn Pakistan Governor," *BBC News*, 5 January 2011, https://www.bbc.co.uk/news/world-south-asia-12116764.

64. "Mumtaz Qadri Charged with Salman Taseer Murder," *BBC News*, 14 February 2011, available http://www.bbc.co.uk/news/world-south-asia-12445519.

65. Dildar and Mughal, *Section 295-C Pakistan Penal Code*, 24–26.

already slight power to protect the religious communities and amend the law of blasphemy. Taseer's daughter, Sarah said "this is a message to every liberal to shut up or to be shot."⁶⁶

Shahbaz Bhatti, a Christian Federal Minister of Minorities, and one of the supporters of the government making efforts to ameliorate the problems of all religious minorities, faced threats to his life for his stand against Pakistan's blasphemy law. He commented during a trip to Canada, recorded on video that:

> I have been told by pro-Taliban religious extremists that if I will continue to speak against the blasphemy law, I will be beheaded . . . As a Christian, I believe Jesus is my strength. He has given me power and wisdom and motivation to serve suffering humanity. I follow the principles of my conscience, and I am ready to die and sacrifice my life for the principles I believe.⁶⁷

On 4 March 2011, Bhatti was murdered in Islamabad and his assassins left leaflets at the scene of his murder, proclaiming that they killed him because he committed blasphemy and warned others to be aware of meeting the same fate if they criticized the law of blasphemy.⁶⁸ It is important to realise that just raising a voice to say that the blasphemy law impinges on the rights of minorities can be regarded as blasphemy. Likewise, Salman Taseer's intention to help a Christian accused, and his commenting on how law affects non-Muslims, was regarded as apostasy and unfaithfulness to Islam. The essence of the crime is that amending the rather recent blasphemy law is seen as an assault on the most sacred values of Muslims; therefore most Muslims defend it even to their death. Maulana Manzoor Ahmed Chinioti, a leader of a right-wing Islamic party, said of Muslims' response to changing the blasphemy law: "They should know that true Muslims will spill their last drop of blood to protect the sanctity of holy personalities and the book."⁶⁹ This kind

---

66. *New York Times*, 4 January 2011 quoted in Marshall and Shea, *Silence*, 99.

67. Bhati's statement recorded from one of his videos, see Ashish Kumar Sen, "Pakistani Government Official Murdered for Criticism of Islamic Blasphemy Law," *Student News Daily*, 4 March 2011, https://www.studentnewsdaily.com/daily-news-article/pakistan-government-official-murdered-for-criticism-of-islam-blasphemy-law/.

68. Gregory, "Under the Shadow of Islam," 204.

69. Muddassir Rizvi, "Pakistan: Abuse of Blasphemy Law," *The Manila Times*, 20 November 2003.

of determination by Muslims makes it difficult to achieve the possibility of reconciliation and peace between religious communities or any reduction in the misuse of the law. Moreover when Muslim and Christian political leaders who raise the question of protecting minorities or changing the law for the sake of peace in society are killed, this affects all potential critics and commentators. After the assassination of Minister Bhatti, President Asif Ali Zardari stated in a local newspaper:

> This is a concerted campaign to slaughter every liberal, progressive and humanist voice in Pakistan. The time has come for the federal government and provincial governments to speak out and to take a strong stand against these murderers to save the very essence of Pakistan.[70]

The government was keen to investigate both murder cases but by and large kept silence over the future implications of the blasphemy law. Yet despite the clear problems attached to change, a bill to amend the law was tabled.

6.5 Amendments to the Blasphemy Laws Act 2010

Sherry Rehman, former minister for information and Pakistan People Party legislator, proposed a bill to amend the blasphemy laws and submitted it to the National Assembly on 30 November 2010. For Rehman, repealing the law would be the ideal situation as "its formulation and mechanisms of implementation have serious implications for social, constitutional and natural justice in Pakistan."[71] To her, such change and amendment is needed for the sake of minorities and this "can be obtained if made politically palatable."[72] She declared that PPP "is the government that can review the blasphemy laws. It is a moment in history that must be seized. Pakistan's identity may be ambiguous, but it is precisely [its] space that can be used

---

70. Quoted in United States Department of State, *International Religious Freedom Report for 2011*, 9.

71. Sherry Rehman, "Gojra and Pakistan's Identity," 13 August 2009, http://sherryrehman.com/gojra-and-pakistans-identity/.

72. Rehman, "Gorja and Pakistan's Identity."

as an opportunity to steer our fragile nation-hood in another direction."[73] Some of the major objectives of the proposed Blasphemy Act were to:

> Avoid miscarriages of justice in the name of Blasphemy . . . and reduce the penalties to each offence so that punishments are proportionate and any incentive to use these laws to settle scores removed. Include the concept of premeditation or intent, which is key to criminal procedure. The terminology of the legislation has been clarified to include in the concept of "*mens rea*" or intent behind the criminal act. Ensure that anyone making false or frivolous accusation under the legislation is penalised as befitting the section under which original claim was made.[74]

Let us see whether these objectives were included in the proposed bill. According to Rehman, the amendment bill, especially Chapter XV: Of Offences Relating to Religion of the Pakistan Penal Code, had their roots in colonial laws. Though she did not mention if the law was misused or not in British India, she admitted that certain laws have become a source of victimisation and persecution of minorities in Pakistan from 1986.

The first change Rehman proposed was to change punishments given under sections, 295-A, 295-B, and 295-C. According to the new Amendment Bill, it was proposed to amend the punishment given under section 295-A, for outraging religious feelings through malicious writing and speech, from ten years to imprisonment of either description up to "two years." Notably, Rehman intended to revive the originally prescribed punishment of two years and fine for outraging the feelings of any class under section 295-A, a clause applied by British in 1927 and amended in 1992 in Pakistan. She also proposed to add the same "malicious and outrageous intention" contained in section 295-A to the new sections: 295-C, 298-B and C. Currently section 295-A, which had been successfully applied to deal with offensive writings in the pre-1980 period, is rarely if ever used.[75] Though it has been said that Pakistan's law of blasphemy protects other religions under section 295-A

---

73. Rehman.
74. Rehman, "Amendments to the Blasphemy Laws."
75. The successful prosecution and judgment given under section 295-A are discussed in detail in chapter 4.

this research clearly shows that this section has been effectively abandoned since the blasphemy laws were added. Therefore, whether changing the punishment of the clause will reduce the current issue of misusing the law is doubtful. However, adding malicious intention to the new sections may be useful and does make a clear statement.

According to the new Amendment Bill, the death penalty inserted in section 295-C for defiling the name of the Prophet should be removed and any words, either spoken or written "should be punished with imprisonment of either description for a term which may extend to 'ten years' or with a fine or with both."[76] Likewise the punishment of life imprisonment for defiling the copy of the Qur'an given under section 295-B should be replaced with "either description for a term which may extend to 'five years' or with fine or with both."

In Pakistan, the death sentence for defiling the name of the Prophet has been regarded as *hadd*, with a fixed punishment as discussed in the fifth chapter. However, nationally this is still contested, especially where it has been maliciously used to persecute the minority. It has also been strongly condemned internationally, although with little effect within Pakistan. For example, in Pakistan death sentences are imposed for homicide. Amnesty International notes that

> There is no reliable evidence to demonstrate that the death penalty helps avoid other serious harm, for example by deterring the crimes for which it is available. Indeed, there is some evidence, albeit inconclusive, that the death penalty can actually contribute to such crimes. It may certainly distract government from seeking more effective means to combat crime.[77]

Amnesty International appealed to the authorities, urging the president to "use his powers under article 45 of the constitution to commute all death sentences."[78]

The second major change according to the Amendment Bill is related to "intention," which is the most important ingredient of the law and has

---

76. Rehman, "Amendments to the Blasphemy Laws," 1.
77. Amnesty International, "Pakistan: The Death Penalty," 21.
78. Amnesty International, 18.

been recognized as an error especially in section 295-C and section 298-A. Notably, these sections do not distinguish between intentional (or deliberate) acts and unintentional acts, which is an important ingredient necessary to convict anyone in criminal law. Section 295 and 295-A, the previous clauses applied by the British, specify the "deliberate and malicious intention" (to punish offensive writing and speech under section 295-A) and deliberate acts (to punish who defiles and damages the place of worship under section 295). The new additions (section 295-C and section 298-B) though containing most of the description of the old law, omit the crucial point of intention in defining the crime. Rehman regards this error as one of the major reasons for the misuse of the law which leaves accusations open to widespread abuse, placing the burden of proving innocence on the accused in the face of prosecution witnesses who tailored their evidence through prejudice or malice.[79] To deal with this issue, Rehman proposed to add intention with words like "malicious and deliberate intention" to secure blasphemy convictions. These terms were originally added in section 295-A in 1927 by the British to convict those who insulted the Prophet Muhammad through offensive publications done with deliberate and malicious intention.[80]

According to Sherry Rehman, the government must reconsider the introduction of the provision that "would make it easier to award punishment to those who file fake cases." To tackle this issue, it was proposed to add a new section, 203, to the legislation on religious offences of the Pakistan Penal Code (Chapter XV) which could punish "anyone making a false or frivolous accusation under any of the sections of 295A, 295B and 295C . . . shall be punished in accordance with similar punishments prescribed in the section in which the false or frivolous accusation was made."[81] Furthermore, anyone making false or frivolous accusations under section 295A, 295B and 295C may be arrested without a warrant and such a person can be tried in Sessions Court.[82] It is important to note, currently these sections according

---

79. Sherry Rehman, "Blasphemy Law Needs Rectification," *The News*, 17 December 2010, available online, https://www.thenews.com.pk/archive/print/275164-blasphemy-law-needs-rectification-sherry.

80. Section 295-A is discussed in detail in chapter 2.

81. Rehman, "Amendments to the Blasphemy Laws," 1.

82. Rehman, "Gojra and Pakistan's Identity."

to the Criminal Procedure Code are cognizable, which give an authority and power to police to register the blasphemy accusation and arrest the accused without warrant. To Rehman, by enforcing this change, the complainants or accusers take full responsibility whether the case is false or true. This change may bring little transformation, however, given that in many cases discussed above people do not wait for any trial or court orders once they hear that someone has apparently committed blasphemy. It is also relevant to mention here that previous sections – 295-A for outraging the religious feelings through speech and writing and section 298, which protected religious freedom of discussion – are non-cognizable. However, people are not only unaware of these sections in contemporary Pakistan but take no responsibility for the proper procedure of law and order.

By reviewing various cases in the Amendment Bill, Rehman argued that the lack of a clear government response gave freedom to accusers to incite acts of violence and intimidation against religious minorities.[83] Rehman further observes that malicious blasphemy allegations have resulted in an exponential rise of blasphemy cases, mostly based on personal reasons such as settling personal scores and grabbing property. She further explains that this "would take away the impunity afforded to malicious accusers and inciters to hate, whose victims may find acquittal but also find that their lives, reputations, security and mobility destroyed by such charges."[84]

To reduce the risk of mob violence Rehman proposed to add a new section 298-E in Chapter XV of the religious offences law which prescribes punishments for seven years with a fine for "any advocacy of religious hatred that constitutes incitement to discrimination or violence . . ."[85] It is indeed the case that people tend to accuse someone for personal reasons yet are rarely punished for a misuse of the law. However, merely saying that the law should not be misused is ineffective as the actual cause of such misuse must be considered before deciding what rule or regulation can be applied to control it. Historically, offensive speeches and publications and inciting the public to violence and to punishment of the accused without trial were

---

83. Rehman.
84. Rehman, "Blasphemy Law Needs Rectification," *The News*, 17 December 2010.
85. Rehman, "Blasphemy Law Needs Rectification."

done even before the blasphemy law was promulgated in the 1980s, and nothing has been done then or since to stop such behaviour.

According to Rehman, initial reports of blasphemy accusations, pre-trial, and trial procedures to convict the accused are frequently incorrectly done at the level of the lower courts. Rehman proposes to amend the Court of Criminal Procedure by adding section 190 (3) to insist that: "all offences falling within sections of 295A, 295B and 295C of Pakistan Penal Code shall exclusively be taken cognizance of by the Court Sessions and Tried by the High Court."[86] The change was proposed to prevent miscarriages of justice in lower courts, because the higher courts afford judges better protection against extremists, as well as place the trial under greater public scrutiny.[87]

Rehman's effort to bring changes to Chapter XV: Of Offences Relating to Religion and procedures of blasphemy prosecution was indeed a significant step with her intention to protect minorities. There are two crucial points which need to taken into consideration: who is opposing this amendment and how can any law be effective if discussing a case, even giving evidence of what occurred, is effectively ruled out? We can reiterate here that historically many clarifications, rules and regulations were declared, if it was clear people had misunderstood the context or purpose of a law. Muslims successfully fought for their right to slaughter a cow, causing the government to extend the meaning and implication of the word "object" to include animate objects such as cows and goats under section 295. The issue of cow slaughter was so sensitive that section 295 was the only clause in which originally the punishment for defiling places and object was seven years, later reduced to two years. Apart from this particular punishment, some procedural changes were made to allow genuine cases to be brought when it was observed that violent Arya Samaj protests over cow slaughter occurred in 1886 and 1890 in Punjab with communal riots. This protest became critical from time to time in various states, and in the 1920s legislative attempts were made to deal with the issue throughout British India[88] as a policy to provide equal

---

86. Rehman, "Amendments to the Blasphemy Laws," 1.
87. Rehman, "Blasphemy Law Needs Rectification," *The News*, 17 December 2010.
88. Thursby, *Hindu-Muslim Relation*, 102–108.

rights to all religious communities.[89] Noting Muslims' minority status in British India, Justice Nawaz Chohan commented that historically Chapter XV was "enacted [and was amended in 1927] by the British to protect the religious sentiments of the Muslim minority in the Subcontinent before the partition against the Hindu majority."[90] However, in Pakistan today, the majority of Muslims protest fervently when minorities and other human rights organizations fight for their rights of protection and freedom. It is critical to see how even discussing changes to the procedure which might reduce misuse of the law has become an offence.

6.6. Reaction to the Amendment Bill

By proposing the changes discussed above, Rehman was aware that it would stir up the community, saying "it's going to be a long haul but I don't think it's impossible. It just looks that way sometimes. If we are to live in Pakistan, to invest in Pakistan's future, then we do have to think about how to find this glass half full."[91] The Amendment Bill brought critical discussions among Pakistan's religious circles. Though it had been under discussion since the law was changed by Zia-ul-Haq, no one had dared formally to submit any such amendment bill or law due to the sensitive matter of blasphemy. The bill was likely to get cross-party support from liberal legislators but the religious parties as well as many other people strongly opposed it, which also threatened the political powers and thus political stability. The government halted the bill's progress after violent protests demanded it be withdrawn, and disbanded the committee set up under the Minister for Minorities, Shahbaz Bhatti, to review the law. Both Rehman and Bhatti were declared "liable for murder" by the rallies.[92] In early 2011, the ruling government lost its two ministers, Salman Taseer and Shahbaz Bhatti as discussed above. Sherry Rehman, who before proposing the amendments had insisted that

---

89. Michael Mann, "Turbulent Delhi: Religious Strife, Social Tension and Political Conflicts, 1803-1857," *Journal of South Asian Studies* 28, no. 1 (2005): 5–34.

90. *Muhammad Mahboob v. The State.*

91. Sherry Rehman quoted by Issam Ahmed, "Could There be a Liberal Resurgence in Pakistan?" 28 January 2011, https://www.csmonitor.com/World/Asia-South-Central/2011/0128/Could-there-be-a-liberal-resurgence-in-Pakistan-Lawmaker-Sherry-Rehman-says-she-s-working-on-it.

92. Faruqi, *Question of Faith*, 42.

repealing the blasphemy laws could protect the citizens of Pakistan later, withdrew her commitment to repealing the law. Though Rehman is still alive, "the blasphemy issue is still haunting [her]" as she was alleged of having committing blasphemy for passing derogatory remarks against the Prophet Muhammad in January 2013.[93] Rehman, according to the petitioner, committed blasphemy on *Dunya* Television program *Dunya Meray Aagay* (The World in Front of Me) on 30 November 2010 while talking about the misuse of the law of blasphemy.[94] However, she was not arrested but the case is under investigation and the court did not declare the exact derogatory words or remarks at issue. It cannot be said whether Rehman will be convicted for blasphemy or not, but it is yet another example that today even Muslims are not secure and free to talk about the law in Pakistan. Many suggestions have been offered to address this very difficult issue but nothing serious has been done to control either the misuse or the law itself. Any endeavour to reduce misuse of the law to protect minorities seems impossible.

Given the subsequent inadequate protection of religious communities in Pakistan, the Human Rights Watch annual report stated that "blasphemy laws have sparked outbreaks of violence against innocent individuals in violation of their rights to freedom of thought, conscience, and religion, as well as lawyers, judges, and others defending the rights of those accused under the laws." The Human Rights Report also notes that "Pakistan's elected government notably failed to provide protection to those threatened by extremists, or to hold extremists accountable."[95] Despite national and international concern, it is clear that Pakistan's minorities, potentially including the 20 percent of its citizens who are Shia, are critically vulnerable citizens, continually struggling for their rights and safety and routinely facing judgment without a fair trial or even without a trial at all, lynched by the mob.

---

93. Azam Khan, "Blasphemy Petition Against Sherry Rehman Accepted," *The Express Tribune*, 18 January 2013.

94. Khan, "Blasphemy Petition."

95. United States Department of State, *International Religious Freedom Report for 2011*, 9.

6.7 Conclusion

It is understood that the issue of the blasphemy law is complicated, and there are no simple solutions. It cannot be said whether the law will be repealed, amended or any criminal procedural change made to protect minorities against religious violence in Pakistan. However, one of the important questions is: who will protect religious feelings which are significantly affecting the life, property and dignity of the citizens of Pakistan?

First it is important to recollect that the political and governing authorities have claimed to protect the communities from religiously motivated violence and hatred by applying and practising Chapter XV: Of Offences Relating to Religion from 1860 until today. Macaulay, the original author of the law, was aware that religious excitement was significant in British India and one of the aims of this law was to protect religious feelings and to control religiously motivated violence. This survey of the historical evolution of the religious offences legislation has shown that, places of worship and objects, religious assemblies, funeral rights and freedom to discuss religious opinions calmly, were protected during the British occupation of the region, although they were threatened by Hindu-Muslim communalism expressed in publications judged offensive in the 1920s. The ensuing revision of religious offences in the 1920s to 1930s clearly reveals that British political power acquiesced to the demands of Muslims by amending the law to prevent the Arya Samaj from writing and distributing maliciously intended attacks on the Prophet Muhammad. However, malicious intent is not evident in the successful prosecution of *Angare*, which appears rather to be part of the British determination to hold on to power to which end they made use of, indeed misused, their own religious offences laws in a prequel to the postcolonial era of present day Pakistan.

Religion and religious offences were and still are areas of significant legislation and a sensitive matter in South Asia especially in the Punjab, evidenced by many apparently religious riots in the region over the decades of Pakistan's existence, which led to the revision of the original 1860 religious conflict laws. This law had been amended a little since its inception, but in Pakistan the outcome of these changes has become especially controversial. Since the founding of Pakistan in 1947, religious groups linked to but not necessarily directly part of the majority Sunni tradition have not stopped trying to reform or amend either the constitution or the law on religious offences. Saeed argues that "the very idea of the Pakistani state was contested and negotiated by different actors in the imagined political community of the nation."[96] Such negotiation, from Islamic parties who once opposed the creation of Pakistan, not only played their part in excluding Ahmadis from the Muslim community but also brought major changes in legal history which later turned the area of religious offences law into a very complex religious conflict. The nature of the 1860 law against "insulting religious feelings" has not only been turned into a blasphemy law, against the intention of the writers, but has also evolved into a set of laws that affect the mode of declaring judgements, by the judiciary and of effecting punishment, legally or not, by the mob, as discussed in the second half of the thesis. Today the reason for officials staying inactive, unable or uninterested in protecting victims is not only religious pressure but politically motivated threats from the local communities and leaders. The socio-political context of this gradual change is clearly shows that "non-Muslim Pakistanis suffer discrimination in infinitely numerous ways both from the state and society."[97]

Today one of the most powerful demands is not to change the law or even touch the laws of the 1980s, intended to protect the Prophet Muhammad, for they have developed a quasi-sacred nature, although the nature of legal processes is in debate by critical Muslim and non-Muslim alike. The first example can be seen in the case *Qureshi v. FSC* in the fifth chapter in which various proposals supporting a lesser punishment than death, and including intention as an important ingredient in Islam, were discussed. This issue has split religious and political leaders, judicial and religious communities. The murders of political leaders have "exposed a deep fissure in Pakistan society between liberal politicians with Western lifestyles and religious leaders who hold to an Islamist view of the world and are gaining influence."[98] Nationally it is still in debate and internationally it has been argued that in the absence

---

96. Saeed, "Politics of Exclusion," 367.
97. Muhammad Badar Alam, "After the Fires Burnt Out," *The Herald*, September 2009.
98. Husain and Wright, "Pakistan: Killers."

of any final theological definition or authoritative Islamic sources the law of blasphemy "remains unsettled."[99]

Of course, it is the case that religion is connected to every part of life, and this connection cannot be ignored, however delicately one treads, in the area of human rights. The more liberal view would see a focus on human rights draws on the good of religions; the more conservative might see human rights opposing eternal truths. Witte asserts in regard to such issues: "The proper response is to castigate the vices and cultivate the virtues of religion, to confirm those religious teachings and practices that are most conducive to human rights, democracy, and rule of law."[100]

Yet the very acknowledging of the illegality within such incidents has started to be accepted. For example, when various *ulama* and members of the Muslim community condemned the misuse of the law and stood with the Downs Syndrome child, Rimsha (non-Muslim), defending her not only as a girl with Downs, but a person who had been wrongly accused. That last point is certainly an important step for the Muslim community as a whole. Yet whether such condemnations of illegality will safeguard future under-age children accused of blasphemy, like Rimsha and Salamat, or other persons unintentionally acting in a way construed as blasphemous, remains to be seen. Unclear, too is whether quiescent Muslims fully realize the implications of the law of blasphemy on non-Muslims, or whether those Muslims who condemn the misuse of the law are ready and willing to suggest ways out of the problem.

The incident of Joseph Colony, mentioned in the introduction, again raised the question minorities have been asking for the last thirty years, of whether it is blasphemy to burn churches, other places of worship, Bibles, and people's property after a blasphemy accusation has been made or even just rumoured. All such acts are still punishable under Chapter XV but are not seen as religious offences in contemporary Pakistan, where people

---

99. Nina Shea, "Pakistan's Anti-Blasphemy Laws," 8 October 2009, Hudson Institute, 2, available at https://www.hudson.org/content/researchattachments/attachment/748/sheapakistan108.pdf.

100. John Witte, Jr. "The Spirit of the Laws, The Laws of the Spirit: Religion and Human Rights in a New Global Era," in *God and Globalization: The Spirit and the Modern Authorities*, vol. 2, eds. Max L. Stackhouse and Don S. Browning (Harrisburg: Trinity Press, 2001), 105–106.

usually refer to Chapter XV as "Qanoon-e-Toheen-e-Rasalat" (the law to protect the Prophet from insult) rather than "Qanoon-e-Toheen-e-Mazhab or Mazahib" (the law to protect religions). Various scholars, in condemning the misuse of the law, imply "Qanoon-e-Toheen-e-Mazhab" is still the basis of the law, arguing that Islam protects other religions in Pakistan: but their view is of limited value given the general confusion.

People often fail to understand the nature of the religious offence and conflict and take immediate action to protect Islam. For example, Samuel Masih was accused of "defiling the mosque" (punishable under section 295 with imprisonment for two years) in Lahore in August 2003 but was murdered in his hospital bed, in the presence of police, by Faryad Ali saying that "it was his duty as a Muslim to kill Samuel [blasphemer]."[101] Does defiling a mosque defile Islam or the Prophet? This misunderstanding can be seen in Rimsha's case, where the local cleric was unable to understand that church assembly and music is a sacred object of Christianity and thus one to be respected under the law; a mob cannot understand that burning a church, temple or any religious place or religious books is likewise a religious offence under section 295. Religious conflict followed by immediate judgements is a well-established pattern in Punjab, outwith the law, and its "control over local population to the detriment of local administration is also well known. The laws mean nothing under these circumstances."[102] People in such cases simply react to protect Islam rather than understanding that Chapter XV: Of Offences Relating to Religion still expects all other religions to be protected: the law is disregarded.

Many suggestions have been offered to address this critical ethical issue. Perhaps the most popular response has been discussed nationally and internationally concerning the religious rights and protection of religious communities which have developed a high profile in order to publicise the issue. Internationally, the implications of the 1980s laws have been condemned, and suggestions made to protect religious communities and religious rights – protections which already exist in the law of Chapter XV of PPC. However, where suggestions merge into sanctions, the situation

---

101. "Pakistani Christian Bludgeoned to Death in Hospital Bed," *Catholic Herald*, 18 June 2004.

102. Rabzon Khan, "Fear and Shame of Gojra," *Daily Times*, 3 August 2009.

would become more difficult for Christians and other minorities. Sanctions imposed by western governments would run the risk of again displaying Pakistani Christianity as a western religion, further alienating indigenous Christians from their Muslim neighbours, who would cause more harm to minorities if the economy suffered. The Danish Cartoon incident of 2005 and an offensive film created in 2012 by an American each critically affected minorities in Pakistan, none of whom had anything to do with the cartoons or film but all of whom were scapegoats. There is no easy solution to prevent personal quarrels being misused through blasphemy accusations unless the issue can be accepted at a political or social level as well as a merely religious level, as Jalal has commented:

> Pakistanis have the "state" if not quite the "nation" of their collective imaginings, and there are ways of overcoming contradictions that cannot be resolved. Without sustained debate on citizenship rights, not just political but also social and economic Pakistan cannot take the elementary steps towards forging a collective ethos as a nation-state.[103]

How can citizens in Pakistan work toward the peaceful co-existence for which Joseph, Taseer, Bhatti, and many accused of blasphemy have already suffered and died? Not only Christians but the blood of thousands of Ahmadis, Shias, and Hindus is at the doors of our churches, temples, mosques and other places of worship, weakening the minorities and Pakistan day-by-day, and threatening those Sunnis who want no part of these attacks. The law has also weakened the state, for "if the government tries to finish it [or even to amend the law for the sake of protection], the government itself will be finished."[104] It has even discouraged those who would "open the door for a dialogue of reason . . . and values of justice and good against hatred and violence."[105] Who will be left to talk on the behalf of religious rights and protection of the religious communities of Pakistan? If it is to continue to be a habitual way of life the country, as the Lahore High Court declared in the Report (1954), it will become a battle field for warning groups and

---

103. Jalal, "Ideology and the Struggle," 136.
104. Marshall and Shea, *Silenced*, 100.
105. Muhammad Sayyad Tantawi quoted in Sookhdeo, *Freedom to Believe*, 13.

religious communities who may perish one by one. As Martin Niemöller put it after World War II,

> First they came for the Socialists, and I did not speak out—
> Because I was not a Socialist.
> Then they came for the Trade Unionists, and I did not speak out—
> Because I was not a Trade Unionist.
> Then they came for the Jews, and I did not speak out—
> Because I was not a Jew.
> Then they came for me—and there was no one left to speak for me.[106]

---

106. Martin Niemöller, "First They Came," available on https://shenandoahliterary.org/blog/2017/08/first-they-came-by-martin-niemoller/.

Bibliography

Abdullah, Abu. "Social Change and Modernisation." In *Bangladesh: Promise and Performance*, edited by Rounaq Jahan, 129–149. Dhaka: University Press, 2000.

Adams, C. J. "The Ideology of Mawlana Mawdudi." In *South Asian Politics and Religion*, edited by D. E. Smith, 371–397. Princeton, NJ: Princeton University Press, 1966.

Ahmad, Ishtiaq. "The Pakistan Islamic State Project: A Secular Critique." In *The State and Secularism: Perspectives from Asia*, edited by Michael S. H. Heng, Ten Chin Liew and C. L. Ten, 185–210. Singapore: World Scientific Publication, 2010.

Ahmed, Akbar S. Jinnah, *Pakistan and Islamic Identity: The Search for Saladin*. London: Routledge, 1997.

———. *Pakistan Society: Islam, Ethnicity and Leadership in South Asia*. Karachi: Oxford University Press, 1997.

Ali, Syed Ameer. *Muhammadan Law*. Vol. 1. Calcutta: Thacker, Spink & Co., 1917.

al-Marghinani, Burhan al-Din. *The Hedaya, or Guide: A Commentary on the Mussulman Laws*. Vol. 1, translated by Charles Hamilton. London: T. Bensley, 1791.

Amritsari, Felix Qasir G. M. *The Blasphemy Law*. Vol. 1. Karachi: Idar-e Amn-O Insaf, 1994.

———. *The Blasphemy Law*, vol. 2, *Death Sentence, Acquittal and Exile*. Karachi: Idar-e Amn-O Insaf, 1995.

———. *The Blasphemy Law*, vol. 3, *From Commitment to Hara-Kiri*. Karachi: Idara-e Amn-O Insaf, 1998.

Anderson, Gerald H., ed. *Biographical Dictionary of Christian Missions*. New York: Macmillan Reference, 1998.

———. *Mission Legacies: Biographical Studies of Leaders of the Modern Missionary Movement*. Maryknoll, NY: Orbis Books, 1994.

Anisuzzaman, M. "The Identity Question and Politics." In *Bangladesh: Promise and Performance*, edited by Rounaq Jahan, 45–64. Dhaka: University Press, 2000.

Arif, Khalid Mahmud. *Working with Zia: Pakistan's Power Politics, 1977-1988*. Karachi: Oxford University Press, 1995.

Asad, Talal. *The Idea of an Anthropology of Islam*. Washington: Centre for Contemporary Arab Studies, Georgetown University, 1986.

Ayoub, Mahmoud M. *Islam: Faith and History*. Oxford: Oneworld, 2005.

Barrier, N. Gerald. *Banned: Controversial Literature and Political Control in British India 1907-1947*. Columbia, MO: University of Missouri Press, 1974.

Bentham, Jeremy. *Essay on the Influence of Time and Place in Matters of Legislation*. Vol. 1. 1843. Available at http://www.laits.utexas.edu/poltheory/bentham/timeplace/index.html

———. *A Fragment on Government*. Oxford: Clarendon, 1776. Available at http://www.efm.bris.ac.uk/het/bentham/government.htm.

———. *The Principles of Morals and Legislations*. Oxford: Clarendon, 1879.

Bhargava, Rajeev, ed. *Secularism and Its Critics*. Delhi: Oxford University Press, 1998.

Bibi, Asia. *Blasphemy: The True Heartbreaking Story of the Woman Sentenced to Death Over a Cup of Water*. London: Virago, 2012.

Binder, Leonard. *Religion and Politics in Pakistan*. Berkeley, CA: University of California Press, 1961.

Black, Antony. *The History of Islamic Political Thought*. Edinburgh: Edinburgh University Press, 2001.

Bodine, Jermaine. "Duncan Black Macdonald, 1863–1943: Preparing Missionaries for the Muslim World." In *Mission Legacies: Biographical Studies of Leaders of the Modern Missionary Movement*, edited by G. H. Anderson, 469–474. Maryknoll, NY: Oribs Books, 1994.

Buckser, Andrew and Stephen D. Glazier. *The Anthropology of Religious Conversion*. New York: Rowman & Littlefield, 2003.

Campbell, Robert D. *Pakistan: An Emerging Democracy*. Princeton, NJ: Van Nostrand,1963.

Cell, John W. *Hailey: A Study in British Imperialism 1872-1969*. Cambridge: Cambridge University Press, 1992.

Chan, Wing-Cheong, Barry Wright, and Stanley Yeo, eds. *Codification, Macaulay and the Indian Penal Code: The Legacies and Modern Challenges of Criminal Law Reform*. Surrey: Ashgate, 2011.

Channan, James. "Human Rights and Situations of Christians in Pakistan." In *Islam in Asia: Perspectives for Christian-Muslim Encounter*, edited by Paul Rajashekar and H. S. Wilson, 105–109. Geneva: Lutheran World Federation, 1992.

Chaturvedi, K. N. *The Constitution of India*. Delhi: Government of India, Ministry of Law and Justice, 2007. Online version available, https://www.wipo.int/edocs/lexdocs/laws/en/in/in023en.pdf.
Chunakara, Mathews George, ed. *The Blasphemy Law in Pakistan and Its Impact*. Hong Kong: International Affairs, Christian Conference of Asia, 1998.
Cleland, John. *The Determinants of Reproductive Change in Bangladesh, Success in a Challenging Environment*. Washington DC: World Bank, 1994.
Clive, John. *Thomas Babington Macaulay: The Shaping of the Historian*. London: Secker & Warburg, 1973.
Cohen, Stephen Philip. *The Idea of Pakistan*. Washington, DC: Brooking Institution, 2004.
Cox, Jeffery. *Imperial Fault Lines: Christianity and Colonial Power in India 1818-1940*. Stanford: Stanford University Press, 2002.
Dacey, Austin. *The Future of Blasphemy: Speaking of the Sacred in an Age of Human Rights*. New York: Continuum, 2012.
DeLong-Bas, Natana J. *Wahhabi Islam: From Revival and Reform to Global Jihad*. London: I. B. Tauris, 2004.
Dildar, Peter Jacob and Aftab Alexander Mughal. *Section 295-C Pakistan Penal Code: A Study of the History, Effects and Cases under Blasphemy Laws in Pakistan*. Faisalabad: National Commission for Justice and Peace, 1995.
Doe, Norman and Russell Sandberg, eds. *Law and Religion: New Horizons*. Leuven: Peeters, 2010.
Esposito, John L. *Islam and Politics*. Syracuse: Syracuse University Press, 1984.
———. *Islam: The Strait Path*. 3rd ed. Oxford: Oxford University Press, 1998.
Everett-Heath, John, ed. *Concise Dictionary of World Place Names*. Oxford: Oxford University Press, 2005.
Faruqi, Mariam, ed. *A Question of Faith: A Report on the Religious Status of Minorities of Pakistan*. Karachi: Jinnah Institution, 2011.
Fyzee, Asaf Ali Asghar. *Cases in the Muhammadan Law of India and Pakistan*. Oxford: Clarendon, 1965.
———. *Outlines of Muhammadan Law*. Delhi: Oxford University Press, 1974.
Friedmann, Yohanana. "Ahmadiyya." In *Encyclopaedia of Islam*, 3rd ed., edited by Kate Fleet, Gudrun Kramer, Dennis Matringe, John Nawas and Everett Rowson. Brill Online, 4 December 2012, http://dx.doi.org/10.1163/1573-3912_ei3_COM_0007.
———. *Prophecy Continuous: Aspects of Ahmadi Religious Thought and Its Medieval Background*. Berkley: University of California Press, 1989; Oxford: Oxford University Press, 2003.
Fry, Michael. *The Scottish Empire*. Berlin: Tuckwell, 2001.
Frykenberg, Robert Eric. *History of Christianity in India*. Oxford: Oxford University Press, 2008.

Gabriel, Theodore. *Christian Citizens in an Islamic State: the Pakistan Experience.* Aldershot: Ashgate, 2007.

Gaur, K. D. *The Textbook on the Indian Penal Code.* 4th ed. New Delhi: Universal Law Publishing, 2009.

Gibb, H. A. R. *Encyclopaedia of Islam.* Leiden: Brill, 1997.

Go, Julian, ed. *Political Power and Social Theory.* Vol. 23. Bingley: Emerald Group, 2012.

Gopal, Priyamvada. *Literary Radicalism in India: Gender, Nation and the Transition to Independence.* London: Routledge, 2005.

Gordon, W. M. and T. D. Fergus, eds. *Legal History in the Making.* London: Hambledon, 1991.

Gour, Hari Singh, Gyanendra Kumar, M. C. Desai and R. B. Sethi. *The Penal Law of India: Being an Analytical, Critical & Expository Commentary on the Indian Penal Code (Act No. XLV of 1860), As Amended Up to Date.* 10th ed. Vol. 1. Allahabad: Law Publications, 1982.

Government of Pakistan. *Qadianis: Threat to Islamic Solidarity.* Islamabad: Pakistan Publications, 1984.

Habib, Irfan. *The Agrarian System of Mughal India, 1526-1707.* 2nd revised ed. Oxford: Oxford University Press, 2000.

Haigh, Christopher. *The English Reformation Revised.* Cambridge: Cambridge University Press, 1987.

Hamid, Kazir Abdul, ed. *The All Pakistan Legal Decisions.* Vol. 12. Lahore: PLD, 1962.

Hamilton, W. R. *The Indian Penal Code with Commentary.* Calcutta: Thacker, Spink and Co., 1895.

Hasan, Mushirul, ed. *Islam, Communities and the Nation: Muslim Identities in South Asia and Beyond.* Delhi: Manohar Publications, 1998.

Hare, Ivan. "Blasphemy and Incitement to Religious Hatred: Free Speech Dogma and Doctrine." In *Extreme Speech and Democracy*, edited by James Weinstein and Ivan Hare, 289–310. Oxford: Oxford University Press, 2010.

Hares, Walter P. *Gojra Jungal Vichch Mangal: The Story of a Canal Colony in the Land of the Five Rivers.* Mysore: Wesley Press, 1934.

Harper, Susan Billington. *In the Shadow of the Mahatma: Bishop V. S. Azariah and the Travails of Christianity in British India.* Grand Rapids: Eerdmans, 2000.

Helmholz, R. H. *The Oxford History of the Laws of England.* Vol. 1. *The Canon Law and Ecclesiastical Jurisdiction from 597 to the 1640s.* Oxford: Oxford University Press, 2004.

Hunter, William W. *The Indian Musalmans.* London: Trübner, 1876.

Hyman, Anthony, Muhammad Ghayur, and Naresh Kaushik. *Pakistan: Zia and After.* London: Asia Publishing, 1988.

Jahangir, Asma. *From Protection to Exploitation: The Laws Against Blasphemy in Pakistan*. Lahore: AGHS Legal Aid Cell, 2008.

———. "Walking Together for Freedom." Lecture presented at the *Breaking Barriers: What it Will Take to Achieve Security, Justice and Peace*, conference hosted by the Joan B. Kroc Institute for Peace & Justice at the University of San Diego, 27 September 2012.

Jahan, Rounaq, ed. *Bangladesh: Promise and Performance*. Dhaka: University Press, 2000.

Jain, Mahabir Prashad. *Outlines of Indian Legal History*. 2nd ed. Bombay: N. M. Tripathi, 1966.

Jan, Tarik, ed. *Pakistan Between Secularism and Islam: Ideology, Issues & Conflict*. Islamabad: Institute of Policy Studies, 1998.

Jalal, Ayesha. "Ideology and the Struggle for Democratic Institutions." In *Old Roads, New Highways: Fifty Years of Pakistan*, ed. Victoria Schofield, 121–138. Karachi: Oxford University Press, 1997. Available online, https://ajalal01.pages.tufts.edu/Articles/schofield.pdf.

———. *The Sole Spokesman: Jinnah, the Muslim League and the Demand for Pakistan*. Cambridge: Cambridge University Press, 1985.

———. *The State of Martial Rule: The Origins of Pakistan's Political Economy of Defence*. Cambridge: Cambridge University Press, 1990.

Jalal, Ayesha, and Sugata Bose. *Modern South Asia: History, Culture, Political Economy*. 2nd ed. New York: Routledge, 2004.

James, Lawrence. *Raj: The Making and Unmaking of British India*. London: Abacus Books, 2003.

———. *The Rise and Fall of British Empire*. London: Abacus Books, 2005.

John, Clement. *Religion, State and Intolerance: Pakistan – 60 Years' Intermix of Religion and Politics*. Geneva: World Council of Churches, 2009.

Jones, J. R., ed. *Liberty Secured? Britain Before and After 1688*. Stanford, CA: Stanford University Press, 1992.

Kamali, Mohammad Hashim. *Freedom of Expression in Islam*. Cambridge: Islamic Texts Society, 1997.

Karim, A. K. Nizamul. *Changing Society in India and Pakistan*. Dhaka, Pakistan: Oxford University Press, 1956.

Karim, Saleena. *Secular Jinnah & Pakistan: What The Nation Doesn't Know*. Belcara, ROI: CheckPoint, 2010.

Kazim, Lubna, ed. *A Woman of Substance: The Memoirs of Begum Khurshid Mirza, 1918-1989*. Delhi: Zubaan, 2005.

Khan, Muhammad Ayub. *Friends Not Masters: A Political Autobiography*. London: Oxford University Press, 1967.

Khan, Hamid. *Constitutional and Political History of Pakistan*. 2nd ed. Karachi: Oxford University Press, 2009.

Khan, Fazal Zada, and Touseef Zada Khan. *Pakistan Penal Code: XLV of 1860*. Lahore: Touseef Zada Khan Publication, 2011.

Khan, M. Zafrullah. *Islam and Human Rights*. 5th ed. Islamabad: Islam International Publication, 1999.

Khan, Mohammad Taimur. *The Pakistan Penal Code (XLV of 1860)*. Lahore: Al-Noor Law House, 2002.

Kim, Sebastian C. H. *In Search of Identity: Debates over Religious Conversion in India*. Oxford: Oxford University Press, 2005.

Laoust, H. "Ibn Abd al-Wahhab." In *Encyclopaedia of Islam*, 2nd ed., edited by P. Bearman, Th. Bianquis, C. E. Bosworth, E. van Donzel and W. P. Heinrichs. Brill Online, 20 June 2013, http://dx.doi.org/10.1163/1573-3912_islam_SIM_3033.

Lau, Martin. *The Role of Islam in the Legal System of Pakistan*. Leiden: Martinus Nijhoff, 2006.

Lal, Nand. *The Indian Penal Code, Act XLV of 1860*. Vol. 1. Lahore: Krishan Lal, 1929.

Nandy, Ashis. "The Politics of Secularism and the Recovery of Religious Tolerance." In *Secularism and its Critics*, edited by R. Bhargava, 321–344. New Delhi: Oxford University Press, 1998.

Lavan, Spencer. *The Ahmadiyya Movement: A History and Perspective*. Delhi: Manohar Book Service, 1973.

Levy, Leonard W. *Blasphemy: Verbal Offense against the Sacred, from Moses to Salman Rushdie*. New York: Knopf, 1993.

Levy, Ruben. *Social Structure of Islam*. Cambridge: Cambridge University Press, 1957.

Llewellyn, J. E. *The Arya Samaj as a Fundamentalist Movement: A Study in Comparative Fundamentalism*. New Delhi: Manohar, 1993.

Lukes, Steven. *Power: A Radical View*. 2nd ed. Basingstoke: Palgrave Macmillan, 2004.

Macaulay, Thomas Babington, J. M. Macleod, G. W. Anderson, and F. Millett. *The Indian Penal Code as Originally Framed in 1837*. Madras: Higginbotham, 1888.

Macaulay, Thomas Babington. *Complete Works of Thomas Babington Macaulay*. Vol. 3. London: Longmans, Green and Co., 1866.

———. *A Penal Code Prepared by Indian Law Commissioners*. Calcutta: Bengal Military Orphan Press, 1837.

Macdonald, Duncan B. *Development of Muslim Theology, Jurisprudence and Constitutional Theory*. New York: Scribner's Sons, 1903.

Madani, Muhammad Asrar. *Verdict of Islamic Law on Blasphemy and Apostasy*. Lahore: Idara-e-Islamiat, 1994.

Mahmood, Shaukat. *The Pakistan Penal Code (XLV of 1860)*. 3rd ed. Vol. 1. Lahore: Legal Research Centre, 1981.

Malik, Iftikhar H. *Religious Minorities in Pakistan*. London: Minority Rights Group International, 2002.

Malik, Jamal. "Ahrar Movement." In *Encyclopaedia of Islam*, 3rd ed., edited by Kate Fleet, Gudrun Kramer, Denis Matringe, John Nawas and Everett Rowson. Brill Online, accessed 4 December 2012, http://referenceworks.brilonline.com/entries/encyclopedia-of-islam-3ahrar-movement-COM_23398.

———., ed. *Perspectives of Mutual Encounters in South Asian History 1760–1860*. Leiden; Boston: Brill, 2000.

Malik, Maleiha. "Angare, the 'Burning Embers' of Muslim Political Resistance: Colonial and Post-Colonial Regulation of Islam in Britain." In *Colonial and Post-Colonial Governance of Islam: Continuities and Ruptures*, edited by Marcel Maussen, Veit Bader and Annelies Moors, 199–210. Amsterdam: Amsterdam University Press, 2011.

Mani, Emanuel Yousaf. *Human Rights Monitor 98: A report on Religious Minorities in Pakistan*. Lahore: National Commission of Justice and Peace, 1999.

———. *Human Rights Monitor 2006: A Report on the Religious Minorities in Pakistan*. Lahore: National Commission of Justice and Peace, 2006.

Marghinani, Ali ibn Abi Bakr. *The Hedaya, or Guide: A Commentary on the Mussulman Laws*. Vol. 1. Translated by Charles Hamilton. Lahore: Premier Book House, 1975.

Marshall, Paul A. and Nina Shea. *Silenced: How Apostasy and Blasphemy Codes are Choking Freedom Worldwide*. Oxford: Oxford University Press, 2011.

Masud, Muhammad Khalid. "The World of Shah Abd al Aziz (1746–1824)." In *Perspectives of Mutual Encounters in South Asian History 1760–1860*, edited by Jamal Malik, 298–314. Leiden; Boston: Brill, 2000.

Maududi, Abul A'la. *Human Rights in Islam*. 2nd ed. Leicester: Islamic Foundation, 1980.

———. *The Islamic Law and Constitution*. 7th ed. Translated by Khurshid Ahmad. Lahore: Islamic Publications, 1980.

Maussen, Marcel, Veit Bader, and Annelies Moors. *Colonial and Post-Colonial Governance of Islam: Continuities and Ruptures*. Amsterdam: Amsterdam University Press, 2011.

Mayne, John D. Commentaries on the Indian Penal Code (Act XLV of 1860). 7th ed. Madras: Higginbotham, 1872.

McChesney, R. D. *Waqf in Central Asia: Four Hundred Years in the History of a Muslim Shrine, 1480-1889*. Princeton: Princeton University Press, 1991.

Mehdi, Rubya. *The Islamization of the Law in Pakistan*. Richmond: Curzon, 1994.

Meri, Joseph W. "Ritual and the Quran." In *Encyclopaedia of the Quran*, edited by Jane Dammen McAuliffe. Brill Online, accessed 12 November 2012, http://dx.doi.org/10.1163/1875-3922_q3_EQCOM_00177.

Metcalf, Barbara D. *Islamic Revival in British India: Deoband, 1860-1900*. New Delhi: Oxford University Press, 2002

Mill, John Stuart. *Utilitarianism: Liberty and Representative Government*. London: Dent, 1909.

Mitchell, John. *An Essay of the Best Means of Civilising the Subjects of the British Empire in India*. Edinburgh: Blackwood, 1805.

Mitchwoch, E. "Ida al-Adha." In *Encyclopaedia of Islam*, 2nd ed., edited by P. Bearman, Th. Bianquis, C. E. Bosworth, E. van Donzel and W. P. Heinrichs. Brill Online, 2010, http://dx.doi.org/10.1163/1573-3912_islam_SIM_3472.

Minault, Gail. "Women, Legal Reform and Muslim Identity." In *Islam, Communities and the Nation: Muslim Identities in South Asia and Beyond*, edited by Mushirul Hasan, 139–158. Delhi: Manohar, 1998.

Morgan, William and A. G. Macpherson. *The Indian Penal Code: Act XLV of 1860*. Calcutta: G. C. Hay, 1861.

Mughal, Aftab Alexander. *Death or Exile: The Story of Salamat Masih's Case*. Multan: National Commission of Justice and Peace, 1995.

Muir, William. *The Mohammedan Controversy: Biographies of Mohammed, Sprenger on Tradition, the Indian Liturgy, and the Psalter*. Edinburgh: T & T Clark, 1897.

Musk, Bill. *Passionate Believing*. Tunbridge Wells: Monarch, 1992.

Murshid, Tazeen M. *The Sacred and the Secular: Bengal Muslim Discourses, 1871-1971*. Calcutta: Oxford University Press, 1995.

Nasr, Sayyed Vali Reza. *Islamic Leviathan: Islam and the Making of State Power*. Oxford: Oxford University Press, 2001.

———. *Mawdudi and the Making of Islamic Revivalism*. New York: Oxford University Press, 1996.

Needham, Anuradha Dingwaney and Rajeswari Sunder Rajan, eds. *The Crisis of Secularism in India*. Durham, NC: Duke University Press, 2007.

Neill, Stephen. *A History of Christianity in India: The Beginnings to AD 1707*. Cambridge: Cambridge University Press, 1984.

Nelson, R. A. *The Pakistan Penal Code: With Commentary*. Vol. 3. Lahore: Law Publishing Company, 1975.

———. *The Indian Penal Code*. Vol. 2. Lahore: Law Publication, 1970.

Newberg, Paula R. *Judging the State: Courts and Constitutional Politics in Pakistan*. New York: Cambridge University Press, 1995.

Nijjar, B. S. *The History of the United Punjab*. Delhi: Atlantic, 1996.
Nizami, M. H. *The Pakistan Penal Code: XLV of 1860*. 5th ed. Lahore: All Pakistan Legal Decisions, 1963.
———. *Supplement to Commentary on the Pakistan Penal Code*. Karachi: Law Book House, 1954.
Normandy, Frank. *A Dictionary and Manual of the Criminal Law*. Madras: Lawrence Asylum Press, 1883.
O'Kinealy, J. *The Indian Penal Code and Other Laws Relating to the Criminal Courts of India*. Calcutta: S. K. Lahiri, 1900.
Pandey, Gyanendra. "The Colonial Construction of Communalism." In *Writings on South Asian History*, Subaltern Studies vol. 6, edited by Ranajit Guha, 132–169. Delhi: Oxford University Press, 1994.
Patel, Geeta. *Lyrical Movements, Historical Hauntings: On Gender, Colonialism, and Desire in Miraji's Urdu Poetry*. Stanford, CA: Stanford University Press, 2002.
Peters, Rudolph. *Crime and Punishment in Islamic Law: Theory and Practice From the Sixteenth to the Twenty-First Century*. Cambridge: Cambridge University Press, 2005.
Pfander, Carl Gottlieb. *The Mizan ul-Haqq: Or Balance of Truth*. London: Church Missionary House, 1866.
Phillips, Henry Arthur Deuteros. *Comparative Criminal Jurisprudence*. Calcutta: Thacker, Spink & Co., 1889.
Pirzada, S. Sharifuddin. *Fundamental Rights and Constitutional Remedies in Pakistan*. Lahore: All Pakistan Legal Decisions, 1966.
Pogson, R. H. "Revival and Refrom in Mary Tudor's Church: A Question of Money." In *The English Reformation Revised*, edited by Christopher Haigh, 139–156. Cambridge: Cambridge University Press, 1987.
Powell, Avril Ann. *Muslims and Missionaries in Pre-Mutiny India*. London: Routledge, 2003.
———. "New Focus on Islam: The Reverend Carl Pfander and the *Mizan Al-Haqq*." In *Muslims and Missionaries in Pre-Mutiny India*. London: Routledge, 2003.
Prakash, Gyan. *After Colonialism: Imperial Histories and Postcolonial Displacements*. Princeton, NJ: Princeton University Press, 1995.
Pratt, Douglas. *The Challenge of Islam: Encounters in Interfaith Dialogue*. Aldershot: Ashgate, 2005.
Qureshi, Muhammad Ismail. *Judgment of Yousaf Kasab Blasphemy Case*. Lahore: Al-Maarif, 2000.
———. *Muhammad: The Messenger of God and the Law of Blasphemy in Islam and the West*. Lahore: Nuqoosh, 2008.

———. *Namoos-e-Rasalat aur Qanoon-e-Toheen-e-Rasalat.* 2nd ed. Lahore: Nashran-o-Tajran Kutub, 1999.

Rahi, Ramnit Lall. *The Invisibles: The Plight of Christians in Pakistan.* Essex: SPS Communication, 2000.

Ranchhoddas, Ratanlal and Dhirajlal Keshavlal Thakor. *The Indian Penal Code.* 20th ed. Bombay: Bombay Law Reporter Office, 1951.

Rashid, Khalid Asi, ed. *A Peaceful Struggle: A Collection of Bishop John Joseph's Writings against Black Laws and Discrimination.* Faisalabad: National Commission of Justice and Peace, 1999.

Rehman, Ata-ur. *Souls on Fire: A Collection of Articles and Editorials Published in Newspapers and Magazines on Gujra Incident.* Lahore: National Commission for Justice and Peace, 2009.

Riaz, Ali. *Faithful Education: Madrassahs in South Asia.* New Brunswick: Rutgers University Press, 2008.

———. *God Willing: The Politics of Islamism in Bangladesh.* Lanham: Rowman & Littlefield, 2004.

Rooney, John. *On Heels of Battles: A History of Catholic Church in Pakistan 1780-1886.* Rawalpindi: Christian Study Centre, 1986.

———. *Shadows in the Dark: A History of Christianity in Pakistan up to Tenth Century.* Rawalpindi: Christian Study Centre, 1984.

Saeed, Sadia. "Political Fields and Religious Movements: The Exclusion of the Ahmaddiyya Community in Pakistan." In *Political Power and Social Theory*, vol. 23, edited by Julian Go, 189–223. Bingley, UK: Emerald Group, 2012.

———. "Politics of Exclusion: Muslim Nationalism, State Formation and Legal Representations of the Ahmadiyya Community in Pakistan." PhD Thesis, University of Michigan, 2010.

Saeed, Abdullah and Hassan Saeed. *Freedom of Religion, Apostasy and Islam.* Aldershot: Ashgate, 2004.

Saiyid, M. H. *Mohammad Ali Jinnah (A Political Study).* 2nd ed. Lahore: Shaikh Mohammad Ashraf, 1953.

Saldanha, Julian. *Conversion and Indian Civil Law.* Bangalore; Theological Publications in India, 1981.

Sarkar, Sumit. "Christian Conversions, Hundutva, and Secularism." In *The Crisis of Secularism in India*, edited by Anuradha Dingwaney Needham and Rajeswari Sunder Rajan, 356–367. Durham, NC: Duke University Press, 2007.

Saxena, N. C. "The Nature and Origin of Communal Riots in India." In *Communal Riots in Post-Independence India*, 2nd ed., edited by Asghar Ali Engineer, 51–67. Hyderabad: Sangam Books, 1991.

Schacht, Joseph. *An Introduction to Islamic Law.* Oxford: Clarendon, 1982.

Schofield, Victoria. *Old Roads, New Highways: Fifty Years of Pakistan*. Karachi: Oxford University Press, 1997.

Seale, Morris S. *Muslim Theology: A Study of Origins with Reference to the Church Fathers*. London: Luzac, 1964.

Siam-Heng, Michael Heng and Ten Chin Liew, eds. *The State and Secularism: Perspective from Asia*. Singapore: World Scientific Publication, 2010.

Simpson, Rick. *Blasphemy and the Law in a Plural Society*. Grove Ethical Studies, no. 90. Cambridge: Grove Books, 1993.

Smith, Donald Eugene, ed. *South Asian Politics and Religion*. Princeton, NJ: Princeton University Press, 1966.

Smith, K. J. M. "Macaulay's 'Utilitarian' Indian Penal Code: An Illustration of the Accidental Function of Time, Place and Personalities in Law Making." In *Legal History in the Making*, edited by W. M. Gordon and T. D. Fergus, 145–164. London: Hambledon, 1991.

Smith, Wilfred Cantwell. *Modern Islam in India: A Social Analysis*. Lahore: Minerva Book Shop, 1943.

Stackhouse, Max L. and Don S. Browning, eds. *God and Globalization: The Spirit and the Modern Authorities*. Vol. 2. Harrisburg, PA: Trinity Press International, 2001.

Stanley, Brian. *The Bible and the Flag: Protestant Missions and British Imperialism in the 19th and 20th Centuries*. Leicester: Apollos, 1990.

Stanley, Brian and Alaine Low, eds. *Missions, Nationalism and the End of Empire*. Cambridge: Eerdmans, 2003.

Starling, Matthew Henry. *Indian Criminal Law and Procedure: With an Appendix of Selected Acts Passed by the Legislative Council, Relating to Criminal Matters*. London: W. H. Allen, 1869.

Stock, Frederick and Margaret Stock. *People Movements in the Punjab*. Bombay: Gospel Literature Service, 1978.

Stokes, Eric. *The English Utilitarians and India*. Oxford: Clarendon, 1959.

Streefland, Pieter. *The Sweepers of Slaughterhouse: Conflict and Survival in a Karachi Neighbourhood*. Assen: Van Gorcum, 1979.

Sookhdeo, Patrick. *Freedom to Believe: Challenging Islam's Apostasy Law*. McLean, VA: Isaac, 2009.

———. *A People Betrayed: The Impact of Islamization on the Christian Community in Pakistan*. Fearn: Christian Focus, 2002.

Swinhoe, Charlton. *The Case-Noted Penal Code: The Indian Penal Code (Act XLV of 1860 as Amended)*. Calcutta: Thacker, Spink and Co, 1909.

Taylor, H. F. Lechmere. *In the Land of the Five Rivers: A Sketch of the Work of the Church of Scotland in the Punjab*. Edinburgh: R. & R. Clark, 1906.

Tharu, Susie, and K. Lalita, eds. *Women Writing in India: 600 BC to the Present*. Vol. 1. London: Rivers Oram Press, 1993.

Thursby, G. R., ed. *Hindu-Muslim Relations in British India: A Study of Controversy, Conflict, and Communal Movement in Northern India 1923-1928.* Leiden: Brill, 1975.

Turner, J. W. Cecil. *Russell on Crime.* Vol. 2. London: Stevens, 1964.

Uddin, Sufia M. *Constructing Bangladesh: Religion, Ethnicity, and Language in an Islamic Nation.* Delhi: Vistaar, 2006.

Usmani, Mufti Taqi, and Moulana Sami-ul-Haq. *Qadianism on Trial: The Case of the Muslim Ummah against Qadianis Presented before the National Assembly of Pakistan.* Karachi: Idaratul-Ma'arif, 2005.

Viswanathan, Gauri. "Coping with Death: The Christian Convert's Rights of Passage in Colonial India." In *After Colonialism: Imperial Histories and Postcolonial Displacements,* edited by Gyan Prakash, 183–210. Princeton, NJ: Princeton University Press, 1995.

———. *Outside the Fold: Conversion, Modernity, and Belief.* Princeton, NJ: Princeton University Press, 1998.

Walbridge, Linda S. *The Christians of Pakistan: The Passion of John Joseph.* London: Routledge, 2003.

Walter, Nicolas. *Blasphemy in Britain: The Practice and Punishment of Blasphemy, and the Trial of Gay News.* London: Rationalist Press Association, 1977.

Watt, W. M. *Islamic Political Thought.* Edinburgh: Edinburgh University Press, 2003.

Webb, R. K. "From Toleration to Religious Liberty." In *Liberty Secured? Britain Before and After 1688,* edited by J. R. Jones, 158–198. Stanford: Stanford University Press, 1992.

Webster, John C. B. *The Dalit Christians: A History.* Delhi: ISPCK, 1992.

Weitbrecht, Mary. *The Women of India and Christian Work in The Zenana.* London: James Nisbet, 1875.

Weinstein, James, and Ivan Hare, eds. *Extreme Speech and Democracy.* Oxford: Oxford University Press, 2010.

Wensinck, Arent Jan. *The Muslim Creed: Its Genesis and Historical Development.* London: Frank Cass, 1965.

Werff, Lyle Vander. *Christian Mission to Muslims, the Record: Anglican and Reformed Approaches in India and the Near East, 1800-1938.* Pasadena, CA: William Carey Library, 1977.

Wilson, H. S., and J. Paul Rajashekar. *Islam in Asia: Perspectives for Christian–Muslim Encounter.* Geneva: Lutheran World Federation, 1992.

Winks, Robin W., and Alaine M. Low, eds. *The Oxford History of the British Empire: Historiography.* Vol 3. Oxford: Oxford University Press, 2001.

Witte, John, Jr. "The Spirit of the Laws, the Laws of the Spirit: Religion and Human Rights in a New Global Era." In *God and Globalization: The Spirit and Modern Authorities*, vol. 2, edited by Max L. Stackhouse and Don S. Browning, 76–106. Harrisburg, PA: Trinity Press, 2001.

Wright, Barry. "Macaulay's Indian Penal Code: Historical Context and Originating Principles." In *Codification, Macaulay and the Indian Penal Code: The Legacies and Modern Challenges of Criminal Law Reform*, edited by, Wing-Cheong Chan, Barry Wright, and Stanley Yeo, 19–56. Surrey: Ashgate, 2011.

Youngson, John F. W. *Forty Years of the Punjab Mission of the Church of Scotland 1855-1895*. Edinburgh: R. & R. Clark, 1896.

Zaheer, Hasan. *The Separation of East Pakistan: The Rise and Realization of Bengali Muslim Nationalism*. Oxford: Oxford University Press, 1994.

Zaman, Muhammad Qasim. *The Ulama in Contemporary Islam: Custodians of Change*. Princeton, NJ: Princeton University Press, 2002.

Journals, News articles and Reports

Abbot, Freeland. "The Jama'at-i-Islami of Pakistan." *The Middle East Journal* 11, no. 1 (Winter 1957): 37–51.

Ahmad, Gulmina Bilal. "A New Order?" *Daily Times*, Pakistan, 7 December 2012, https://dailytimes.com.pk/104916/a-new-order/.

Ahmad, Imtiaz. "The Ashraf-Ajlaf Dictionary in Muslim Social Structure in India." *Indian Economic and Social History Review* 3 (1966): 268–278.

Ahmad, Mumtaz. "The Crescent and the Sword: Islam, the Military, and Political Legitimacy in Pakistan: 1977-1985." *The Middle East Journal* 50, no. 3 (Summer 1996): 327–386.

Ahmed, Akbar S. "Pakistan's Blasphemy Law: Words Fail Me." *The Washington Post*, 19 May 2002. Available, https://www.washingtonpost.com/archive/opinions/2002/05/19/pakistans-blasphemy-law-words-fail-me/c1cd08f4-b34d-442b-a1ad-73ec1815a2be/?noredirect=on&utm_term=.f7b309cbfeec.

Ahmed, Issam. "Could There be a Liberal Resurgence in Pakistan?" 28 January 2011, https://www.csmonitor.com/World/Asia-South-Central/2011/0128/Could-there-be-a-liberal-resurgence-in-Pakistan-Lawmaker-Sherry-Rehman-says-she-s-working-on-it.

Alam, Muhammad Badar. "After the Fires Burnt Out." *The Herald*, September 2009.

Ali, Ahmad, and N. M. Rashed. "The Progressive Writers' Movement in its Historical Perspective." *Journal of South Asian Literature* 13, no. 1/4 (1977–1978): 91–97.

Ali, Syed Mohammad. "Repeal Discriminatory Legislation." *Daily Times*, 11 August 2009.

American Centre for Law and Justice. "'Religious Freedom Acts': Anti-Conversion Laws in India." 26 June 2009, available at http://media.aclj.org/pdf/freedom_of_religion_acts.pdf.

Amjad-Ali, Charles. "Islamisation and Christian-Muslim Relations in Pakistan." *Al-Mushir* 29, no. 3 (1987): 71–79.

Amnesty International. "Country Report: Pakistan." 2007, available at http://www.refworld.org/docid/46558edb25.html.

———. "Pakistan: Blasphemy Acquittal Welcome but Law Must be Amended." 16 August 2002, AI Index: 33/026/2002.

———. "Pakistan: Insufficient Protection of Religious Minorities." 1 May 2001, Al Index: 33/008/2001.

———. "Pakistan: The Death Penalty." September 1996, AI Index: ASA 33/10/96.

———. "Pakistan: Use and Abuse of the Blasphemy Law." 26 July 1994, Al Index: ASA 33/08/94.

———. "Pakistani Woman Sentenced to Death." 18 November 2010, AI Index: ASA 33/011/2010.

Anant, Aripta. "Anti-Conversion Laws." *The Hindu*, 17 December 2002. Available at http://www.hinduonnet.com/thehindu/op/2002/12/17/stories/2002121700110200.htm.

Bauman, Chad M. "Postcolonial Anxiety and Anti-Conversion Sentiment in the Report of the 'Christian Missionary Activities Enquiry Committee.'" *International Journal of Hindu Studies* 12, no. 2 (2008): 181–213.

Brown, Kevin Smullin. "Reforming England's Blasphemy Law to Protect the Individual." *Islam and Christian-Muslim Relations* 14, no. 2 (2003): 188–203.

"Changing Name of Rabwah." *The Persecution of Ahmadis*, 31 December 2010, http://www.persecutionofahmadis.org/change-of-name-of-rabwah/.

"Chilling Act." *Dawn*, 5 December 2012, https://www.dawn.com/news/768976.

"Christian's Homes Burnt Over Desecration." *Dawn*, 1 August 2009. Available at, https://www.dawn.com/news/964049.

Coppola, Carlo and Sajida Zubair. "Rashid Jahan: Urdu Literature's First 'Angry Young Woman.'" *Journal of South Asian Literature* 22, no. 1 (Winter, Spring 1987): 166–183.

Evans, Stephen. "Macaulay's Minute Revisited: Colonial Language Policy in Nineteenth-Century India." *Journal of Multilingual and Multicultural Development* 23, no. 4 (2002): 260–281.

Forte, David F. "Apostasy and Blasphemy in Pakistan." *Connecticut Journal of International Law* 10, no.1 (Fall 1994): 27–68.

Goodall, Kay. "Incitement to Religious Hatred, All Talk and No Substance?" *Modern Law Review* 70, no. 1 (2007): 89–113.

Government of India, Law Commission of India. "Report on Conversion/Reconversion to Another Religion – Mode of Proof." Report no. 235, December 2010, available online http://lawcommissionofindia.nic.in/reports/report235.pdf.

Gregory, Shaun. "Under the Shadow of Islam: The Plight of the Christian Minority in Pakistan." *Contemporary South Asia* 20, no. 2 (2012): 195–212.

Hasan, Mahmudul. "Free Speech, Ban and 'Fatwa': A Study of Taslima Nasrin Affair." *Journal of Post-Colonial Writing* 46, no. 5 (December 2010): 540–552.

Hashmi, Arshi Saleem. "Bangladesh Ban on Religious-Based Politics: Reviving the Secular Character of the Constitution." *Spotlight on Regional Affairs*, Electronic Journal (12 February 2011). Available at http://www.ssrn.com.

Human Rights Commission of Pakistan. "State of Human Rights in 1998." Lahore, Pakistan, 1999.

Husain, Zahid and Tom Wright. "Pakistan Killer Had Revealed Plans." *The Wall Street Journal*, 5 January 2011. Available at https://www.wsj.com/articles/SB10001424052748703675904576063581434623072.

Hussain, Zahid. "Eight Christians Mercilessly Burn to Death in Pakistan." *The Times*, 3 August 2009.

Huff, James Andrew. "Religious Freedom in India and Analysis of the Constitutionality of Anti-Conversion Laws." *Rutgers Journal of Law & Religion* 10, no. 2 (2009): 1–36. Available at https://lawandreligion.com/sites/law-religion/files/Religious-Freedom-Huff.pdf.

"Innuendo." *Burton's Legal Thesaurus, 4E* (2007), accessed 26 March 2013, http://legal-dictionary.thefreedictionary.com/Innuendo.

"Insinuation." *A Law Dictionary, Adapted to the Constitution and Laws of the United States*, John Bouvier (1856), accessed 26 March 2013, http://legal-dictionary.thefreedictionary.com/Insinuation.

Islam, Shamsul. "Police Removed Quranic Verses from Ahmadi Graves to 'Avert Clashes.'" *The Tribune Express*, 18 August 2012, available, https://tribune.com.pk/story/423802/police-remove-quranic-verses-from-ahmadi-graves-to-avert-clashes/.

Jalal, Ayesha. "Conjuring Pakistan: History as Official Imagining." *International Journal of Middle East Studies* 27, no. 1 (1995): 73–89.

Jenkins, Laura Dudley. "Legal Limits on Religious Conversion in India," *Law & Contemporary Problems* 71, no. 2 (Spring 2008): 109–127.

Jeremy, Anthony. "Practical Implications of the Racial and Religious Hatred Act 2006." *The Ecclesiastical Law Society* 9, no. 2 (2007): 187–201.

Jilani, Annes. "Blasphemy Law and the Minorities." *The News*, 14 May 1998.

Kabir, Shahriar. "Multidimensional Communal Repression and Proposed Blasphemy Law." 6 February 2010, http://www.secularvoiceofbangladesh.org.

Kennedy, Charles H. "Repugnancy to Islam: Who Decides? Islam and Legal Reform in Pakistan." *The International and Comparative Law Quarterly* 41, no. 4 (October, 1992): 769–787.

Khan, Azam. "Blasphemy Petition Against Sherry Rehman Accepted." *The Express Tribune*, 18 January 2013.

Khan, Rabzon. "Fear and Shame of Gojra." *Daily Times*, 3 August 2009.

Lahore High Court. *Report of the Court of Inquiry Constituted under Punjab Act II of 1954 to Enquire into the Punjab Disturbances of 1953*. Lahore: Government Prinitng, Punjab, 1954. Available online, http://www.thepersecution.org/dl/report_1953.pdf.

Larkin, Barbara, ed. *Annual Report on International Religious Freedom 2000*. Washington: US Governing Printing office, 2000.

Leader-Elliott, Ian D. "Macaulay's Penal Code, Adam Smith and the Jurisprudence of Resentment." Working paper (January 2012), available at: http://www.works.bepress.com/ian_leader-elliott1/1.

Madan, T. N. "Secularism in Its Place." *Journal of Asian Studies* 46, no. 4 (1987): 747–759.

Mahmud, Shabana. "Angāre and the Founding of the Progressive Writers' Association." *Modern Asian Studies* 30, no. 2 (1996): 447–467.

Malik, Iftikhar H. "The State and Civil Society in Pakistan: From Crisis to Crisis." *Asian Survey* 36, no. 7 (July 1996): 673–690.

Malik, Saira. "The Social Transformation of the 'Ulama' in British India during the 19th Century." *Journal of Islamic Law and Culture* 12, no. 1 (2010): 54–57.

Mann, Michael. "Turbulent Delhi: Religious Strife, Social Tension and Political Conflicts, 1803–1857." *Journal of South Asian Studies* 28, no. 1 (2005): 5–34.

"Mumtaz Qadri Charged with Salman Taseer Murder." *BBC News*, 14 February 2011. Available, http://www.bbc.co.uk/news/world-south-asia-12445519.

Munir, Mohammad and M. R. Kayani. *Report of the Court Inquiry Constituted under Punjab Act 11 of 1954 to Enquire into the Punjab Disturbances of 1953*. Lahore: Government Print, Punjab, 1954.

Narula, Smita. "Overlooked Danger: The Security and Rights Implications of Hindu Nationalism in India." *Harvard Human Rights Journal* 16 (Spring 2003): 41–68.

Nasr, S. V. R. "The Rise of Sunni Militancy in Pakistan: The Changing Role of Islamism and the Ulama in Society and Politics." *Modern Asian Studies* 34, no. 1 (January 2000): 139–180.

National Commission for Justice and Peace. *Human Rights Monitor 2008: A Report on the Religious Minorities in Pakistan*. Lahore: NCJP, 2008.

———. "News Letter of National Commission for Peace and Justice." *The Mirror* 13, no. 1 (January-March 2010).

Niazi, M. A. "Blasphemy Case Shakes the Nation." 3 December 2010, https://nation.com.pk/03-Dec-2010/blasphemy-case-shakes-the-nation.

"No Evidence Against Pakistan 'Blasphemy Girl,'" *BBC News Asia*, posted on 22 September 2012, https://www.bbc.co.uk/news/world-asia-19686941.

Oommen, George. "The Emerging Dalit Theology: A Historical Appraisal." *Indian Church History Review* 34, no. 1 (June 2000): 19–37.

"Outlawed Terrorists in Gorja." Editorial in *Daily Times*, 4 August 2009.

Raman, Kartik Kalyan. "Utilitarianism and the Criminal Law in Colonial India: A Study of the Practical Limits of Utilitarian Jurisprudence." *Modern Asian Studies* 28, no. 4 (October 1994) 739–791.

Ranveer, Rana. "Asma Targeted in Ahmadi Hate Campaign." *The Express Tribune*, 27 October 2010.

Rehman, I. R. "The Flaw of the Law of Blasphemy." *Newsline*, June 1998.

———. "Jumping the Gun: Award of Death Penalty Without Establishing Intent Contradicts the Federal Shariat Court Ruling." *Newsline*. June 1998.

Rehman, Sherry. "Amendments to the Blasphemy Laws Act 2010." 30 November 2010. Available at https://www.jinnah-institute.org/images/amendments%20to%20the%20blasphemy%20laws%20act%202010.pdf.

———. "Blasphemy Law Needs Rectification." *The News*, 17 December 2010. Available online, https://www.thenews.com.pk/archive/print/275164-blasphemy-law-needs-rectification-sherry.

———. "Gorja and Pakistan's Identity." 13 August 2009, http://sherryrehman.com/gojra-and-pakistans-identity/.

Rizvi, Muddassir. "Pakistan: Abuse of Blasphemy Law." *The Manila Times*, 20 November 2013.

Pirzada, Syed Sharifuddin. "Quaid-i-Azam Mohammad Ali Jinnah as a Lawyer." *Pakistan Journal of History & Culture* 28, no. 1 (2007) 7–21.

"Pope Pleads for Life of Condemned Pakistani Woman." *BBC News*, 17 November 2018. https://www.bbc.co.uk/news/world-south-asia-11777482.

"Profile: Pakistan's New US Envoy Sherry Rehman." *BBC News*, 23 November, 2011, https://www.bbc.co.uk/news/world-asia-15858462.

"Salman Taseer: Thousands Mourn Pakistan Governor." *BBC News*, 5 January 2011. https://www.bbc.co.uk/news/world-south-asia-12116764.

Sen, Ashish Kumar. "Pakistani Government Official Murdered for Criticism of Islamic Blasphemy Law." *Student News Daily*, 4 March 2011, https://www.studentnewsdaily.com/daily-news-article/pakistan-government-official-murdered-for-criticism-of-islam-blasphemy-law/.

Shea, Nina. "Pakistan's Anti-Blasphemy Laws." 8 October 2009, Hudson Institute. Available at, https://www.hudson.org/content/researchattachments/attachment/748/sheapakistan108.pdf.

Shekh, Younas. "Blasphemy: My Journey." http://www.muktomona.com/Articles/Younus_Sheikh/blasphemy.

Siddique, Osama and Zahra Hayat. "Unholy Speech and Holy Laws: Blasphemy in Pakistan – Controversial Origins, Design Defects, and Free Speech Implications." *Minnesota Journal of International Law* 17, no. 2 (2008): 303–385.

Sobhan, Rehman. "Growth and Contradictions within the Bangladesh Bourgeoisie." *Journal of Social Studies* 9 (July 1980): 1–27.

Toffolo, Cris E., and Charles Amjad-Ali. "Christians in Pakistan Confront Charges of Blasphemy." *The Christian Century* 115, no. 21 (July 1998). Available online, https://www.christiancentury.org/article/2012-04/christians-pakistan-confront-charges-blasphemy.

"Ulama Council Chief Demanded Bail for Rimsha." *The Express Tribune*, 4 September 2012.

United States Department of State, Bureau of Democracy, Human Rights and Labour. *International Religious Freedom Report for 2011*. Available at http://www.state.gov/documents/organization/193145.pdf.

Upadhyaya, Prakash Chandra. "The Politics of Indian Secularism." *Modern Asian Studies* 26, no. 4 (October 1992): 815–853.

Usmani, Faizman. "Blasphemy Law: To Repeal or Not to Repeal?" Posted on 2 December 2010.

"Violence Brings Pakistan's Women Advocates to Aid Religious Minorities." *Women News Network*, 19 August 2011. Available at, https://womennewsnetwork.net/2011/08/19/violence-pakistans-women-religious-minorities/.

Wiederhold, L. "Blasphemy against the Prophet Muhammad and his Companions (*sabb al-rasul, sabb al-sahabah*): The Introduction of the Topic into Shaf'i Legal Literature and Its Relevance for Legal Practice under Mamluk Rule." *Semitic Studies* 42, no. 1 (March 1997): 39–70.

Zafar, Emmanuel, ed. "The Minorities View." *Hamsookhan* 7, no. 9 (September 2009).

Zafar, Muhammad Imtiaz. "Can Pakistan be a Secular State?" *Research Journal of South Asian Studies* 28, no. 1 (January–June 2013): 165–185.

Primary Legal Cases of British India

Abdul Kader v. Abdul Kasim, AIR (1932) Calcutta 459.
Bechan Jha v. Emperor, AIR (1941) Patna, 492.
Burhon Shah v. Emperor, (1887) P. R. N0. 26.

Devi Sharan Sharma and another v. Emperor, AIR (1927) Lahore 594.
Dhalu Ram v. Emperor, 10 Cr. LJ 445 (1909).
Imam Ali and others v. Queen Empress, (1887) ILR Allahabad, 152.
Illam Din v. Emperor, AIR (1930) Lahore, 157.
Jailal Jha v. King Emperor, ILR 256 (1925) Patna 537.
Jan Muhammad v. Narain Das, (1883) AWN 39.
Jhulan Sain v. Emperor, 40 C. 538=18 I. C. 677.
Kali Charan Sharma v. King Emperor, AIR (1927) Allahabad, 654.
Kolimi Mahabub v. Sri Sidheswaraswami, AIR (1945) Madras 496.
Khoja Muhammad Hamid Khan v. Emperor, (1881) ILR 3 Madras 178.
Maqsood Hussan v. Emperor, AIR (1940) Patna 4141.
Mangat v. Emperor, AIR (1919) Lahore 433.
Masit v. Emperor, (1912) ILR 34 Allahabad 78.
Mir Chittan v. Emperor, AIR (1937) Allahabad 13.
Moti Lal v. Emperor, (1901) ILR 24 Allahabad 155.
Muhammad Hussain v. Emperor, AIR (1919) Allahabad 188.
Muhammad Jalil Khan v. Ram Nath Katua, AIR (1931) Allahabad 341.
Queen Empress v. Ramazan, (1885) ILR 7 Allahabad 461.
Queen Empress v. Rehman, (1893) 13 AWN 144.
Queen v. Subhan, (1896) ILR Allahabad 395-6.
Ratna Mudali, ILR (Indian Law Reports) 10 Madras 26.
Ram Prasad and others v. Emperor, (1911) ILR 33 Allahabad 773.
Rajpal v. Emperor, AIR (1927) Lahore 590.
Peary Lal v. State, AIR (1917) Allahabad 317.
Shive Sharma v. Emperor, AIR (1941) Oudh 310.
Sheo Shankar v. Emperor, AIR (1940) Oudh 348.
Shiv Ram Das Udasin v. Punjab State, AIR (1955).
The Public Prosecutor v. Sunuku Seethiah, (1911) ILR 34 Madras 92.
Umer Din v. Emperor, AIR (1915) Lahore 409.
Vijairaghava Chariar v. Emperor, (1903) ILR 26 Madras 554.

Post-Colonial Legal Cases of India
A. I. R. Allahabad, (1960), 718.
Baba Khalil Ahamad v. The State of UP, AIR (1960) All 715; (1960) Cr. LJ 1528.
Ramji Lal Modi v. The State of UP, AIR (1957) SC 623.
Sant Das Maheswari v. Babu Ram Jodoun, AIR (1969) Allahabad 436.
Shiv Ram Das v. The Punjab State, AIR (1955) 28.
Siva Ram Das v. The State of Punjab, AIR (1955) Punjab 28.
Veerabadran Chettiar v. E. V. Rama Swami Naiker, AIR (1958) SC 1032.

Post-Colonial Legal Cases of Pakistan (1947–1979)
Abdul Karim v. The State, PLD (1963) Karachi 669.
Abdur Rahman Mobashir v. Amir Ali Shah, PLD (1978) Lahore 133
"Jesus in Heaven on Earth" and in the matter of Woking Muslim Mission and Literary Trust, Lahore and of the Civil and Military Gazette, Limited, Lahore v. The Crown, PLD (1954) Lahore 724.
Major General Fazal-i-Raziq, Chairman WAPDA v. Ch. Riaz Ahmad, PLD (1978) Lahore 1082.
Muhammad Khalil v. The State, PLD (1962, West Pakistan) Lahore 850.
Noor Muhammad v. Fiaz Ahmad, PLD (1960, West Pakistan) Lahore 567.
Okil Ali v. Behari Lal Paul, PLD (1962) Dacca 487.
Public Prosecutor v. P. Ramaswami, AIR (1964) Madras 258. Available online, https://indiankanoon.org/doc/764762/.
Qaisar Raza v. The State, (1979) P. Cr. LJ 758 (Khairpur, Sindh).
Shafiqur-Rehman v. The State, (1976) P. Cr. LJ (Pakistan Criminal Journal) 1456 Lahore.
The Punjab Religious Book Society v. The State, PLD (1960, West Pakistan) Lahore 629.
Taj Muhammad and others v. The State, PLD (1971) Peshawar 162.

Cases from 1980s of Pakistan
Ayub Masih v. The State, PLD (2002) Supreme Court 1048.
Muhammad Ismail Qureshi v. Pakistan through the Secretary of Law and Parliamentary Affairs, PLD (1991), FSC 10.
Muhammad Mahboob v. The State, (2002) 54 PLD, SC 587, 16 (Pakistan).
Mujibur Rehman v. Federal Government of Pakistan, PLD (1985) FSC 8.
Muzaffar Iqbal v. The State, (1993) P. Cr. LJ 1993.
Riaz Ahmad v. The State, PLD (1994) Lahore 504.
Salamat Masih v. The State, (1995) 28 P. Cr. LJ 813 (Lahore).
Syed Ijaz Husain Alias Tahir Pir v. The State, (1994) MLD 15 Lahore.
Ubaid Ulla v. The State, (1991) SCMR 1734.

Newspapers
Catholic Herald, UK
Dawn, Karachi
Jang, Rawalpindi
Nawa-e-Waqt, Lahore
The Express Tribune, Pakistan
The Manila Times, Philippine
The Muslim, Islamabad
The New York Times, New York

The Pakistan Times, Lahore
The Times, London

Web Search
http://www.amnesty.org.uk
http://www.bbc.co.uk/news/world-south-asia
http://www.brillonline.nl
http://www.indiankanoon.org
http://www.jinnah-institute.org
http://wwwjournals.cambridge.org
http://www.lawcommissionofindia.nic.in
http://www.muktomona.com/Articles/Younus_Sheikh/blasphemy
http://www.pakteahouse.net
http://www.persecutionofahmadis.org
http://www.thecounterpunch.hubpages.com/hub/Martin_Niemoller
http://www.hartsem.edu/macdonald

Langham Literature, with its publishing work, is a ministry of Langham Partnership.

Langham Partnership is a global fellowship working in pursuit of the vision God entrusted to its founder John Stott –

> *to facilitate the growth of the church in maturity and Christ-likeness through raising the standards of biblical preaching and teaching.*

Our vision is to see churches in the majority world equipped for mission and growing to maturity in Christ through the ministry of pastors and leaders who believe, teach and live by the Word of God.

Our mission is to strengthen the ministry of the Word of God through:
- nurturing national movements for biblical preaching
- fostering the creation and distribution of evangelical literature
- enhancing evangelical theological education

especially in countries where churches are under-resourced.

Our ministry

Langham Preaching partners with national leaders to nurture indigenous biblical preaching movements for pastors and lay preachers all around the world. With the support of a team of trainers from many countries, a multi-level programme of seminars provides practical training, and is followed by a programme for training local facilitators. Local preachers' groups and national and regional networks ensure continuity and ongoing development, seeking to build vigorous movements committed to Bible exposition.

Langham Literature provides majority world preachers, scholars and seminary libraries with evangelical books and electronic resources through publishing and distribution, grants and discounts. The programme also fosters the creation of indigenous evangelical books in many languages, through writer's grants, strengthening local evangelical publishing houses, and investment in major regional literature projects, such as one volume Bible commentaries like the *Africa Bible Commentary* and the *South Asia Bible Commentary*.

Langham Scholars provides financial support for evangelical doctoral students from the majority world so that, when they return home, they may train pastors and other Christian leaders with sound, biblical and theological teaching. This programme equips those who equip others. Langham Scholars also works in partnership with majority world seminaries in strengthening evangelical theological education. A growing number of Langham Scholars study in high quality doctoral programmes in the majority world itself. As well as teaching the next generation of pastors, graduated Langham Scholars exercise significant influence through their writing and leadership.

To learn more about Langham Partnership and the work we do visit **langham.org**

www.ingramcontent.com/pod-product-compliance
Lightning Source LLC
Chambersburg PA
CBHW051537230426
43669CB00015B/2631